Current Perspectives in Psychology

Current Perspectives in Psychology presents the latest discoveries and developments across the spectrum of the psychological and behavioral sciences. Each book in the series focuses on critical advances in research, theory, methods, and applications and is designed to be accessible and informative to nonspecialists and specialists alike.

Alan E. Kazdin, editor

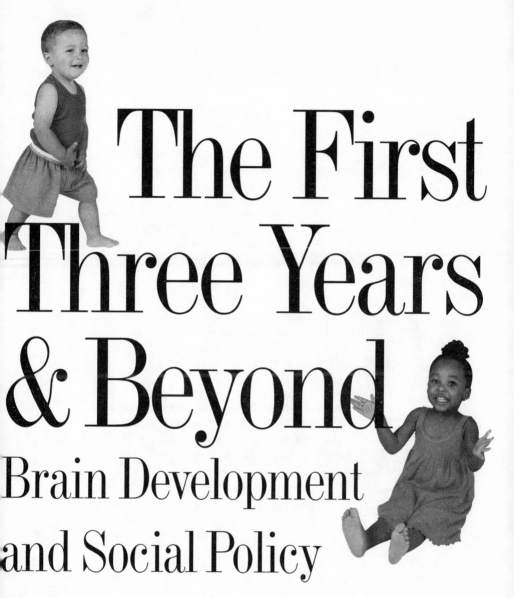

The First
Three Years
& Beyond

Brain Development
and Social Policy

Edward F. Zigler, Matia Finn-Stevenson, and Nancy W. Hall

YALE UNIVERSITY PRESS   NEW HAVEN AND LONDON

Designed by Sonia L. Shannon.
Set in Adobe Garamond with Gill Sans display type by
The Composing Room of Michigan, Inc.
Printed in the United States of America by
R. R. Donnelly & Sons.

Library of Congress Cataloging-in-Publication Data
Zigler, Edward, 1930–
    The first three years and beyond : brain development and social
policy / Edward F. Zigler, Matia Finn-Stevenson, and Nancy W. Hall.
        p.   cm. — (Current perspectives in psychology)
    Includes bibliographical references and index.
    ISBN 0-300-09364-0 (cloth : alk. paper)
    1. Child development.   2. Infants—Development.   3. Brain—
Research—Social aspects.   4. Child welfare—United States.
5. Family policy—United States.   6. United States—Social
policy—Evaluation.   I. Finn-Stevenson, Matia.   II. Hall, Nancy
Wilson.   III. Title.   IV. Series.
HQ767.9Z543   2002
305.231—dc21
2002011146

A catalogue record for this book is available from the British Library.

The paper in this book meets the guidelines for
permanence and durability of the Committee on
Production Guidelines for Book Longevity of the Council on Library
Resources.

10 9 8 7 6 5 4 3 2 1

To Marilyn ("Mickey") Segal
In recognition of her lifelong commitment
to the study of child development and her
advocacy and philanthropic support
of our nation's children

Contents

Acknowledgments

This book was made possible by the support of the Smith Richardson Foundation and Marianne Gerschel of the Spunk Fund, to whom we extend our appreciation. We also gratefully acknowledge the contribution of Paul J. Lombroso for his review of some of the chapters and from whose insight and study of the brain we benefited. Our heartfelt thanks to Julie Nark for coordinating various activities associated with writing the book, to Valerie Vergato Zielinski for assisting in production, to Nicole Wise and to Laura Jones Dooley for editing the manuscript, to Sally Styfco for editorial assistance, and to Elizabeth Gilman for her contributions to some of the chapters.

1

The More Things Change
Politics and PET Scans

At the turn of the century, traditionally a time for reevaluation and setting priorities, the United States of America put children and parents in the spotlight, focusing media and policy efforts on the importance of giving families the supports they need to thrive. The public's attention was drawn to attempts, some more successful than others, to balance the needs of children, parents, and society as a whole with supportive programs in education, health care, and child welfare. To promote the most effective use of tax dollars, the latest research from child study, pediatrics, education, law, and other disciplines was offered. In this way programs could be built on a scientific understanding of what children and families need and with consideration of the consequences of ignoring those needs. Through these efforts was spawned a host of family support programs—some successful, some less so, some popular, others not at all. And controversy arose over the level—personal or governmental, whether federal, state, or local—at which responsibility for meeting the children's needs should be addressed and who should bear the associated costs of family-support programs.

The time period in question? The transition from the nineteenth to the twentieth century.

Of course, these very statements might well be made today, in the early years of the twenty-first century. Child study embodies, as do few other fields, the maxim "The more things change, the more they remain the same." Since its inception in the late nineteenth century, the field of developmental psychology has been dominated by changing paradigms and pendulum swings over many issues—most prominently, perhaps, question of nature versus nurture, or the relative importance of children's innate nature, as opposed to their experiences, in shaping their lives.

During the later decades of the 1900s, many scholars began to focus on the intersection of child development study and its applications to social policy issues of child and family health, development, and welfare. The study of child development as it relates to social policy development—and vice versa—has become an important discipline, enriched by the contributions of scholars and practitioners from fields ranging from developmental and clinical psychology, pediatrics, and medicine, to law, sociology, anthropology, and education.

In the 1990s, another paradigm shift introduced the language of neurobiology and neurochemistry to the discussion. Spurred in large part by technological advances in neurological imaging, the notion that brain activity could be observed and brain development mapped gained near-instant prominence through widespread media coverage of high-visibility conferences devoted to the findings of brain research.

This focus has come at a time of growing concern about the health, well-being, and education of children, and it presents new opportunities for supporting policy responses to address children's and parents' needs. Brain research has caught the attention of scientists in such disciplines as developmental psychology who are finding that discoveries in neuroscience enhance our understanding of how children acquire the ability to think, understand, and use language.

One difference between how the field of child development has changed since early twentieth century and today (and we might well argue about its significance) concerns the nature of the research tools at our disposal. Then and now, most of what we know about child development comes from observational and behavioral studies. What variables support—or impede—healthy growth and development? What supports can legitimately enhance parents' ability to provide optimal environments for their children? The answers to questions like these have largely come, and will likely continue to come, from observing children and talking with parents; from conducting rigorously designed studies of the effects of interventions and prevention efforts; and by tracking over time and across groups of children the effects of demographic change and society's responses to them.

Even in 1900 it was true that increasing medical and technical understanding was boosting children's welfare. Advances in bacteriology slashed infant mortality rates in the early years of the twentieth century by improving the safety of the nation's milk supply and drinking water. Increasing sophistication in the medical care of children saved yet more lives through the development of vaccination programs, the introduction of antibiotics, and the treatment of cancers and other diseases. Radiologic developments enhanced our diagnostic skills and, not insignificantly, became an important tool in the detection of physical child abuse.

In the last quarter of the twentieth century, advances in medical technology opened windows into the workings of the human brain. Research on the brain, often touted as "new," actually began several decades ago in an attempt to understand and treat neurological disorders. This research blossomed during the 1990s, spurred by the application of techniques such as functional magnetic resonance imaging (fMRI) and positron-emission tomography (PET) to neuroscience. Just as remarkable as the introduction of the microscope and the development of X-ray technology, these techniques have tremendous potential to enhance our understanding of human development. Such technologies improve our ability to intervene effectively when disease, injury, or environmental or genetic insult damages the brain or central nervous system. And, not incidentally, the ability to take a relatively noninvasive, detailed look at human brain development over the lifespan fundamentally changes the way we view our children and ourselves (see box, "Neurological Imaging Techniques").

In the 1930s, behavioral scientist B. F. Skinner shocked us with his notion that we need not understand or even examine what takes place in "the black box" (the brain) in order to grasp the basics of, predict, or even control human behavior. Back then, of course, the point was largely moot, since none of the imaging technology extant allowed

Neurological Imaging Techniques

The tools we use to gather information about the brain are many and varied. In addition to drawing inferences from animal studies, researchers are increasingly able to view what goes on inside the human brain. Most of the tools now available produce the equivalent of a snapshot—a moment frozen in time—of the state of the brain in question. Useful for diagnosing injury or illness related to tumors, lesions, and congenital defects, these images can also provide information about brain size at a given time. More recently developed imaging techniques, such as positron-imaging tomography (PET), described below, give us more of a sense of the brain at work by showing us how neurological tissues use chemicals like hormones and neurotransmitters or metabolize sugars when different structures within the brain are working at various levels of intensity.

Computed tomography, or CT scanning: Information from multiple X-ray images of areas as thin as one to ten millimeters in thickness is "stacked" and then displayed on a video monitor to yield the equivalent of a cross-sectional view of the area being scanned. Obtaining these images typically takes thirty to sixty minutes. This procedure is also known as computerized transaxial tomography (CAT).

Functional magnetic resonance imaging, or fMRI: In this procedure, a magnetic field is created around the subject, who reclines on a narrow table inside a tunnel-shaped tube. Radio waves directed at the area under study create detailed pictures of the brain and neurological tissues. The procedure is safe, noninvasive, and painless (unless dyes need to be injected for contrast studies), but it can be problematic for patients who suffer from claustrophobia or anxiety or for children who may need sedation to help them stay still during the typical sixty-to-ninety-minute screening; the equipment also makes loud humming and hammering sounds that many patients find unnerving. The test is costly to administer.

Positron-emission tomography, or PET: In this scanning technique, a natural or synthetic substance such as a metabolite or neurotransmitter marked with positron-emitting radioisotopes is injected into the patient. These radioactive tracers help researchers to monitor and map brain activity. Shortcomings in both the temporal and spatial resolution of PET scan images have been noted, as has the expense of the procedure (Shonkoff and Phillips 2000).

Several caveats apply to the interpretation of studies based on these relatively new and still-evolving technologies. First, our database of findings derived from neurological imaging studies is still extremely small. Studies of the brains of children are rare, and likely to be based on autopsy studies or clinical images of children with neurological illnesses or injuries. The ethical issues arising from the use of imaging studies to learn more about healthy developing brains are myriad: even techniques that are not in and of themselves painful may in some cases be associated with uncomfortable procedures related to the injection of dyes and isotopes.

Because obtaining clear and exhaustive images with most of these techniques can take anywhere from thirty to more than ninety minutes, infants and young children are likely to require sedation in order to remain still enough for the procedure to work; sedatives themselves involve a small but not entirely insignificant level of risk. Although there are no documented side effects of the magnetic fields or radioisotopes used, the jury is still out on whether these may yet be identified, particularly in connection with repeated exposure to imaging technology. Few committees charged with approving research are likely to sanction the large-scale use of these techniques on healthy children for even one-time participation, let alone longitudinal study. Until more sophisticated imaging techniques that are faster, less invasive, and guaranteed to present little or no risk to participants evolve, we must draw conclusions carefully from the brain images available to us, acknowledging their limitations.

us access to the mysteries of the working brain anyway. Findings from neurobiology and neurochemistry suggest outcomes unimaginable to a scholar of childhood in 1900 (and no doubt will seem curiously primitive to the psychologist or child advocate of 2100).

Today, however, we know many things about how the brain works that we did not know in 1900 or even in Skinner's heyday. We know, for instance, that synaptic density (the number of neural connections that enable the brain to do its work) increases more rapidly in the first year of life than in any other period of human development. We also know that many of these dendritic connections—the ones, we presume to be less ingrained by experience and repetition—disappear, literally pruned away by our bodies during the second and third years of life. At the peak of brain development, between one and two years of age, these synaptic connections, which "define the limits of intellectual capacity" (Goldman-Rakic, Bourgeois, and Rakic 1997, 29), are 50 percent higher in the frontal cortex of the child than they are in an adult (Bruer 1999). After a period of relative stability, this rich connectivity *declines* until, at some point during adolescence, synaptic connections appear to settle into an adult level.

We now know that the brain is far more adaptable than ever believed possible and that this plasticity persists well beyond the childhood years. Studies indicate that adult brains, as well as those of young children, are capable of complex learning and even of dramatic adaptations in response to stress or injury. Brain development, therefore, does not cease after early childhood or even after we reach physical maturity.

Other issues, however, have been disputed as a result of the hubbub surrounding these developments in neurology. The mechanisms responsible for brain development are not fully understood, nor are the influences that optimize, impede, or otherwise mediate normal growth. For our present purposes, though, the most important questions asked in the wake of this focus on brain research concern early childhood, its significance in the life of a human being, and the role parents and others play during this period.

Social scientists and practitioners of "hard" sciences have not always understood one another's methods, nor have they made the effort to develop a framework encompassing a broader view of child development. The time is ripe to integrate brain-related physiological studies into the developmental science canon. Just as we have come to take for granted that neither a strict environmental nor a narrowly focused genetic position explains the course of individual development, we must make room for neurons in our lexicon, alongside nature and nurture, and in so doing so strengthen both our understanding and our ability to meet the needs of children and families.

Nature, Nurture, and Neurons

Most of us are inexperienced in the arts of masonry and bricklaying. Yet few of us would dispute the notion that a stone wall with a well-built, strong foundation will—except in the face of exceptional circumstances—stand straighter and stronger and last longer than a wall in which stones are piled willy-nilly on the ground without concern for the uniformity, breadth, or alignment of its first course. So it seems surprising as we enter this millennium that there is considerable controversy brewing over how best to lay the foundation of a human being's life, how to optimize the chance that an individual will grow and develop into a whole, healthy person capable of living a loving, productive life that might someday include raising other children into similarly socially and cognitively robust and vigorous individuals.

This controversy centers around the conflict between the theories of those who have been characterized as the "zero to three-ers" (for example, National Association for the Education of Young Children 1997; Ounce of Prevention Fund 1996; Zero to Three 1999) and a splinter group of scientists and science writers who emerged in the late 1990s to challenge what one educator has called the "myth of the first three years" (Bruer 1997, 1999; see also Gladwell 2000 and Holland 1998).

Parallel to the growth in our understanding of child development and family functioning have always been efforts to intervene in the lives of children on both an immediate level by offering help and support directly to individuals and families and by designing legislation and implementing programs intended to address their needs on a larger scale. Legislation promoting early intervention and developmentally appropriate early childhood education (Head Start, for example), adequate nutrition during the prenatal and early childhood period (WIC, the Women, Infants, and Children program), health care for children (for example, CHIP, the Children's Health Insurance Program, which expands health care coverage to low-income children ineligible for Medicaid), family cohesiveness and continuity of care in the first months of life (family and medical leave legislation), and other family-friendly programs, have been shown not only to benefit individual children but also to be cost-effective means of enhancing social competence in large groups of children while minimizing the need for future remedial services.

Those who promote a view of human development in which the prenatal period and first few years of life play a diminished role have made several important points, chiefly that zero-to-three-ers (among whom the authors count themselves) have been guilty, from time to time, of exaggerating the claims and implications of brain research for child development study and program development. The metaphor of a pendulum swinging between extreme points of view (chiefly between nature and nurture) could not be applied to this new research. For a year or two, debate raged over the importance of brain research and its implications for child development, then the field cleared somewhat as moderate and more integrative positions (many of which we discuss in this book) were developed.

These debates, however, fostered unease between policy makers and scientists who were divided over the implications of neurological research for infants and children. Scholars disagreed over the interpretation of dramatic findings related to rapid brain growth in early childhood and the subsequent pruning of certain neurological connections during toddlerhood and the preschool years. What did this apparent explosion and retooling in neural growth say about the first few years of life? Were the events of these years critical to future development? Was this period unique in its importance? What role did environmental input—especially from parents—play in development at this stage, and what consequences existed for those children deprived of rich environments?

Other scholars, often the neurochemists and neurobiologists around whose work this controversy centered, were uncomfortable with how their research was being interpreted. Neuroscience itself, they argued, was in its infancy, and brain research conducted on adults, on neurologically impaired patients, or even as a function of autopsy findings was not necessarily applicable to normally developing infants and young children. Many raised caveats regarding the extrapolation of the findings of animal-based studies to human beings.

Although much of this brain research remains in its early stages, the popular media widely disseminated the preliminary findings. In 1996, for example, *Newsweek* published a cover story entitled "Your Child's Brain" that detailed the growth of the brain during the early years and showed the remarkable sensory and other capabilities of infants. Another major newsweekly cover story in 1998, in *U.S. News and World Report,* focused on how, in light of brain research, we are reshaping our thinking about how children acquire language. The research and accompanying media exposure has also had a phenomenal impact in the policy arena. Several conferences, including one held at the White House in 1997, and related conference proceedings captured the interest of policy makers at all levels of government and resulted in policy initiatives that highlight the importance of the early years of life.

The policy focus on the early years derives from neuroscientific evidence that indicates, first, that there is a period, starting before birth and continuing for the first three years of life, during which there is rapid synapse formation, and second, that both brain size and brain function depend on environmental stimulation. These findings support the notion that children's experiences during infancy and early childhood are fundamental for their health and well-being and contribute to their ability to learn. Because parents and other adults in the child's life mediate these early experiences, knowledge about the developing brain, as well as policies that provide supportive services during the early years, have the potential to enhance the lives of children and their ability to achieve later academic success.

Media coverage of brain research had promoted the alleged implications of these findings for child-rearing. Early intervention was touted as essential to the young child's optimum development (and the precept "the earlier the better" became widely accepted). The interventions being promoted at this time, however, were not of the well-researched, broadly based, two-generation variety (which we describe in Chapter 4) that has been so effective in recent decades in promoting school readiness, social competence, parenting skills, and child health.

Although the "gourmet baby" movement (Zigler and Lang 1991) first gained ascendancy in the 1980s, the trend flowered as popular understanding (and misunderstanding) of brain research grew in the 1990s.

No longer was playing on the kitchen floor with a saucepan and a wooden spoon or being sung a simple lullaby at bedtime considered adequate stimulation for deriving peak performance from a human being. Baby music classes, gymnastics sessions, history flashcards, and "educational" toys were promoted by entrepreneurs eager to cash in on the brain wave and embraced by parents made to feel guilty (especially if they were separated from their children each day by their jobs) for not giving their baby every possible advantage. Mozart in the crib, museum-quality architectural building blocks, pint-sized violins, and stark black-and-white graphics in the nursery were the hallmarks of good parenting in the 1990s. These children were being given a leg up on development, promoted to the Ivy League track before they were out of their designer diapers.

Or were they? In the late 1990s, a small group of scholars and reporters questioned both the applicability of this brain research to early childhood and, indeed, the special significance of the first three years of life. Neurological research findings, they argued, did little to demonstrate that the first three years represented a *critical period* in human life, nor did they prove the merits of weighting highly specific intervention efforts so heavily during the early years. Faster than they could don their strikingly printed visual-stimulation t-shirts (promoted by one merchant as a means to "increase concentration skills, stimulate the creation of synapses, increase an infant's attention span, calm a baby, [and] enhance curiosity"; Happy Baby 1998), parents were left wondering whether they were helping their children at all through these efforts.

Parents were not the only ones shaking their heads in confusion. Policy makers, too, began to wonder whether brain research provided an appropriate basis for the family support and intervention programs they had been urged by their constituents to support and had helped to develop and fund. If environmental inputs are of little consequence in the neurological development of the child, for instance, as one anti-zero-to-three-er suggested (Bruer 1999), then what use, some legislators wondered, are programs like Head Start and Early Head Start or home visitation programs designed to increase social competence or parent education programs designed to enhance the very parent-infant interactions now being devalued by some?

The Pendulum Swings

That a controversy should arise over the nature of child development itself—and over the role parents and policy makers should play in it— should come as no surprise to anyone familiar with the hundred-plus year history of developmental psychology. The modern field of child study has always been subject to polarizations of theory, simplistic versions of which have often trickled down (typically through the popular media) to parents and other laypersons concerned with children. Consider, for instance, the furor that arose in the 1960s, when the perennial nature versus nurture debate flamed with particular heat. Empirical evidence gathered at this time pointed to the influence of early experiences on intelligence.

One perspective was provided by Joseph McVicker Hunt, who, in his influential book *Intelligence and Experience* (1961), argued that human intelligence is in large measure an environmental product. Hunt contended, based on the findings of animal research and other studies, that we could promote a faster rate of intellectual growth in children, increasing infant IQ by thirty to seventy points, by "governing the encounters that children have with their environments, particularly during the early years of their development" (Hunt 1961, 35). The condensed and simplified version of this already extreme notion raised the expectations of eager parents. *Readers' Digest* titled an interview with Hunt "How to Raise Your Child's IQ by 20 Points." A *Life* magazine cover story at this time turned psychologist Burton White's suggestion that hanging a mobile over a child's crib was an appropriate form of stimulation into the "finding" that exposing infants to crib mobiles could significantly increase their developmental quotients (Early Learning Right in the Crib 1967; Zigler and Muenchow 1992).

The debates continued in the 1970s. Consider, for instance, the following:

> During the last twenty-five years the impact of new biological and social knowledge has caused revision or reformula-

tion of many theories about the development of behavioral processes. In particular, the complexity of the interactions and transactions between nature and nurture are now more fully appreciated. There remains, however, one theory which is particularly resistant to change: that the environment in the early years exert a disproportionate and irreversible effect on a rapidly developing organism, compared with the potential for later environmental influences. [Clarke and Clarke 1977, 4]

Pioneering child psychologists Ann and Alan Clarke were skeptical about this view of development. Their consequent doubts regarding the justification for broadly based early intervention programs, is reflected with great precision in the proposals put forth by educator John Bruer in *The Myth of the First Three Years* (1999). Bruer's criticisms of what he terms "brain-based policy" are disparaging indeed—for instance, he derides support for strengthening family leave policies, child care standards, and early intervention programs (he, like the Clarkes before him, singles out Head Start as an example) because, in essence, brain research does not directly support such legislative efforts.

Such arguments, then and now, are spun of straw. They are based on misunderstandings or misinterpretations of developmental science, which has provided overriding support for these and other productive, cost-effective programs long before the Carnegie Corporation published *Starting Points* in 1994, the first report to propose that findings from brain research bolstered support for such efforts.

If a little knowledge is a dangerous thing, a little *more* knowledge has thoroughly muddled popular beliefs about child development. Today we might describe that nature versus nurture debate as nature versus nurture versus neurons. To the lenses through which we viewed the children of the nineteenth and twentieth centuries, the microscope and the X-ray machine, we've added neurological imaging devices. Though they seem incredibly high-tech and sophisticated to most of us, we need to recognize that they are still in the earliest stages of development. Even so, they have brought us glimpses into the living, dynamic functioning of the human brain and in so doing have introduced new controversy into the fields of child study and family policy over the applications of the growing body of neurological research to social policies relevant to child and family health, development, and welfare.

PET Scans and Policies

Research has long played an important role in child advocacy. The White House held its first conference on children's needs and interests in 1909. Such conferences were held every decade until the Reagan administration discontinued them during the 1980s. In the first half of the twentieth century, child advocates focused largely on issues of physical health and mortality, bringing science to bear on public health policy. Many also brought children's interests to the attention of academic institutions and philanthropists who founded child study institutes at many leading universities.

Under the administration of President Lyndon B. Johnson in the 1960s, advocates both promoted the establishment of intervention programs for disadvantaged children and guided the implementation of these efforts. A number of changes at the time stimulated researchers' interest in social policy. As state and federal governments contributed more resources and attention to the development of social programs, social scientists discovered new opportunities to use their knowledge to shape decisions made on behalf of children. Although there were significant tensions between purely academic research in this area and the applications of that research to real situations involving children and their families, more and more scholars began not only to believe that they could apply their understanding to improving children's quality of life but to feel ethically compelled to do so (Stipek and McCroskey 1989).

Practical considerations prompted policy makers to seek the advice of experts in child development, education, and child health. Even when moral and ethical concerns drive policy considerations, however, economics remains the driving force behind the distribution of human and material resources. Government bodies eager to find the most effective ways to spend their funds sought the expertise of scholars familiar with child health and development. These academicians and researchers in turn studied the outcomes of intervention programs, and many became advocates themselves, appealing to local, state, and federal governments to set high standards and continue funding for the best programs. From their studies of child and family programs and the needs of children and families, scholars derived "childhood social indicators," data that paint a picture of the conditions of children.

Acceptance of the notion that scientists and legislators can work together for the benefit of children and families has come slowly (and with periodic resistance from both sides), but it is now clear that research plays a critical role in policy development. No matter what the issue at hand may be, policy development goes through a predictable series of stages beginning with the identification of a problem and continuing with exploration of what might be done about it. This exploratory step leads to a search for reasonable solutions, which are then implemented, sometimes on a limited basis at first. An evaluative stage follows, in which legislators review data on the efficacy of the steps taken to combat the original problem; adjustments, revisions, or intensification of promising efforts and abandonment of ineffective steps then follow. In reality, this process is less streamlined, complicated by the number of interests vying for representation in the finished policy product, by the scope and nature of the problem itself, and by the availability of the resources needed. In any case, however, it is clear that the process will be the most effective when each stage of the process is based on solid empirical research describing the nature of the problem and how it is (or is not) mediated by proposed solutions. Research has an irreplaceable role to play in child and family policy formation.

The new focus on brain research has not only sparked discussion but generated controversy—often heated—over some of the most basic issues in child development. What implications are there for our understanding of early development and its consequences relevant to later outcomes? Exactly what role does early experience play in determining how a child's cognitive and social development will proceed? What role do parents play? Is it possible to ameliorate or reverse the ill consequences of early developmental deficits? These questions have profound implications for the preservation and continued development of family policy. Some theorists, decrying what they perceive as the lack of clear implications of brain research findings for policy development (Bruer 1999; Gladwell 2000), have suggested that without clear directives arising from neurological findings, policy development efforts have rested and will continue to rest on shaky theoretical ground. If Early Head Start has no demonstrable effect on synaptic development or the Family and Medical Leave Act of 1993 cannot be shown to change the brain's architecture, why should we spend money, time, and effort to mount and promote these supportive efforts?

New Questions, New Answers

We believe that the answers to questions like these can be found in the chapters that follow, though they may not always come from the voxels, pixels, and digitized images arising from today's brain-imaging machines. Decades of debating nature versus nurture have finally ended. No longer do we believe that these spheres of influence are separable. Most scholars of child development, whether they design parenting questionnaires, observe mothers and infants together in lab or home settings, seek the origins of behavior in gene-mapping protocols, or examine environmental influences on synaptic development, champion a *whole child* approach to development. No longer do we view the child as a disembodied cognitive system or a developmental quotient. Each and every behavior appears to represent some reflection of both genetic and environmental factors.

With this volume we propose that it is not only possible but essential for the growth of child study and child and family policy study that we, as a field, eventually reach a comparable conclusion with respect to the integration of neurological findings into the canon of what we know about how children develop and why they behave as they do. If we are careful and thoughtful, we may even be able to avoid repeating earlier errors. Representatives of the media and education, for instance, have already—perhaps unwittingly—shaped a good deal of the early discussion of brain development in terms of what it means for cognitive development. We commit a serious error when we equate the brain only or primarily with cognitive development. Every human behavior—physical, cognitive, or social—originates in the brain. Others have described more eloquently than we can the emotional context of all learning and cognitive development (Pruett 2000b); in later chapters in this volume we'll discuss research findings on the role played by the social and emotional ecology of family and child development in mediating learning, social competence, and the results of child abuse and neglect, among other topics.

Not only does brain research have profound implications for sustaining and continuing to promote sound social policies, but, as again we will demonstrate in the chapters that follow, no brain findings to date have diminished the impact of the body of traditional observational and behavioral research in child development. Emerging neurological work is entirely supportive of and consonant with the protection and promotion of social policy responses to the needs of children, families, and communities in a variety of spheres, including medical, educational, and social realms. The Early Head Start program, for instance, which was launched in 1995 and is designed to serve economically disadvantaged infants and toddlers from birth to age three, promotes the environments and interactions that set the scene for healthy brain development. Interest in brain research and the early years present an opportunity for renewed focus on the Family and Medical Leave Act, and many states are investigating how to take this important piece of family support policy a step further by providing both longer and paid leaves of absence following the birth or adoption of a child.

These examples of policy efforts that have resulted from media exposure of the research on the brain are positive. Brain research may also influence child care, health care, education, and other child-oriented policies. As researchers concerned with how child development study can both promote and benefit from sound policy development, we are concerned about several current trends as neurological research takes its rightful place alongside genetic, clinical, and behavioral studies of the child and the family in the trends century.

First, as often happens at the intersection of scientific study and journalism, necessary simplification of the research in question has led to unintentional skewing and overstatement of many findings emerging from neurochemical and neurobiological studies of the infant and developing child. Later we'll look not only at how this misunderstanding developed but at how it was virtually inevitable that it should have and at what we can do to bridge the gap between science and journalism.

Second, as we've noted here, we hope to clarify misunderstandings from this media coverage that might have negative implications for social policy development. Decades of research have shown that children, families, and communities benefit demonstrably from legislation providing for parental leave, early intervention, parent support, early and continued comprehensive health care, early education, and high-quality child care. Even the barest bones of such programs have been hard-won. Now there looms before us the possibility that legislators and their supporters could misunderstand the very brain science that promises to *support* these policy efforts and could withdraw or weaken their backing for these important child and family policies.

In the pages ahead, we'll cover each of these areas with an eye to explaining how the contributions of brain science represent not so much a paradigm shift in developmental psychology as new tools to speed us along our established trajectory. Earlier in this chapter we compared getting a child off to a healthy start in life with building a stone wall. The foundation stones of our design are the following themes, which help to frame our understanding of the critical areas of child policy:

- Brain research, still in its own infancy, has so far confirmed what decades of observational and behavioral research have told us, that the young child's experience of the world has a profound impact on early and continuing development.

- Parents play a vital role in the development of their child, but a caregiving situation emphasizing warmth, continuity of care, love, and respect gives infants and young children all the elements they need for healthy and sound cognitive, social, and physical development.

- Growth and development do not stop after infancy, toddlerhood, or even the school-age years. Everything we continue to learn about human growth and development —through a combination of traditional and imaging-based research—confirms our previous understanding that the early years of life are crucial in laying the foundation for a lifetime of learning and loving but that development and learning continue throughout our lifespan.

- Sound, empirically derived social policy providing for safe and appropriate early care, education, health care, and parent support is a critical component of the way we can strengthen families, communities, and the nation as a whole, and the neurobiological evidence gathered to date simply supports earlier research from which this conclusion is derived.

Three things have happened since reports of brain research and its purported implications for learning and development began to appear in the popular press. First, as we have noted, the research findings have been oversimplified and often misunderstood—leading, in many cases, to our second concern, that parents began to express fears and questions about what this research meant for them. Third, and perhaps most alarming, were the implications of media portrayals of critical or sensitive periods for learning, leading parents to worry that they needed to implement musical instruction, math games, or foreign-language lessons in the playpen or even the crib. Adoptive parents fretted that they might have missed crucial opportunities to nurture children who came to them late in infancy or as toddlers or preschoolers. At least two recent books have stated boldly that parents are not even critical players in their child's development, leading some to wonder whether they should do anything special at all with their children (Bruer 1999; Harris 1997).

We believe that it is appropriate, therefore, to explore how new research and old can be integrated into a foundation on which we can build effective family policy that will promote the healthy development and learning of all children. Change almost always engenders confusion at first, and to a great extent the messages emerging from interpretations and misinterpretations of brain research have bewildered not only parents and caregivers but teachers, child advocates, and policy makers. In the chapters ahead we hope to clarify points of confusion and bolster the foundation upon which so many important components of our nation's family support system have been built. Like the foundations of child development itself, straightening out the basics upon which family policy is built can only help our efforts to endure and remain effective means of strengthening families and enhancing child development.

2

The Science of Brain Research

"In recent years, enormous advances have been made in the understanding of human development. We have learned that intelligence is not fixed at birth, but is largely formed by environmental influences of the early formative years. It develops rapidly at first, and then more slowly; as much of that development takes place in the first four years as in the next thirteen. We have learned further that environment has its greatest impact on the development of intelligence when that development is proceeding most rapidly—that is, in those earliest years."

This quotation could have been taken from a recent publication on brain development, but it is actually excerpted from a letter written in 1975 to the journal *American Psychologist* (Moynihan 1975, 940). Its words aptly capture our rationale for writing this book and what we show in this chapter in particular: brain studies are adding to our understanding of child development, but—although what we know from neuroscience research still has limitations—studies on the brain corroborate and build on much of what we have long known about cognitive, emotional, and behavioral development from other disciplines.

Research on the brain is progressing at a phenomenal pace today. Yet brain studies actually began decades ago with researchers focusing on the anatomy, physiology, chemistry, and molecular biology of the central nervous system. Early researchers worked to understand how the central nervous system, and in particular the brain, functions. More recently, researchers have directed their attention to discovering how brain activity relates to behavior and cognition, and they have sought to find out not only how the brain develops, matures, and maintains itself but also answers to such questions as, Are there critical periods in brain development? And how do environmental factors and experience influence brain development? This line of research and especially its application are controversial, as we indicated in Chapter 1. The genes play a critical role in development, as we shall see in this and other chapters. Nevertheless, there is no question that very early in life the brain is receptive to environmental influence and is ready to take in information. Perhaps even more important, research is revealing that experiences shape the brain physically.

The Biological Roots of the Study of Child Development

This line of research is adding to our store of knowledge, yet we have known for some time that infants are born not with a "blank slate" but with sensory and perceptual skills that enable them to interact with and learn from the environment (Diamond 1988; Stern 1977, 1985). In addition, as we have discussed, interest in the biological bases of growth and development and the debate over the relative roles of experience (nurture) and our biological heritage (nature) are as old as is the history of the study of child development.

The current link between the study of child development and neuroscience echoes some of the assumptions of the founding fathers of developmental psychology (Johnson 1999b). Although many theorists have speculated about children's development, the British naturalist Charles Darwin is credited with launching child study as a scientific endeavor. Darwin theorized that complex species evolve from simpler forms of life and that evolution occurs through an interaction between genetic variations and mutations and the demands of the particular environment. The publication of *On the Origin of Species* in 1859 sparked an immediate debate on the possible link between human beings and other species, as well as in the biological roots of behavior and development, and this line of thinking dominated the field for years (Kessen

1965). Darwin also established the observation of children in their natural environment as a scientific method of study when he published his biography of his son. Numerous baby biographies by various authors followed, providing insight into children's early growth and development and leading to theoretical formulations about human development.

The Swiss psychologist Jean Piaget, who revolutionized the understanding of how children think, also took a biological approach to explaining development. Piaget's work was based on the premise that intelligence is a "biological adaptation of a complex organism to a complex environment" (Chen and Siegler 2000, 95). In his theory of cognitive growth, Piaget underscored the role of the environment in human development, noting that the individual, at every stage of development, is actively engaged in acquiring knowledge and constantly exploring the environment in an attempt to understand it. Central to Piaget's theory are the notions that it is human nature to organize experiences and adapt to what is being experienced and that it is through these processes of organization and adaptation that infants and children progress from one stage of development to the next.

Subsequent research has shown that Piaget underestimated infants' and children's cognitive abilities. In addition, whereas Piaget presented a linear and orderly progression of the growth of intelligence, cognitive development is now thought to be more complex. And it is worth pointing out that Piaget did not study the brain (see box, "Research on Developmental Differences in Cognitive Development: Then and Now").

Several aspects of current brain research do build on Piaget's theory, however (Johnson 1999b). For example, Piaget contended that the child's ability to imitate involves several cognitive functions: the child must fix in his or her mind the memory of the action, compare it with a mental representation, and then direct a series of actions that match the two mental constructs, making imitation a complex skill that does not develop until late in infancy. This notion of imitation was challenged when researchers found that imitation occurs much earlier, but questions remain as to whether this early imitation is distinct from the more mature imitation Piaget described (Anisfeld 1991). Neuroscientists are now working on studies that may eventually offer

Research on Developmental Differences in Cognitive Development: Then and Now

Jean Piaget opened our eyes many years ago to the fact that children not only know less than adults but also actually think differently. He based his findings on observing children and noting the answers they gave to questions he asked. Depending on their age, children gave different answers, which led Piaget to conclude that children undergo developmental changes in cognition. New research that seeks to explain how the brain develops confirms that children do indeed think differently, actually using different parts of the brain than do adults when performing similar tasks. Bradley Schlaggar and his colleagues at the Washington University in Saint Louis conducted imaging studies using fMRI scans on children ages seven to ten as they worked on word-processing tasks. They compared the scans with those taken of adults working on similar tasks. Both the adults and children were required to think about the task, which involved saying a word out loud in response to a written word. The findings: children and adults had different responses, and the children used sections in the back of the brain known to be reserved for visual processing, whereas adults used the frontal cortex. These findings are not surprising, as we describe later in the chapter: the frontal cortex undergoes structural change during adolescence and is the last part of the brain to develop.

answers to that question: in one line of research, there are indications that single nerve cells, or neurons, in an infant monkey cortex appear active when the monkey is matching an action to one it is observing, in other words, when the monkey is imitating an action (Gallese et al. 1996).

Bert Touwen (1998), who underscores developmental psychology's roots in the biological bases of development, highlights the work of two other founding members of the field of child study, Arnold Gesell (1928) and Myrtle McGraw (1943), noting their interest in brain maturation and locomotor development. Gesell and McGraw conducted observational studies and described stages of motor development, such as sitting up and walking, as well as children's behavior and their social and emotional development.

The assumption underlying Gesell's maturational theory (1928) is that development is guided from within and unfolds according to a predetermined, sequential timetable. Although he noted that both heredity and experience influence development, he believed that environmental influence was decidedly secondary (Crain 1985). Contemporary methods of parenting began to evolve as mothers and fathers found Gesell's predictive information (for example, the "terrible twos," the "lively threes") useful in giving them an idea of what to expect of their children at different stages of development.

Although she is generally considered to have adhered to a maturational theory, McGraw (1943) disagreed with Gesell about a maturational unfolding of a developmental sequence of behavior. Like Gesell, McGraw derived her ideas from meticulous observations of children, but she constructed various methods to show how infants and young children act upon, as well as react to, the environment. She also viewed the role of the environment as important to development: this conclusion was derived, in part, from studies comparing training provided to fraternal twins, early in life to one twin and later in life to another, with the twin who received early training clearly becoming more proficient in the particular skill later in life (Dalton and Bergenn 1995).

McGraw is also known for her work on reflexology. She showed, for example, that changes in the structure of early reflexes are evidence of how the maturation of higher brain centers change behavior. Although some contend that McGraw's work was largely speculative (Johnson 1999b), others, such as Thomas Dalton (1995, 1998) note that she and her colleagues (notably Smith 1941) conducted more complex analyses of neurobehavior than is generally acknowledged. Touwen (1995), too, considers her to be far ahead of her time in explaining that variations in locomotion among infants were not indications of abnormalities, as Gesell would have described, but as having occurred as a result of the neural mechanisms underlying motor functions. This is also a focus of Touwen's current research, using evidence from pre- and postnatal neurological data (Touwen 1995).

A Closer Look at Nature Versus Nurture

The study of children is now based on increasingly complex scientific methodologies and a variety of theories that attempt to answer different questions. As we noted in Chapter 1, a new frontier in the field is the link of child development to neuroscience. Throughout the history of the field scientists have debated the relative roles of nature and nurture in growth and development. As we describe elsewhere in the book, this debate continues today in relation to brain development.

Although most scientists today have moved away from the acrimony associated with the controversy, viewing both genetic endowment and environmental influences as important, theorists historically have tended to extreme views, at one time favoring environmental influences and at other times emphasizing the role of genetic inheritance. Most research today looks not at either nature or nurture but, rather, at the interplay of the two during normal development; at times, it is clear, genetic factors disrupt normal development regardless of how supportive the environment is. And at times when the environment is severely deprived—as we shall see in the next section—development can be compromised despite normal genes (Lombroso and Pruett 2002).

The main topic of discussion in the nature-nurture controversy has been, over the years, cognitive development and its close cousin, intelligence. Interest in early experience and the impact of the environment on intelligence was evident in the work of Joseph McVicker Hunt (1961) and Benjamin Bloom (1964), both of whom took an extreme environmental position in the controversy. As we note elsewhere, the extreme environmental position has led to simplistic expectations about outcomes of early interventions and has dominated recent attempts to provide "conclusions" that are based on preliminary and inconclusive findings in neuroscience.

Although interest in intelligence long dominated the nature-nurture controversy and was indeed the original focus of the debate, in recent years the debate has shifted to other aspects of development. Growth in the field of behavioral genetics and, more generally, in funding for such global efforts as the Human Genome Project, have fueled renewed work in this area, with the realization that genetic factors exert a pervasive influence on health, development, and behavior. As in the field of developmental psychology, there are some exceptions, but overall, most researchers in behavioral genetics and related disciplines see both biological inheritance and environmental experiences as providing important contributions to human development. Using as their starting point the notion that individual differences in behavior, as well as many psychopathological disorders, have a genetic component, scientists are taking the research to another level, adding a new dimension to our understanding of human development.

Consider, for example, current research on autism. Autism is a developmental disorder evident early in life and characterized by the inability to establish social interactions, impaired communication and attention, and, often, repetitive patterns of behaviors and movements. The etiology of the disorder was at one time discussed in relation to parental psychopathology, which is, of course, an environmental factor. In the past several years, however, researchers have conducted genetic studies using monozygotic (identical) and dizygotic (fraternal) twins, finding that genetic factors play an important role in the etiology of the disorder. In identical twins, if one has autism, 90 percent of the time the other twin will also have the disorder (Lombroso and Pruett 2002). Researchers have isolated several genes that contribute to autism (Risch et al. 1999), and as we describe later, some have examined brain development in autistic children and adults, finding abnormalities in certain regions of the brain. This line of research is contributing to new theories about autism and may lead someday to new interventions.

Research in behavioral genetics is progressing in other areas as well, revealing that researchers are rethinking previous explanations and making linkages across disciplines. Take as an example the research on divorce. Longitudinal studies in the social sciences have shown that individuals whose parents divorced have difficulties establishing and maintaining relationships, many often divorcing themselves (Wallerstein, Lewis, and Blakeslee 2000). Matt McGue and David Lykken (1992), testing the long-held notion that divorce is entirely influenced by environmental factors, found that among monozygotic twins, who are genetically similar, the risk for divorce is significantly higher than is the case with dizygotic, or fraternal, twins or those who had first-degree relatives who were divorced. Because this area of research is still very much in its infancy, it cannot be said that one is genetically pre-destined to divorce, but the findings challenge the view that the environment alone is at play, indicating the need for studies to document if and how genes are implicated and ascertain how genetic influence may be mediated by multiple factors that may be biological, environmental, or both (McGue 1994). It may be that genetic predisposition may explain why some children suffer long-term consequences associated with their parents' divorce while others do not (McGue and Lykken 1992).

We make this point in view of findings that reveal a complex gene-environment transaction in many aspects of human development. The complexity of development is noted when we look at the research as a whole, rather than studies in specific areas, a point well worth keeping in mind later when we discuss research on the brain. For example, reviews of studies both on twins reared apart and on adoptive siblings unrelated biologically but reared together often reveal little environmental impact, pointing to a significant genetic contribution to development. But these studies cannot be regarded in isolation; a frequent limiting factor is that individuals reared in extreme poverty or other adverse circumstances are rarely, if ever, included in twin and adoptive studies (McGue 1994), making it unsurprising that such studies fail to find an environmental effect.

The role of the environment, however, is strongly evident in many other studies. Neurological studies of infants reared in orphanages in Romania are especially instructive. Many orphanages in Romania were appalling institutions where infants were given minimal custodial care: they were confined to cots, fed with propped-up bottles, having almost no interactions with adult caregivers. These infants were rarely picked up, never hugged or smiled at. Researchers found that the babies' psychological deprivation affected their brain development and resulted in compromises in stress hormone regulation as well as other consequences (Carlson and Earls 1999). The longer the Romanian infants stayed in the orphanages, studies have found, the greater were the developmental consequences. Michael Rutter and his colleagues studied a group of Romanian orphans brought to England and adopted before age two, some before six months. Assessed on arrival, the babies were found to be severely developmentally impaired and severely malnourished. When tested again at age four, after several years in the adoptive environment, these children evidenced immense developmental and physical progress, especially those adopted before they were six months of age (Rutter 1998). Although these studies reveal the negative outcomes of severely deprived environments, the optimistic finding is that such outcomes can be reversed if the environment improves early in life, highlighting the critical influence of the environment and the value of early intervention.

Although some of these studies of orphanages focused in part on the brain and are relatively new, they are similar to studies from the social sciences conducted in an earlier era on infants in orphanages. Those studies, conducted several decades ago, yielded similar findings, alerting us to the critical role of the environment and providing the basis for many intervention and prevention programs early in the life of the child (Dennis 1960, 1973; Provence 1989; Skeels 1966).

Environmental factors are also important in richer environments and for older children, though it can be hard for researchers to pull apart the complex interactions between the genes and environment (Lamb 1997; Shonkoff and Phillips 2000). The research on parenting styles illuminates this point. Some studies have found that parental behavior and parents' interactions with children are important factors in the socialization of children (Maccoby 1992, 2000). Although parents clearly influence children, it is also evident that children influence parents, leading us to appreciate the reciprocity of the parent-child relationship. For example, children are born with certain traits or temperaments as part of their biological heritage—that is a genetic given. Their temperament, in turn, evokes different responses from those around them. Hence two children may grow up in the same family but experience very different social environments depending in part on their temperament and the way their parents react and relate to them. Sandra Scarr and Kathleen McCartney (1983) thus state that children, and adults, actually take part in shaping their environment.

Some of the studies on child abuse provide a clear example of this point. The studies indicate that whereas in many cases parental ignorance and pathology are involved, some children actually bring out the worst in their parents. Thus infants who are hard to calm, or low birthweight and premature infants whose cries are piercing and whose parents are unable to comfort them, could bring otherwise rational parents to a point of exasperation that may result in abuse (Egeland and Brunquell 1979; Liederman 1983). Gerald Patterson (1982) and his colleagues (1990) also found that parents' reaction to a difficult child may cause continued difficulty on the child's part and eventually may lead to a cycle of coercion and family dysfunction. Further complicating the picture are findings that show that the brains of children who experience chronic abuse early in life are structurally altered, which may in part explain abused children's inability to cope with stress later in life and to experience other educational, social, and emotional problems (Glaser 2000; Kaufman and Charney 2001). However, the extent of structural change in the brain may differ owing to several factors, one being that individual children react differently to stress (Lewis 1992). Clearly these interactions and relationships are highly complex and interrelated.

The Growth and Development of the Brain

The intricately complex gene-environment transaction in development, known for many years, is also evident in current studies in neuroscience. The studies are showing that brain development is not simply a predictable biological process, nor is it entirely the result of a response to experience. Rather, it is an outcome of a bidirectional process in which both the genes and the environment interact.

Underscoring the complexity of the process, William Greenough and James Black (1992) note that in brain development there are: (1) intrinsic forces that provide the scaffolding essential for later development; (2) another kind of intrinsic force, evident in synapse overproduction (discussed later), that is designed to capture information from experience; and (3) a separate mechanism that is responsible for input from the experiences unique to each individual. They contend that in view of the existence of this latter mechanism, the quality of the child's experiences is important, a point that will become evident in this as well as subsequent chapters.

The Brain's Structure and Organization

Although the infant's experiences after birth and their role in brain development have captured widespread interest in recent years, brain development begins, and is subject to environmental influence, during the prenatal period. Before discussing this point, it is important that we review the structure and organization of the brain. Given the limited scope of this chapter, our review is selective and is elaborated upon in subsequent chapters. Here we provide highlights of what is currently known about how the brain is built.

The brain is often described as looking rather like a very big walnut. It is made up of the forebrain (the upper cortex), and mid- and hindbrain (the subcortex), the latter of which is the brain stem. Connecting the brain stem to the rest of the body is the spinal cord, which carries fibers from the brain to connect with muscles and organs in other parts of the body. The entire system is referred to as the central nervous system. Although the brain is associated with such activities as thinking, learning, and remembering, it actually governs all functions, from basic but vital ones such as breathing and reflex activity to voluntary activities such as walking and those that are entailed in receiving, processing, and storing information from the environment.

The brain does all this and more remarkably efficiently. It is organized into right and left hemispheres. These are not mirror images of each other; rather, they contain regions within which are "centers" that control different functions and activities (Kolb and Wishaw 1985). The right hemisphere controls the left side of the body and contains the areas responsible for visual processing. The left hemisphere controls the right side of the body and contains the areas responsible for language processing. The two hemispheres are connected by fiber tracts, known as the corpus callosum, which may serve to transfer information across the division that separates the two parts of the brain (Kinsbourne and Hiscock 1983). Although pictorial renditions of the brain necessarily depict a two-dimensional view, the brain is three-dimensional and its various regions are highly interconnected. The location and function of each region are known, but the regions' defining limits—that is, where each begins and ends—are at this point difficult to establish (Siegel 1999).

The foundation of the brain's development is laid down as billions of neurons are generated, migrate, and form appropriate connections beginning in the third week of gestation (see box, "Early Brain Development"). Neurons, or nerve cells, are one of two types of cells that make up the brain and they receive and send impulses, or signals. Neuroglia, or glial cells, feed and support the neurons, some transferring nutritive matter to neurons, others having a role in the development of myelin insulation, described later, or in guiding neural migration (Janowsky and Carper 1996). Like other cells, neurons consist of a cell body, or nucleus, and cytoplasm. However, in neurons, the cytoplasm is drawn out into large numbers of fine, wirelike dendrites and axons. The dendrites receive impulses, whereas the axons send impulses. Chemicals transmit these impulses, or messages, from one neuron to another. The connectivity of the neurons (that is, the number of connections made by the dendrites and axons with other cells) accounts for the brain's functional maturity and governs even the most basic of actions. The activation of one neuron can influence thousands of neurons at the receiving end. The pattern of growth and connectivity is not random, but it is also not wholly based on the unfolding of a genetic blueprint; cells need environmental input to function properly, but they are genetically guided in making the appropriate connections. The process of making connections is at its most active during fetal life and continues during the first few years of life.

The junctions through which electrical impulses, or messages, pass from one neuron to another are called synapses. A relatively small proportion of synapses is present at birth and the rest are formed after birth. Synaptic connections are added to the brain through a process that includes overproduction and selective pruning. The nervous system inherently has a large number of connections, a genetic given, and then environmental experiences play a role in maintaining and strengthening some of these once they are established and some synapse elimination occurs as part of normal development. The outcome is a refined form of what constitutes the bases for later phases of development, eventually making the brain highly specialized, with specific activities confined to particular areas in the brain.

Critical or Sensitive Periods: The Timing of Experience

Both the genes and the environment interact in complex ways in building the brain. But is there a critical period associated with brain development? This question is not only of interest to researchers but

Early Brain Development

During the period from conception until the third year of postnatal life, the brain grows at a rate unmatched by any later developmental stage. The intense activity in the brain can be understood as directed at the achievement of several tasks necessary for normal development (Shonkoff and Phillips 2000). The first task, beginning in the embryonic period (three to eight weeks after conception), is the development of brain cells and their migration to where they belong and where they will eventually function within the central nervous system. This occurs so quickly that by birth, most of the one hundred billion brain cells that form the adult brain are already in existence. In fact, during the prenatal period, many more neurons are produced than are eventually needed, and many of them are shed in utero. When the brain cells have reached their location, they begin the second task of sprouting axons and dendrites used for sending and receiving signals. The growth of synapses, the connections between the cells that allow information to travel, extends well into postnatal life through a process of over-production and pruning, described in this chapter. The forming and strengthening of these connections are important aspects of brain de-velopment. Each neuron is connected to thousands of other neurons, forming neural pathways that some call the brain's wiring. Eventually, a protective, fatty substance called myelin develops around the nerve axons, increasing the speed of communication between cells.

has policy implications as well, examples of which we show through-out this book.

A critical period is a specific developmental time during which the organism is especially sensitive to environmental influences. The same influence before or after the critical period may have little or no impact on development, a phenomenon clearly evident during the prenatal period in relation to the maturation of sensory systems. As we shall see in Chapter 8, genetic factors guide development, but malnutrition, various drugs and alcohol, and maternal diseases can disrupt normal development.

Infancy has been described as a critical period because at birth, the human brain is the most undifferentiated organ in the body. The genes and experiences shape how the neurons connect to one another, in this way "form[ing] the specialized circuits that give rise to mental processes" (Siegel 1999, 14). The differentiation of circuits within the brain involves several processes that include more extensive synaptic connections and the growth of protective myelin sheaths along the lengths of neurons. Myelin is a fatty substance that insulates neurons, producing stronger, enhanced connections and increased speed of nerve conduction. Increased myelination, which is affected by experiences and nutrition during the early years, correlates with increased brain function. It occurs most rapidly during the first two years of life then more slowly until adolescence and possibly later. We know that some regions in the brain begin myelination before other regions, but there is no consensus about the course of completion for myelination.

Also, although the sheer exuberance of synapses during early life has led infancy to be labeled a critical period, Peter Huttenlocher notes that in the human cerebral cortex, the period during which there are large numbers of connections goes beyond infancy and "extends from the second half of the first year of life to late childhood or early adolescence" (1994, 50).

This points to a critical period that is more extended than infancy. Take the school-age years as an example. We know from cross-cultural studies as well as the social sciences that a developmental transition, known as the "five to seven year shift," enables children to benefit from schooling and is associated with changes in behavior and cognition (White 1965, 1996). Although the exact age frame is sometimes debated (some researchers suggest that it begins at three and ends at ten, for example), there is agreement that children do indeed experience a developmental transition that affects their emotional as well as cognitive functioning (Sameroff and Haith 1996), thereby contributing to their ability to profit from schooling. Although brain development during the middle childhood years has not captured the public interest, Jeri Janowsky and Ruth Carper see this age period as crucial in brain development: "Regardless of the exact moment of synaptogenic peak, or the completion of dendritic growth, the early school age years are a time of connective or synaptic exuberance. The exuberance, at a time of increasing behavioral fine-tuning and behavioral complexity, sets the child up with ample neural material. . . . It may, in fact, be a time of the greatest availability of neural hardware in one's lifetime" (1996, 44).

That a critical period in brain development is not confined to infancy does not diminish the importance of environmental experiences, especially early in life, in shaping the brain. Traumatic experiences that result in stress have shown the possibility of damage to the deeper structures of the brain (Lombroso and Sapolsky 1998; Sapolsky 1996), as noted earlier in our example of abused children. In Chapter 8 we show that during prenatal and early postnatal periods, the presence of environmental hazards can have devastating consequences on development in general and the development of the brain in particular.

Positive experiences in the physical and psychological environment, and not only traumatic ones, also affect the brain by activating pathways and stimulating existing connections (Brown 1999; Siegel 1999). Such experiences need not be elaborate, as in the installation of mobiles over the child's crib or the broadcasting of musical recordings. Rather, simple and routine aspects of the physical environment such as noise, light, and temperature variations stimulate brain activity. Of significance also is the social and psychological environment—touching the baby, cooing and smiling at the baby, or otherwise responding to and playing with him or her—contribute to development. This offers an explanation for the developmental delays found among children who grew up in orphanages who were deprived of routine experiences and interactions.

Two points regarding environmental influences and the notion of critical periods should be underscored. First, although the neuroscience research provides much information about how the absence of experiences or the presence of hazards can negatively affect development, "it says virtually nothing about what to do to create enhanced or accelerated brain development" (Shonkoff and Phillips 2000, 183). Second, the sense of urgency associated with the notion of critical periods must be placed in context. The developing brain is open to influential experiences across a broad period of development. Critical periods have an abrupt ending, but there are also sensitive periods, which have a less abrupt ending.

To illustrate the abrupt ending characteristic of a critical period, consider the classic work of David Hubel and Torsten Wiesel (1970). These researchers studied the influence of early experience on visual cortex organization immediately after birth. They showed that animals, in this case kittens, whose eyes were deprived of normal visual experience during a specific and brief period of time were never able to obtain normal vision. The researchers arrived at the precise timing by undertaking shorter and shorter periods of time during which they placed a patch over one of the eyes in the study animals and by using animals of different ages. In older animals, deprivation of light and visual experience had no effect on the visual cortex, whereas in younger animals, visual deprivation resulted in irreversible damage. Lombroso and Pruett (2002) describe these studies, also noting that similar conclusions can be drawn from natural experiments with human infants and older individuals with cataracts; an infant born with a congenital cataract (which effectively restricts light and visual experience) that remains undetected or untreated during the first years of life will be blind in the affected eye even after the cataract is removed. However, when cataracts develop in adults, whose visual system is mature, normal vision is restored once the cataracts are removed.

In language acquisition, the critical period is not only longer but also more flexible: unlike with vision, the window of opportunity is not completely and abruptly shut at the end of the critical period. Hence it is easier for very young children to learn a second language, but it is not impossible for children to do so in later years, a point we cover in a later chapter. The same is true for other aspects of development, which leads to the preference for the term "sensitive period" when infancy is discussed in broad terms, since it implies less rigidity in the nature and timing of early experience (Shonkoff and Phillips 2000).

The Plasticity of the Brain

Regardless of whether we describe infancy as a critical or sensitive period, studies on the consequences of environmental deprivation support the notion that infancy and early childhood are important times during which to intervene with programs that ensure that all children have developmentally appropriate experiences. Also revealed in these studies is the plasticity, or malleability, of the brain; insults to the brain during critical periods can have possibly permanent consequences (see box, "The Brain in Adolescence"). Although it is vulnerable, the brain is thought to have the capacity for reorganization and can at times compensate for loss caused by injury or other trauma (Jansen and Low 1994).

Although the brain's capacity for reorganization and compensation remains unclear, animal and human studies provide insight. These show that the cerebral cortex in particular can reorganize. Hubel and Wiesel's studies (1970) showed that depriving one eye of light results in not only a failure of neural pathway formation in that eye but also an increase in neural connections in the other eye. Similarly, some victims of stroke can eventually recover some brain functions thought to be lost, leading researchers to note that there is hope in eventually finding effective therapies for many illnesses of the brain, such as Parkinson's disease and Alzheimer's (Blake 1997; Morris and Worsley 2002). Studies reviewed by Elizabeth Jansen and William Low (1994) and Harry Chugani (1998) reveal cortical reorganization following brain injury or trauma to the brain of children; this not only shows us how the brain works but also opens the way for thinking about new possibilities for intervention when damage has occurred.

The Brain in Adulthood

Although the findings relating to the brain's plasticity appear to have huge potential, brain plasticity does have limits. The brain cannot compensate, for example, in all cases of severe injury. Also, at times, the brain's ability to shift functions to another area in the brain comes at a cost: whereas rehabilitative progress may compensate for loss in one area of the brain, there may be a concurrent deterioration of abilities that previously belonged to this new area (Grafman and Littman 1995). Additionally, although cortical reorganization has been shown in both adults and children, the brain is more resilient and reorganization is therefore more effective at a younger age, before the central nervous system has matured (Jansen and Low 1994).

The Brain in Adolescence

Much of the lay interest in neuroscience has focused on brain development in infancy and early childhood. Some of the most exciting findings, however, come from imaging studies that show that substantial changes in the human brain's structure occur later in life. We have seen that changes in the brain occur during the middle childhood years. It is also becoming evident that the brain undergoes substantial changes during the teenage years.

Researchers do not yet know what accounts for the changes to the adolescent brain. But they are finding that the changes are based on the same "use it or lose it" principle that governs brain development early in life. That is, neural connections that are used are retained and those that are not used are discarded. Jay Giedd and his colleagues at the National Institute of Mental Health conducted imaging studies, repeatedly scanning the brain of the same 145 children as they grew up. They found that an overproduction of neurons and dendrites—once thought to be evident only very early in life—occurs just before puberty and is followed by a decline after adolescence, indicating that pruning had taken place (Giedd, Blumenthal, and Jeffries 1999; Thompson, Giedd, and Woods 2000).

Of significance with regard to this second wave of pruning is where in the brain it takes place. The brain does not develop as a whole all at once; rather, various regions within the brain develop in spurts at different times (Siegel 1999). The changes taking place in the adolescent's brain occur in the prefrontal cortex. The prefrontal cortex (it is right above the eyes, extending past the forehead) is the area responsible for "executive functions," such as planning, reasoning, controlling impulses, and understanding the consequences of behavior. The pruning in the prefrontal cortex that occurs during adolescence coincides with the time that the individual is experiencing physical and anatomical changes, forming relationships, and exploring his or her emerging independence. With the prefrontal cortex not yet mature and clear thinking difficult, the adolescent is vulnerable to making decisions or taking unnecessary risks that can have lifelong negative consequences (Lerner 2002).

Consider, for example, teenage drinking or abuse of other drugs. We have long known that teens are susceptible to peer pressure in this regard. What we are now finding from brain research on both animals and humans is that the impact of alcohol and drugs on the brain may be different during adolescence than it is later in life (Brown et al. 2000; Swatzwelder 1998). This sensitivity can result in injury to the developing region of the brain and eventual impairments to such mental processes as memory. It may also be at the root of the addiction that plagues many teens, an addiction so devastating that it is hard for some to overcome (Spear 2000).

In addition to increasing our understanding of brain changes that underlie teen behaviors and the vulnerability of teens to the effects of alcohol and other drugs, the research is leading to increased knowledge of brain diseases. Neuroscientists, for example, are taking a closer look at schizophrenia, a disease that lies dormant until after the frontal cortex has developed. Such studies will ultimately lead to more effective treatment options and, we hope, to prevention strategies. For now, what is significant to child development experts is that the new findings show that even during adolescence the brain is a work in progress.

Nevertheless, the brain keeps changing, especially in response to new experiences, throughout life. Most of us know this intuitively—we keep learning new things, changing our perceptions and understanding, maybe even becoming wiser—but until recently, this view was not reflected in brain research. In one of the most startling and controversial studies to date, researchers found that the adult brain actually produces new neurons. This is hotly debated and is quite a departure from previous findings of a mere decade ago that indicated that in the adult brain, the number of neurons remains static, with changes

occurring only in their connectivity (Rakic 1985). In the study, Elizabeth Gould and colleagues (1999) found that new neurons are generated daily in the cerebral cortex, which houses centers for higher intellectual functions. Although the study was done with monkeys (whose
use in research is found to be quite predictive of what happens in humans), it could have—if the results are replicated—far-reaching implications not only for the treatment of diseases of the brain but also
for our understanding of psychological development. The authors
note, for example, that the findings may eventually explain that one
function of the new neurons in the adult brain might be to encapsulate
new information as it is learned, perhaps recording and storing experiences into memory much like a moving tape. Keep in mind, however,
that the findings that the adult brain produces new neurons are as yet
preliminary and that other researchers have contested them (for example, Nowakowski and Hayes 2000).

Contributions of the Research
Research Methods

These and other exciting findings, which are transforming our understanding of the brain, are made possible by increasingly sophisticated
study methods. Many of the strategies we use for studying the brain
were developed centuries ago. In the 1860s, for example, French surgeon Paul Broca presented a case study of an individual with brain
damage, noting the localization of a specific area for aspects of language, to this date still called "Broca's area." Improvements to the microscope in the nineteenth century and the subsequent introduction of
techniques in staining neural tissue enhanced the study of the brain,
eventually enabling researchers to provide a phrenological map that
shows various regions and distinct mental functions within the brain
(Mundale 1998). Classic studies using animals have shown the impact
of the environment on brain development, and studies based on dam-
aged and dead human brains have, over the years, added to our store of
knowledge.

However, the recent development of new techniques is enabling
enormous progress, opening new opportunities for the study of the
brain. For example, advances in molecular genetics make it possible
not only to identify specific genes but to separate genes from an ani-

mal's genome and study the effect on brain development (Johnson 1999a). Using this approach, researchers have found, for example, that the deletion of a certain gene prevents rats from learning specific tasks (Silva et al. 1992).

Not only in genetics but in neuroscience the development of sophisticated tools is enabling researchers to study brain activity in individuals, through both recording and imaging techniques. Electrophysiological recording techniques are used to record the electrical activity of neurons and are often useful in studying information processing in the brain. Several electrophysiological recording techniques exist. One example is event-related potentials (ERPs), which measure the electrical activity generated as neuronal groups fire, either in response to stimuli or in reaction to spontaneous, natural brain rhythms. Other recording techniques for tracking the brain's electrical activity from the outside include electroencephalograms (EEG) and magnetoencephalography (MEG). In studies using such techniques, an individual wears a cap with electrodes that pick up brain waves during certain events, such as looking at a picture. Even infants can be tested with such techniques because they are not invasive (Gopnik, Meltzoff, and Kuhl 1999). In addition to these non invasive methods, invasive applications of recording techniques are used in animal studies (and in humans undergoing neurosurgery) to gain insight into what is happening at the basic unit of information processing—that is, the individual neuron (Stein, Wallace, and Stanford 1998)—in which case an electrode must actually penetrate the neuron.

Perhaps the most widely acclaimed of the new techniques is neuroimaging, which allows researchers to observe brain activity in healthy individuals, often as they are performing cognitive tasks. Two widely used imaging techniques are positron-emission topography (PET) and functional magnetic resonance imaging (fMRI). Both are based on the principle that when areas of the brain increase in activity, a series of physiological changes takes place. Both imaging techniques measure these changes, but in different ways, PET by tracking increased blood associated with increased activity in a brain region and fMRI by tracking changes in the concentration of oxygen in the blood (Buckner and Petersen 1998). Imaging techniques have limitations. At this time, for example, they have poor resolution, hence our inability, noted earlier in the chapter, to ascertain the defining limits of brain regions. Also, as Peter Huttenlocher (1990) points out, interpretations of imaging studies must be made cautiously; development is an ongoing, dynamic process, but imaging studies provide a glimpse of only one point in time. Nevertheless, these and other sophisticated research techniques not only provide a window into the function of the brain, they corroborate what we know about human development from other disciplines, expanding areas of study and adding to our knowledge (see box, "A Focus on the Problem, not the Technique").

Expanding Areas of Inquiry

Recent research in psychology reveals that three stages of memory include encoding information, storing the information, and retrieving it in recall. Although previous techniques in studying the brain have been of limited use in studying memory, imaging techniques are useful in this regard. For example, individuals may be presented with information before a brain scan, and brain areas that are active when the individual is asked to recall (retrieval stage) the information can reveal which areas of the brain are being used. Using such techniques, interesting findings emerge. For example, whereas it was previously thought that areas in the brain's medial temporal lobe were involved in long-term memory, imaging studies are showing that areas in the prefrontal cortex are actually activated in some tasks associated with memory retrieval, thus significantly expanding the area of inquiry and leading researchers to pose a new set of questions with regards to memory (Buckner and Petersen 1998).

Forming New Theories

As new brain studies present findings, they not only change our understanding about development but also help us form new theories. An example is the research on autism. Leo Kanner (1942) first identified autism about sixty years ago. As we discussed earlier in this chapter, early studies on autistic children focused on environmental explanations, some noting that the parents of autistic children were cold and unresponsive. However, since researchers have been sleuthing for a bi-

---

A Focus on the Problem, not the Technique

Space precludes our discussing all the new techniques used today in brain research. Yet it is important to note that although a great deal of attention is paid to the development of sophisticated means of studying the brain, neuroscientists are, as Barry Stein, Mark Wallace, and Terrence Stanford write, "problem-oriented rather than technique-oriented" (1998, 434). In other words, as useful as each individual technique is, it provides only part of the picture. Scientists therefore typically combine the information from several studies using several methods. In addition, they derive insight into the brain, and often a starting point for their studies, using research findings from the behavioral and social sciences.

---

ological explanation, having found that several genes contribute to the expression of autism, no consensus exists as to how environmental conditions contribute to gene malfunction or to when in development malfunction occurs. Some researchers (Bauman and Kemper 1985, 1994; Courchense 1991) contend that gene malfunction leading to autism occurs early during the prenatal period, specifically either during the first month, when the genes lay down the basic body and neural structures, or during the second trimester, when certain circuits are wired. However, with brain studies showing that a significant part of brain development occurs after birth, there are now hypotheses suggesting that something can go awry postpartum rather than prenatally. That autistic children appear to be normal until their second year of life lends some support to this hypothesis.

In the meantime, brain studies continue to increase our understanding of the disorder. Margaret Bauman and Thomas Kemper (1985), for example, studied brain tissues obtained from autopsies of autistic children and adults and found abnormalities in three areas of the brain: parts of the frontal lobe were thicker than normal; cells in the limbic system were smaller but more numerous; and immature cells with stunted connections were present in the cerebellum. Symptoms of autism can be traced to each of these areas of the brain. There are other brain studies. Some, for example, show that autistic children are more sensitive, rather than less sensitive, to environmental stimuli, which provides new information on the disorder as well as an understanding that autistic children may be overwhelmed by environmental stimulation. In addition, armed with the recent understanding of the plasticity of brain (that is, its ability to restore function and regenerate cells), researchers are developing therapeutic techniques in the hope of figuring out how to intercept the errant wiring that is evident in the autistic brain.

Collaborations

The research in neuroscience, and especially the techniques developed to study the brain, is being applied to studies in developmental psychology, leading to collaborations among researchers across disciplines. This is evident in such emerging areas of study as cognitive neuroscience as well as in individual studies that elucidate our understanding of aspects of development and contribute to the development of new theories.

The investigation of infants' ability to recognize faces early in life is an example. In the 1960s developmental psychologists developed complex techniques to study the newborn's ability to see, as well as to ascertain visual scanning patterns in newborns. Using such tools as infrared cameras, researchers found that some objects, especially facelike objects, are of special interest to newborns and that even shortly after birth babies prefer to track facelike patterns as opposed to scrambled patterns. Although such findings were used to provide support for the notion that the infant's preference to faces is innate, other studies have shown that face processing may be an acquired skill developed only after several months' exposure to faces in the environment (Cohen and Salapatek 1975). Mark Johnson (1999b) reviews neuroimaging studies showing that a particular region in the cortex is activated when infants are shown faces. He also reviews biological data that indicate that not only one but two brain systems are used in visually guided behavior in human infants. Subsequent neuroimaging and other studies by Johnson and his colleagues (de Haan, Oliver, and Johnson 1998; Morton and Johnson 1991) have led to the conclusion that at least three factors are involved with respect to infants' preference for faces: first, the primitive tendency of newborns to orient toward facelike patterns; second, the presence of many faces in the infant's normal environment; and third, the activation of cerebral cortical circuits when faces are within the infant's visual field. Johnson notes that these three factors acting in concert result in the "inevitable outcome" of the brain's developing the specialization for processing faces: "This specialization is not 'coded for' by the genes, or is not just the result of passive exposure to faces, but it is the result of an active process in which the infant's own behavior selects the appropriate input for its still-developing brain" (1999b, 156).

From this brief example of face recognition in infants it becomes clear how the research in developmental psychology is advanced when imaging techniques and brain studies are used to explore aspects of child development. Not only is the information of interest in and of itself, but it also shows how genes and experiences interact in brain development. It seems unlikely that any neuroscientist working in isolation would have chosen to study face preferences in babies, but because scientists are building on the research from the social sciences and collaborating with researchers in developmental psychology, contributions and advances in knowledge are occurring in both fields. In this chapter we've presented only a small portion of what we are learning about the brain, and in many ways, much of this knowledge, while corroborating what we know, is a work in progress. New lessons are being learned, and implicit in these are applications for programs and policies, which is our focus in the chapters that follow.

3

Family Leave

The transition to parenthood, no matter how joyful, is one of the most stressful experiences in the life of a family. It is only over time that a mutually satisfying parent-infant relationship begins to emerge, time that is often unavailable to the many parents who must return to the workplace too soon after the birth or adoption of a child. Some infants are placed in out-of-home care as early as two weeks after birth, and there is widespread concern that placing a child in substitute care at this age may be detrimental to both child and parents.

Although most new parents immediately cherish their infant, it takes time to develop the emotions and behaviors that ensure a strong sense of mutual attachment and form the critical underpinnings for healthy social and cognitive development, especially for first-time parents unaccustomed to reading and responding to an infant's behavioral cues. Learning that even the tiniest babies are active participants in this new relationship, shaping their parents' behaviors as parents influence theirs, is strongly facilitated when the members of this new family can spend as much time together as possible (Belsky, Spanier, and Rovine 1983; Brazelton and Greenspan 2000; Stern 1974). The earliest days and months of life, in which parent or parents and child read each other's signals and respond in a timely and loving fashion, over and over again, represent a sensitive period in the development of reciprocal relationships (Bronfenbrenner 1988; Pruett 1999; C. T. Ramey and

S. L. Ramey 1999; Zigler, Hopper, and Hall 1993). The child's development of a sense that the world is a stable, predictable place depends largely on a sense of continuity and responsiveness provided by the presence of a small number of consistently present caregivers.

The demands of the workplace, however, often conflict with parents' needs during this time. Women who must return to employment outside the home before they feel ready to do so report feeling stressed, guilty, and cheated out of an important experience (Farber, Alejandro-Wright, and Muenchow 1988; Zigler and Frank 1988). Not only the mother but often the entire family will pay a high price for forgoing time at home with a new infant.

A Policy Response

Policy makers at all levels of government and business administration have been made aware of, if they are not always willingly or rapidly responsive to, changes in family life and the evolving family-work relationship (Frank and Zigler 1996). The context within which U.S. families grow and develop changed radically during the second half of the twentieth century for a large proportion of our nation's children. The most striking change stems from an increase—beginning during World War II and continuing to the present day (Coontz 1997; Skolnik 1991)—in the percentage of women in the out-of-home workforce, a change attributable in part to the economic need for two incomes in most families, and in part to the rise of single-parent households, the vast majority of which are headed by women.

Women's patterns of employment in the United States increasingly resemble those of men. Most American women participate in the labor force; whether single or married, they enter into paid labor for the same reasons that men do: to support themselves and their families. In 1960, fewer than one woman out of five returned to the workplace once she had children; today almost three-fourths of women who take maternity leave return to work and do so within six months of giving birth (Kamerman and Kahn 1991). Fifty-eight percent of women in the labor force today have a child younger than twelve months of age, and 65 percent of single mothers of infants are in the out-of-home workforce (U.S. Department of Labor 2000).

What Are the Provisions of the FMLA?

Your job—or, under certain circumstances, a comparable job with equal pay and benefits—will be protected while you take leave:

- If you are having or adopting a baby or your spouse is having a baby
- If you are caring for a child, parent, or spouse with a serious health condition
- If you yourself have a serious health condition or are pregnant
- For up to twelve weeks in any year (leave may be taken intermittently as needed; two parents are *each* entitled to twelve weeks of leave unless they work for the same employer, who may require that they take no more than a total of twelve weeks of leave)

You are covered under FMLA if:

- Your employer has had fifty or more employees on the payroll for at least twenty work weeks during the current or previous year, working within seventy-five miles of *your* worksite
- You have worked for your employer for at least twelve months and have worked at least 1,250 hours during the previous year

During your job-protected leave:

- Your employer is not obligated by the law to pay you
- Some employers may provide some pay through disability insurance programs

■ Your employer must continue to pay for your health insurance coverage

Note: The complete text and provisions of the Family and Medical Leave Act can be found at www.dol.gov/dol/allcfr/ESA/Title_29/Part_825/Subpart_B.htm

The most significant policy response to this demographic reality has been the passage and implementation of the Family and Medical Leave Act, or FMLA (see box, "What Are the Provisions of the FMLA?"). Parental leave legislation came before Congress in 1985. Versions of this bill came before Congress again in 1987 and in 1989 before both houses finally passed it in 1990. President George Bush, however, vetoed it. Congress passed the bill again in 1991, and although the bill enjoyed overwhelming popular support, opposition from business and industry groups prompted President Bush to veto it again. The Family and Medical Leave Act was finally signed into law by President Bill Clinton in 1993 as one of the first official acts of his first term in office (see box, "The History of Family Leave in the United States").

The United States was among the last of the world's industrialized nations to establish a national parental leave policy; among advanced industrialized countries, only the United States, Australia, and New Zealand lack a paid parental leave (see box, "Family Leave: The International Context"). The Family and Medical Leave Act has allowed more than twenty million families to take leave following childbirth or adoption (Lichtman 1999). Over twice that many families, however, are ineligible for leave under the FMLA. Only about half of U.S. workers meet eligibility criteria for taking a family leave after the birth or adoption of a child, and far fewer can actually afford to do so (Commission on Family and Medical Leave 1996; National Partnership for Women and Families 1999a, 1999b, 2000). In addition, only 2 percent of full-time workers are employed by companies that voluntar-

The History of Family Leave in the United States

1908 The first federal legislation mandating maternity leave is specifically tied the purpose of the leave, to protect women's health

1978 The Pregnancy Disability Amendment to Title VII of the Civil Rights Act is passed, prohibiting workplace discrimination based on pregnancy

1985 The Yale University Bush Center in Child Development and Social Policy releases the results of two years' work by a multidisciplinary committee on infant care leave, which recommends six months' job-protected leave with partial income replacement

1985 The predecessor of the Family and Medical Leave Act is introduced in the 99th Congress by Senator Christopher Dodd (D-Conn.); the bill is never reported out of committee in the Senate

1987 Connecticut becomes the first state to pass a family and medical leave bill; Minnesota, Oregon, and Rhode Island soon follow suit

1990 The FMLA, studied and proposed since the 1970s, is passed by Congress and vetoed by President George Bush

1991 The 102d Congress again passes the FMLA; again President Bush vetoes it

1993 Congress passes the FMLA a third time; President Bill Clinton signs it into law

1999 President Clinton proposes to allow states to use unemployment insurance and/or temporary disability insurance to cover wage replacement during parental leaves

ily provide paid family leave (Harris 2001). The United States differs from most other developed—and many developing—nations in that federal family leave policy covers only a small percentage of workers and provides no wage replacement (see table 1). Although 79 percent of Americans support the development of plans to provide income replacement in association with family leave-taking, policy makers have been slow to respond to this demand (National Partnership for Women and Families 1999a).

Has the FMLA Been Effective?

Almost a decade after the original implementation of the Family and Medical Leave Act, there is good news and bad news. Dire scenarios envisioned by business groups opposed to the original passage of the act have not materialized. The provisions of the plan have been, as a rule, both easier and more cost-effective to administer than most private-sector groups had anticipated (Commission on Family and Medical Leave 1996; Galinsky and Bond 1998). The news for families, however, has been less positive. Although the FMLA has achieved for millions of families what Congress and President Clinton, aided in their endeavors by policy experts, developmental psychologists, pediatricians, and business analysts (for example, National Partnership for Women and Families 1999a–d and Zigler and Frank 1988), originally intended, millions more are left out in the cold, either ineligible to take leave because of the size or nature of the business for which they work or because (as is most often the case) taking an unpaid leave is not a viable option. Even with the FMLA in place, American parents are often forced to chose from a limited range of less-than-optimal alternatives: one parent, usually the mother, must stay home, at the risk of the family's economic stability, or parents must place their infant in substitute care long before they feel ready to do so.

This is not simply a matter of squeamishness or sentimentality on the parents' part. Given the parlous state of child care in the United States and the potential for detrimental effects related to both cognitive and social development, as we have described earlier (Belsky 1986; Lamb et al. 1992; Phillips et al. 1987; Sroufe 1988), it is not surprising that many families feel that their only choice is between placing a child

Family Leave: The International Context

As in the United States, rising rates of maternal employment in the second half of the twentieth century have spurred policy architects to seek creative solutions for families—and nations—worried about the consequences of having to juggle work and family life. Concern about the cognitive and developmental outcomes of early and persistent placement in supplemental child care has also motivated other nations who are traditionally more child-oriented than the United States to develop a set of effective policy responses to these issues.

Almost all industrialized nations now have a cohesive policy mandating paid maternity leaves, parental leaves (which may be taken for extended periods by either or both the mother or father of a new baby), and, in some nations, other child-related leave (for example, for parents to attend school events or see to a child's medical care). The European Union now has in place a mandated fourteen-week maternity leave (Kamerman 2000b). These nations have put a number of funding mechanisms in place, among them temporary disability insurance, unemployment insurance, the use of a family allowance, and a social insurance benefit.

The provisions of each country's parental leave plans vary, but throughout the European Union, parental leaves are increasingly normative and are increasingly long enough to be a realistic substitute for the use of supplemental infant care. The United States remains among the few countries to have no paid leave and is the only advanced industrialized nation to have such a short leave. Among member nations of the Organization for Economic Cooperation and Development,* only the United States, Australia, and New Zealand lack a paid parental leave (Kamerman 2000b).

Sheila Kamerman notes that the main differences underlying U.S. and foreign parental leave policies are ideological: in the United States the policy is conceived largely as an employee benefit, one which, because it typically provides no wage replacement and because of narrow restrictions on small businesses, is inaccessible to most parents. In Europe, by contrast, family leave programs are specifically designed to encourage employees to remain at home with their young infants (Kamerman 2000b). Alternatively, because European programs include significant wage replacement, they offer parents the choice to remain within or to return to the paid labor force and still be able to afford high quality infant care.

This notion of parental choice in the area of infant care is strongly tied to European parental leave policies, though little has been made of this connection in the United States (Kamerman 2001a; Kamerman and Kahn 1991). The availability of adequate parental leave programs in Europe is clearly one variable in their less frequent (compared to that of U.S. parents) use of infant care programs (Kamerman 2000b).

In sharp contrast to the standard in the United States, parental leave in the other OECD countries is available to virtually every new mother, and nearly all mothers take the opportunity to stay home with their infants for some or all of the time permitted. The average childbirth-related leave in the OECD is thirty-six weeks, which sometimes includes predelivery time off. In all OECD nations but the United States, health care coverage is guaranteed for the childbirth. The average wage replacement during leave in OECD nations ranges 70 percent to 100 percent, with slightly lower wages available for more extended parental leaves in some nations. The only eligibility criterion for new mothers in most nations is a history of employment; in Sweden, Norway, and Denmark, this standard can be waived. And although parental leave was originally extended only to the biological parents of a child, the trend in OECD nations is to make leave available to adoptive parents as well. Paternity leaves tend to be shorter than leaves for mothers, ranging from a few days to a few weeks, but a great many fathers (up to 90 percent in Sweden) take advantage of them.

* *OECD member nations:* Australia, Austria, Belgium, Canada, Czech Republic, Denmark, Finland, France, Germany, Greece, Hungary, Iceland, Ireland, Italy, Japan, Korea, Luxembourg, Mexico, Netherlands, New Zealand, Norway, Poland, Portugal, Spain, Sweden, Switzerland, Turkey, United Kingdom, and United States

Table 1. Sample parental leave provisions of OECD nations

Nation[a]	Time off	Income Replacement (%)
Austria	16 weeks	100
Belgium	15 weeks	75–80
England	18 weeks	100
France	16 weeks	100
Germany	14 weeks	100
Italy	20 weeks[b]	80
Luxembourg	16 weeks	100
Norway	52 weeks	100[c]
Spain	16 weeks	100
Sweden	78 weeks	80[d]

Source: Kamerman 2000b

Notes: [a] In some nations listed, a longer parental or child rearing leave is also available and is typically paid at a lower rate than the initial maternity leave
[b] Two months before birth
[c] The first 42 weeks are paid at 100%; remaining weeks at 80% of income
[d] Twelve additional weeks are available at a flat rate, and twelve more with no income replacement

in substandard child care and risking the family's economic stability by taking an unpaid leave of absence from work during the earliest weeks or months of the child's life. Of particular relevance here is Sheila B. Kamerman's (2000a, b) observation that the use of infant care is significantly lower in nations with a paid infant care leave.

A bipartisan federal Commission on Family Leave (1996) has reported to Congress its findings relevant to the outcomes to date of the FMLA. This report includes an in-depth analysis of family leave policy and extensive survey data containing information on the effect of implementing the FMLA on employers and employees. Among the highlights of the commission's findings are the following employer-related outcomes:

- Employers have found implementation of the FMLA easier and less costly than many had anticipated

- Over 90 percent of employers comply with key provisions of the FMLA and call the regulations "very easy" to implement; many employers voluntarily implement more generous benefits than the law requires (Galinsky and Bond 1998)
- Between 89 percent and 98.5 percent (depending on type of business) report no cost or only small costs involved with implementing the FMLA
- Smaller businesses have incurred relatively smaller, not larger, FMLA-related expenses, contrary to predictions made by business groups before the FMLA was passed
- Many larger firms (250 or more employees) report cost *savings* associated with the FMLA, mostly from reduced employee turnover and training; these firms also report enhanced productivity and goodwill among employees because of job-protected family and medical leaves (see also National Partnership 2001)
- Only 53 percent of employers provide any form of income replacement during leaves (Galinsky and Bond 1998)

The commission also reported the following family-related outcomes:

- More than twenty million families have been able to take advantage of the provisions of the FMLA since its implementation in 1993.
- Far too many families are either ineligible for leave under the provisions of the FMLA or cannot take leave because no provision is included for income replacement during their leave. Of new mothers surveyed who were eligible for but did not take maternity-related leave under the FMLA, 100 percent cited lack of replacement income as the main reason.
- Over 11 percent of female leave-takers are forced to rely on public assistance during at least part of their leave.
- Accurate information about eligibility requirements and provisions of the FMLA are not always readily available to employees. Only 27.5 percent of leave-taking employees

surveyed had heard about the FMLA from their employer; they were more likely to have obtained the necessary information from family members, the media, or their union.

The Science of Family Leave Policy

Social science adds an important component to our understanding of the time parents need with newborn infants. Decades of research on parent-infant interaction (Brazelton 1986; Stern 1974) demonstrate that parents and their infants need time to establish a pattern of interaction that will enable them to recognize and respond to each other's signals. This attunement to each other's rhythms provides an important foundation in the infants' developing sense of self. Through their interaction with their parents, infants come to realize that they can influence and affect their environment. Infants then begin to build a sense of security and trust within the family relationship and environment.

Even during an infant's earliest weeks, research shows that the interactions between infants and parents are reciprocal and bidirectional, meaning that infants influence the nature of these interactions rather than being passive objects of parental behaviors. These early interactions, which have been compared to an intricate dance in which the partners take cues from one another to synchronize their steps (Brazelton, Koslowski, and Maine 1974), enable babies to accomplish the most fundamental developmental task of all: forming trusting relationships (Erikson 1959, 1963).

It is through these interactions—brief and minor, but occurring hundreds, even thousands of times over the course of the first days and weeks in the life of the new family—that infants come to trust that their needs will be met. For this to occur, however, a certain level of continuity must be achieved. Should the caregiving environment change too radically, or should the infants' cues not bring consistent, rapid, nurturing responses, the child's sense that the world is a stable, predictable, loving place may be impaired (Hopper and Zigler 1988). Because this stability is critical as a foundation from which the infant feels safe enough to explore and learn about his world (Bretherton 1985; Parke 1981), the ramifications for both social and cognitive development are profound.

Research on the family system also supports the need for granting parental care leaves. The period immediately following birth has been described as significant for the redefining of family roles (Belsky 1985; Goldberg and Easterbrooks 1984; Minuchin 1985). Following the birth or introduction of a new child, all family members—mothers, fathers, siblings, and grandparents—need time to adjust and renegotiate their family relationships and roles. Each member of the family feels disruption at the entrance of a baby. Time is needed to allow for a comfortable transition and to regain family equilibrium. Although these relationships are dynamic and do continue to change, the introduction of a newborn into the family is one of the most important transitional periods in a family's life (see box, "Laying the Groundwork: The Infant Care Leave Project").

The time new parents must spend at work can interfere significantly with parent-infant interaction. The more hours parents spend at work, the fewer hours they spend engaging in play, as distinct from other caregiving activities, with their babies (Goldberg and Easterbrooks 1984). Parents who attempt to compensate for time away from their babies by forcing "quality time" during their hours together may actually become less responsive, ignoring their infants' social cues and responses, which may cause their infant to withdraw from interaction in an effort to avoid over-stimulation (Brazelton et al. 1974; Cohen 1982). When parent-infant time must regularly be squeezed into the afterwork hours, interaction between fathers and babies, and between the two parents, also tends to be crowded out (Pederson et al. 1982).

A solid body of behavioral and observational research clearly supports the notion that this is a critical time in the life of a child, not the *only* important time, but one that will lay the groundwork for later growth and development. The need for continuity of care, for an environment in which an infant can reasonably expect its needs to be met, appropriately, with warmth and affection and respect for the infant's active role in the thousands of tiny interactions that form the basis for his or her relationships with others, is beyond question (Brazelton and Greenspan 2000; C. T. Ramey and S. L. Ramey 1999).

The new note sounding in this discussion is that contributed by fledgling neurological research. Far from demonstrating that the rou-

Laying the Groundwork: The Infant Care Leave Project

In 1983, a multiphase project designed to explore the rationale for and feasibility of a national infant care leave law was launched at Yale University's Bush Center in Child Development and Social Policy by Bush Center director Edward Zigler. As the first comprehensive evaluation of the need for such a leave, the mechanisms by which it might be achieved and funded, and the potential implications of adopting a large-scale infant-care leave policy, this work formed the foundation of what eventually became the Family and Medical Leave Act.

The research undertaken as a part of this broad-based study included surveys of new mothers, psychological and sociological analyses of the family and of the state of infant care in the United States, historical analysis of maternity leave job-protection policies, demographic analysis, a look at comparable or potential model programs from other nations, investigations of private-sector leave policies being used by both large and small employers, national and state perspectives on the need for legislation, possible mechanisms for funding a paid leave program, and the legal ramifications of implementing a national family leave policy.

Once these individual pieces of research were complete, they were submitted for study to the Advisory Committee on Infant Care Leave, an interdisciplinary group made up of noted experts in the fields of child development, social policy, medicine, law, sociology, business, finance, government, and labor. After careful review of the broad body of research produced by the Bush Center, this committee issued national policy recommendations on 10 December 1985. In recognition of the urgent need for leave to care for a newborn, the committee recommended a six-month, job-protected infant-care leave for working parents, three of those months with partial wage replacement and three of them unpaid (Zigler and Frank 1988). In spite of this recommendation, Congress was able to pass only a twelve-week unpaid leave during its last session of 1992; even this minimal proposal was vetoed—twice—by President George Bush.

tine, quotidian events that transpire in an infant's world are unimportant, investigations of the workings of the brain and the neurochemistry associated with social interactions and cognitive events provide the strongest support for what we have long known: these early interactions are critical to the child's well-being, ability to explore and learn, and ability to negotiate effectively the stresses associated with everyday life. Research into the biochemistry of stress reactions, for instance (Gunnar et al. 1996; Hertsgaard et al. 1995; Nachmias et al. 1996; Tout et al. 1998), indicates that potential stresses, such as those associated with negotiating novel situations, are mediated by a child's secure attachment to her caregivers. Toddlers in one study (Nachmias et al. 1999) were invited to play with a live clown. Even though they showed every indication of being frightened by the experience, children who were securely attached to the parent with them (as measured earlier, on a different day) experienced no rise in stress hormones. In contrast, equally frightened children whose attachment to the parent with them had been rated less favorably showed a marked rise in stress hormones when approached by the clown.

The study of the relations among environmental inputs, experience, and neurological change is still in its infancy (Shonkoff and Phillips 2000), but there is already a solid body of research that shows strong correlations between experience and not only transient changes in the body's neurochemistry but profound and lasting changes to the actual architecture of the brain and central nervous system (recall, for instance, the persistent neurological impact of abusive experiences mentioned in the preceding chapter). As our ability to assess more easily and with greater sensitivity the impact of early experience on the whole child—behavior, neurochemistry, and brain physiology—matures, we feel certain that this body of data will support what observational research has shown us all along: that responsiveness and consistency in infancy are essential components of optimal development.

Making the Transition from an Unpaid to a Paid Family Leave

The report to Congress on outcomes accruing from the implementation of the Family and Medical Leave Act included a number of recommendations for strengthening and broadening the accessibility of family and medical leaves under the act. The National Partnership for Women and Families and other groups have also proposed improvements to family leave legislation. These include:

- Establishing a narrower exemption. The FMLA is currently applicable only to businesses employing fifty or more individuals. The commission's report to Congress proposed extending the benefits of the FMLA to businesses with twenty-five or more employees (at least one commissioner has suggested that the number be lowered to fifteen employees). Critics argue that the costs of administering the FMLA at this level would be prohibitively expensive for small business owners, but data collected on the impact of the FMLA on employers actually indicates that small businesses spend proportionately *less* on FMLA administration than do larger employers.

- Amending both tenure and hour requirements for FMLA eligibility. The act requires that employees have been on the job for at least twelve months before becoming eligible to take leave under the FMLA and that they have worked at least 1,250 hours during the previous twelve months. The report to Congress included recommendations that both of these requirements be changed to expand eligibility.

- The development of model systems for FMLA record-keeping.

- The enforcement of health benefit protection. Nine percent of employees surveyed by the commission reported having lost some form of health benefits during their leave.

- Increasing public education on family and medical leave. Most employees surveyed had not obtained information about their rights under the FMLA from their employers, citing instead as information sources friends and family members; television, newspapers and magazines; and unions. The commission recommended the establishment of a toll-free information number, public service announcements in different media, employer education, and other actions to increase overall public awareness of the act and its provisions.

- The expansion of leave-qualifying events. This recommendation of the National Partnership for Women and Families (1999a) would extend coverage under the FMLA to include more family needs, such as attending parent-teacher meetings and other school functions, and to help victims of domestic violence care for themselves and their children.
- The provision of wage replacement of some kind.

Each of the commission's recommendations was to some extent controversial. Few were made unanimously. No issue before the commission was as thorny, however, as that concerning income replacement during the leave. Senator Larry Craig (R-Idaho), for instance, voiced his opposition to providing income replacement to leave-takers: "Of course there are employees who do not take unpaid leave because they cannot afford to do so. This is a simple fact of life. Of course those employees that do take such leaves may well suffer financial hardships when they take an unpaid leave. This, too, is a simple fact of life. These factors, alone, do not justify leaves provided under the act becoming paid in whole or in part in the interest of uniformity of justice" (Commission on Leave 1996, 233).

It seems highly unlikely that a federal mandate for wage replacement during FMLA leaves will be enacted in the near future. Impediments to such a plan include not only differences of political and philosophical opinion such as that expressed by Senator Craig but also issues related to the rights of various branches of government to make changes in laws governing the use of funds set aside for other purposes. In May 1999, for instance, President Clinton announced his intention to allow states to use funds earmarked for unemployment insurance (UI) or temporary disability insurance (TDI) to provide partial income replacement during family leave (Wisensale 2001). Questions immediately arose over whether the executive branch had the legal right to rewrite federal jobless aid policies to extend the use of these monies for this purpose when they had previously been tied specifically to job-seeking behavior (Pear 1999). Business groups argued that such a move would lead to an increase in employer taxes (though others, like the National Employment Law Project, responded that unemployment trust fund accounts are healthy enough to shoulder the additional burden). Conservative policy makers like William Archer (R-Tex.) argued that such a move would "pit out of work Americans against their neighbors who have jobs" (Heymann 2001; Pear 1999; Wisensale 2001). Supporters of the president's plan noted that costs to the UI and TDI programs would be offset in large part by obviating the need for some FMLA employees (9 percent overall and 11.6 percent of women) to rely on public assistance during leaves. Such reactions evoke the concerns of policy analysts like Gil Steiner, who predicted several decades ago that the development of a coherent family policy system in the United States would be, even if achievable, characterized by turf wars and the conflicts which inevitably arise when the groups affected by a policy or proposed policy face off over its potential consequences (Steiner 1981).

Temporary disability insurance is the most common means of providing salary replacement during a family or medical leave. TDI policies replace some or all of the employee's salary during periods of disability (including time off related to pregnancy and childbirth). These salary reimbursement systems are in use throughout the nation, having been applied by both large and small businesses for more than half a century. TDI coverage is offered by many private companies and mandated in at least five states: California, Hawaii, New Jersey, New York, and Rhode Island. The New York and New Jersey programs offer employers the option of subscribing to a state-administered disability insurance plan, an approved private plan, or an approved self-insured plan. Hawaii provides TDI coverage through private insurance carriers, and the California and Rhode Island TDI plans are administered by the state. Most TDI plans are funded through regular employee contributions, sometimes in concert with employer contributions (mandated or voluntary, depending on individual state regulations). TDI programs, for which administrative procedures are already in place, are notable for their low cost and capacity to see families through times of income crisis; coupled with the FMLA's health care coverage and guarantee of employment following parental leave, wage replacement or partial wage replacement through TDI could make the taking of a leave following the birth or adoption of the child a reality for a significant proportion of parents.

Initiatives proposed in several states, including Massachusetts and Illinois, would offer leave benefits through the UI system, typically for the twelve weeks presently provided for under the FMLA, but in at least one case (Vermont) for up to twenty-six weeks. Opponents of this use of UI benefits argue, however, that the law as written does not allow funds to be allocated for those who are on leave from actual employment; proponents of the plan believe that legal precedent exists giving individual states the flexibility to define plan eligibility more broadly.

New Department of Labor regulations, however (Connecticut Task Force on Family and Medical Leave 2000), propose to permit states to use just these funds or others of their choosing or devising, to help close the income gap represented by unpaid leave offered under the FMLA. Individual states have been given considerable discretion in designing individual programs, which will be evaluated (with a focus on cost effectiveness and impact on employers) after four years. The Department of Labor will then decide whether to make such plans permanent. As of this writing, at least eleven states (Connecticut, California, Iowa, Maryland, Massachusetts, Minnesota, New Hampshire, New Jersey, New York, Vermont, and Washington) are considering and costing out a number of income replacement plans. Average costs of various plans have been lower than anticipated by critics. A number of plans under consideration in Connecticut, for example, are projected to cost employers between $.04 and $1.45 per leave-taking employee per week; estimated weekly per-employee costs of expanding state UI or TDI programs to cover family and medical leaves in a sample of other states range from $.11 in Washington to $1.25 in Massachusetts (see table 2).

Family leave is but one important part of a package of public policy initiatives that support children and their families from birth through old age (Steiner 1981). In addition to a more comprehensive family leave policy than the FMLA, parents need the kinds of options that are afforded to parents in other countries in the form of family allowance policies and high-quality, affordable child care.

Table 2. State initiatives under consideration for financing family and medical leaves

One of the ironies of family leave legislation is that individual states moved more quickly and more decisively than did the federal government to research and pass family leave legislation; Connecticut, for instance, became the first state to pass a family leave law (in 1987). As of 1999, nineteen states had passed and implemented family leave laws that were in one or more ways more generous than the FMLA (for example, concerning employers covered, more generous definitions of family members covered or events for which leave can be taken, and so on). With respect to the passage of legislation permitting income replacement during a family-oriented leave, states are again taking the lead over federal policy-making. The following states are considering plans that would implement wage replacement plans based on a variety of funding mechanisms.

Temporary Disability Insurance: California, Massachusetts, New Jersey, and New York and Puerto Rico have TDI systems in place or are conducting studies of the cost of permitting the use of TDI benefits for families taking parental leave.

Unemployment Compensation: Arizona, Connecticut, Florida, Georgia, Hawaii, Illinois, Indiana, Kansas, Louisiana, Maryland, Massachusetts, Minnesota, Mississippi, Missouri, Nebraska, New Jersey,* New Mexico, Oregon, Pennsylvania, Texas, Vermont, and Washington have evaluated the costs of permitting leave-taking employees to collect income through unemployment insurance, or have such programs in place.

TANF Overruns: Massachusetts is exploring the use of Temporary Assistance to Needy Families block grant surpluses for wage replacement during family and medical leaves.

Other: Colorado, Connecticut, Hawaii, Iowa, Illinois, Maine, Maryland, Minnesota, New Hampshire, Oklahoma, New Jersey, Vermont, Virginia, and Wisconsin are investigating other options, including the use of general tax revenues, the creation of special trust funds or other accounts, or making use of UI/TDI hybrid programs.

*States considering multiple initiatives are listed under more than one category
Sources: Jordon 1999; Lichtman 1999; Women's Statewide Legislative Network 1999

In addition to the human costs and benefits of family leave (see, for example, Commission on Leave 1996), the economic ramifications—both positive and negative—must be carefully and creatively considered. Innovative approaches to financing family leave must be developed. New initiatives should target programs that benefit employees and employers, parents and children alike. New research should focus on leave programs that provide the most comprehensive benefits to the greatest number of employees, with priority given to identifying leave programs that support those families most in need.

Once in place, leave policies need to be monitored continually and evaluated both with respect to the processes involved (for instance, ease of implementation, availability of information, and employee and employer satisfaction with plan provisions) and to the outcomes. These, in the short term, could include (but would not be limited to) employee satisfaction with the nature and duration of the plan, availability of income replacement and the adequacy of the same to meet families' needs, and the impact of the availability of leave on the use of infant care. Employer-related variables might include the effect of leave availability and affordability on employee turnover costs associated with replacement and training. Long-term evaluations could assess the likely significance of continual parental care during the early months on the quality and stability of the child-parent relationship and on a host of developmental variables. Outcome and process evaluations by unbiased scholars with no stake in the programs under consideration is essential for determining whether programs have achieved their desired ends, whether unanticipated benefits have accrued to participating families (or employers or communities), and whether unexpected *disadvantages* have emerged. Such research is an important part of a cycle that relies on solid information to define the type of policy needed, how effective changes can be made, and how new policies or adjustments to existing policies can be implemented most effectively.

At the heart of the baby brain battle as it applies to parental leave legislation, however, is a question about the impact of policies that permit infants and parents to be together during the earliest months or years of the infant's life, and only continued research will answer this question. We anticipate that, no matter how quickly neurobiological imaging advances technologically, we will be largely dependent in answering this question—at least for the foreseeable part of the twenty-first century—on the same kinds of behavioral and observational research on which we have already relied and on which parental leave policies are already solidly built.

4

Early Intervention
and Child Care

The storm of controversy surrounding neuroscience and brain research focuses in particular on the efficacy of early interventions and experiences during infancy and the early years of childhood. There are two very different views: some believe that the quality of experiences early in life is a vital cornerstone for later brain development, whereas others argue that early interventions make little or no difference.

But, as we have indicated in previous chapters, it is clear that early life experiences *do* matter in the course of a child's healthy development. There is dynamic interaction between genetic makeup (nature) and experience (nurture); if children experience difficult life circumstances, there will be developmental consequences. Intervening early on can help protect children from the effects of these adverse experiences.

The research on the brain is just emerging, but as we have discussed, we know a great deal about early development from studies in the social sciences. For instance, there is clear evidence that for some children, intervention programs during the early years can be quite effective, and for all children, the timing of experiences and the quality of their environment and social interactions during the early years is important to healthy development.

These are important points to emphasize. The demographics of today's society indicate that many families and children are in need of, and can benefit from, a range of support and services. For children raised in socioeconomically disadvantaged families, one form of support is delivered through early childhood intervention programs such as Head Start. Such intervention programs focus on children at risk for developmental delays and educational failure. Our concern, however, extends to all children, regardless of socioeconomic circumstance, because many children from all backgrounds are in child care facilities, which (because many are known to be of poor quality) can have an adverse impact on development.

These points have become more critical and relevant given the current debate about whether society should support early intervention and child care programs during the preschool years in the same way we now support the education of all school-age children. Some advocates argue for programs that begin in infancy and toddlerhood, while others contend that support services should be available to all families, as early as possible, starting even in the prenatal period (see Karr-Morse and Wiley 1997.) Although universal access (that is, services for all children and families) is optimal, prevention and early intervention are vital for children at risk due to environmental and biological disadvantage, because these are the conditions where positive early experiences can make an important difference for later success.

The terms "early childhood intervention programs" and "child care" are sometimes confused with each other, since both focus on the young child. Each has distinct characteristics, however. Early intervention and child care both share the potential for providing young children with appropriate and nurturing experiences. One major difference is the focus in early intervention on at-risk children only, whereas child care applies to all children. Another difference is the length of time the child spends in the setting: early intervention is often a part-day program, whereas child care can be used as an all-day, year-long program (see box, "Defining Early Intervention").

At times, interventions may also include child care. The Carolina Abecedarian Program, for example, designed to help ameliorate the ef-

Defining Early Intervention

Early childhood intervention encompasses a number of strategies used to assist families and promote children's well-being. The RAND Corporation provides the following comprehensive definition in a review of several early intervention programs: "Early childhood interventions are formal attempts by agents outside the family to maintain or improve the quality of life of youngsters, starting with the prenatal period and continuing through entry into school (i.e., kindergarten or first grade). Naturally, much of the support children receive during these early years will come from their families, relatives and friends. The intent of early intervention is to work with the family to enhance or supplement this support and thus lay the best possible foundation for future health, and for future academic and social functioning" (Karoly et al. 1998, 4).

fects of poverty on children's development, was both an early childhood intervention and a child care program because full-day, full-year educational child care was provided (Campbell and Ramey 1994). The High/Scope Perry Preschool Program and the federal Head Start program are early intervention programs offering half-day preschool, in addition to other services, for only the length of the school year (Zigler and Styfco 1993).

Early intervention programs vary. They range from ensuring adequate prenatal care and screening newborns to parenting education for pregnant adolescents and preschool for children with identified developmental disabilities or low-income children who are at risk for educational failure. Some programs are categorized as "one generation" because their services are delivered directly to the child or parent; other programs are "two generation" in nature by intervening with the child and parent(s) simultaneously (St. Pierre and Layzer 1998; Smith 1995). Most intervention programs attempt to address goals in at least three broad areas: enhancing educational readiness, improving child health and development, and supporting parents in an attempt to improve a range of outcomes.

Child care, by contrast, refers to various facilities where children spend their time in the care of someone other than a parent. Child care in the United States generally falls under one of three categories that vary in the setting, number, and ages of children in the arrangement and in regulatory features (Zigler and Hall 2000).

In-home, or "kith and kin" care, is usually provided by a relative (other than a parent) or an unrelated person (such as a neighbor, babysitter, au pair, or nanny) for the child(ren) of only one family at the child's own home.

Family child care is provided by the caregiver, who may be either a relative or an unrelated person, in the home, for about four to six children. The caregiver can be licensed (in some cases, the requirement is for registration rather than licensure) by the state or not.

Center-based care consists of group care arrangements for at least a dozen children in one of three age groups: infants and toddlers (zero to two years), preschoolers to kindergartners (three to five years), and school-aged children (six to twelve or thirteen years). Sometimes high-school students receive center-based care, particularly when crime prevention is the focus.

Early Childhood Intervention Efforts

Before examining the evidence, it is important to consider the general assumptions that guide early childhood intervention programs (Reynolds et al. 1997). First, poverty is a risk factor, because it typically does not provide favorable conditions for children's health and well-being. Poverty is associated with lack of prenatal care and poor nutrition (McLoyd 1998), which can have devastating consequences on brain development. Second, interventions will help compensate for or even offset the potentially negative effects of risk factors by giving children educational and social experiences that they may not otherwise have. Third, intervening earlier rather than later in life is more effective. And, almost as important, an intervention is more likely to lead to long-lasting positive change if it continues beyond the early childhood years. An intervention's impact can also vary by family and child characteristics and the quality of the postintervention environment in which families and children must function (Reynolds et al. 1997; Zigler and Styfco 1993).

The importance of early childhood intervention and the influence of the first three years of life on subsequent years have recently been questioned (Bruer 1999; Farran 2000; Gomby, Culross, and Behrman 1999; St. Pierre and Layzer 1998). Efficacy as a goal is not in question, but rather efficacy in relation to our high expectations. Critics and supporters alike have argued that the expectations for many early interventions were too grandiose, such as with the Head Start program (see U.S. General Accounting Office [GAO] 1997, 1998a; Zigler 1998). Evaluation studies of interventions have also posed problems. In some program evaluations, sample sizes were too small and follow-up studies were affected by attrition, making it difficult to learn from the findings. In some cases, gains in characteristics such as intelligence found in the studies of some interventions did not prove long-lasting. Another problem is that today's society is very different than when the programs were first conceptualized, some as early as the 1960s (Farran 2000; St. Pierre and Layzer 1998; U.S. GAO 1998b).

These criticisms of the potential of interventions and problems with evaluation of the programs are valid. Yet recent studies demonstrate that when early childhood interventions are of high quality, sufficient duration, and subjected to rigorous evaluation, they do indeed have a positive impact, not only during the childhood years but into adulthood, too (see Barnett 1995; Bryant and Maxwell 1997; Consortium for Longitudinal Studies 1983; Currie 2000; Guralnick 1997; Halpern 2000; Karoly et al. 1998; McCall, Larsen, and Ingram, in press; Reynolds et al. 1997; and Yoshikawa 1995).

A historical perspective on the evaluation of interventions is useful in understanding the impact of early intervention programs. Initial evidence in support of early childhood intervention programs comes from the Consortium for Longitudinal Studies (Lazar et al. 1982). The consortium investigated the effects of eleven programs designed for low-income, minority infants and preschoolers in the 1960s and early 1970s, from early childhood to young adulthood. In these evaluations, researchers looked at changes in children's intelligence as an indication of program success. For most of the programs, there were initial differences in intelligence (as measured by intelligence quotient, or IQ, tests) between children who participated in the program and a control group, which did not participate. However, this tapered off, and then vanished altogether, by the time children were nine to nineteen years old (Darlington et al. 1980). Still, program children in comparison to control group children continued to perform better on mathematics achievement tests from third to sixth grade, they had more positive attitudes toward educational achievement, and their mothers had higher occupational aspirations for them (Darlington et al. 1980). Significant findings in favor of program participants were also evident at thirteen to twenty-three years of age (Royce, Lazar, and Darlington 1983). For most programs, significantly more participants than nonparticipants had met their school's basic requirements for normal progression (that is, they were never placed in special education classes or retained in grade). The participants old enough to have completed high school were more likely to have attained a high-school diploma and to hold higher occupational aspirations than were nonparticipants. Children's positive attitudes toward educational achievement also positively predicted their future educational expectations and attainments and their eventual employment status.

Steven Barnett (1995) reviewed the effects of several early childhood intervention programs serving low-income preschool children. He concluded that "early childhood programs can produce large short-term benefits for children on IQ and sizable long-term effects on school achievement, grade retention, placement in special education, and social adjustment" (25). Likewise, Arthur Reynolds and his colleagues (1997) examined reviews of a large number of evaluations (published between 1983 and 1997) and found "very strong evidence that most programs of relatively good quality have meaningful short-term effects on cognitive ability, early school achievement, and social adjustment" and "increasing evidence that interventions can produce middle- to longer-run effects on school achievement, special education placement, grade retention, disruptive behavior and delinquency, and high school graduation" (6). Both Barnett and Reynolds and colleagues found that most of the studies provided support for both short-term and long-term (that is, lasting for more than three years) improvements, with effects ranging from medium to large in size, especially in comparison to most social programs. Both reviews suggest that the general program features that seem to make a difference for achieving positive results are intensity, comprehensiveness, and quality of implementation.

Evaluations of three individual programs—the High/Scope Perry Preschool Program, the Carolina Abecedarian Project, and the Chicago Child-Parent Centers—also provide convincing data on how children's early experiences can influence later development and on the importance of high-quality experiences for children.

In 1962, the High/Scope Perry Preschool Program enrolled 123 African-American three- to four-year-old children, all of whom scored below 90 on the Stanford-Binet Intelligence Scale (indicating risk of school failure) and came from low-income families (Schweinhart and Weikart 1998; Weikart and Schweinhart 1997). Fifty-eight children were randomly assigned to attend a high-quality, cognitively oriented preschool program, and sixty-five children were assigned to a control group that did not attend the program. The program lasted for two-and-a-half hours a day, five days a week, for either one or two school years. Teachers used the High/Scope Curriculum, the focus of which is to give children opportunities to take the initiative—to help plan, carry out, and review their own learning experiences—thereby encouraging autonomy and independence. It is important to note that, in addition to the preschool experiences, teachers made weekly home visits of up to ninety minutes to keep parents involved as partners in their children's education. To date, the program has been found to have important positive outcomes that last well into adulthood (Schweinhart, Barnes, and Weikart 1993):

- Over time, children were found not only to perform better in school but also to have more positive attitudes toward school. As a group, children who participated in the program had lower rates of grade retention and placement in special education than children who did not participate in the program and were more likely to have higher performance on achievement measures, school grades, and standardized tests (Schweinhart and Weikart 1998).
- From ages four to seven, program children scored

higher than control children on tests of intellectual performance. Although this difference was not sustained over time, by age fourteen, program children improved in school achievement, general literacy, and attitudes toward school, seven years after intellectual performance had faded out.

▪ By age nineteen, program children demonstrated higher graduation rates and college attendance than did control children (Schweinhart et al. 1985).

▪ At age twenty-seven, program participants showed higher levels of income, higher rates of employment and home ownership, were married longer, and had lower rates of teenage pregnancy, arrests, and welfare utilization, in comparison to those who did not attend the program (Schweinhart et al. 1993).

The Carolina Abecedarian Preschool Program began in 1972 as an attempt to ameliorate the effects of poverty on children's cognitive development. This program demonstrates how an intensive intervention delivered from infancy can produce lasting social, cognitive, and academic benefits. Using a prospective, randomized design, 111 infants and their families (primarily African-American) were assigned to a program group (57 children) or to a control group (54 children). Program group children received five years of high-quality educational intervention consisting of year-round, full-day educational child care and/or preschool, five days a week. The program used low child-staff ratios, had appropriately paid staff, and provided stable care. Nutritional supplements and social support services were also provided to the families. The control group received everything but the educational intervention. When the children reached school age, one-half of the program group was randomly assigned to continue receiving the intervention (eight years of preschool and school-age intervention), while for the other half, the intervention ceased (five years of preschool intervention). For the initial control group, one-half was assigned to receive the school-age phase of the intervention (three years of school-age intervention), whereas the other half continued without the intervention. Program and control group children have been compared at several points up to age five, and at ages eight, twelve, fifteen, and twenty-one years of age (Campbell and Ramey 1994, 1995; Ramey and Campbell 1984, 1991; Ramey, Yeates, and Short 1984):

- By twenty-four months of age, and throughout the preschool period, program children scored significantly higher on cognitive development tests and were more responsive to and engaged with their surroundings (Ramey and Campbell 1984; Ramey, Yeates, and Short 1984).

- At the end of the school-age phase, reading and mathematics scores were found to increase as the number of years of intervention increased (Ramey and Campbell 1991).

- By age fifteen, preschool program children, when compared to control children, demonstrated better academic performance, modestly higher IQ scores, higher levels of retention in the appropriate grade for the child's age, and less need for social or remedial services (Campbell and Ramey 1994, 1995).

- Recent evidence indicates that some effects have persisted through age twenty-one (Campbell et al. 2002). Young adults who had received the program continued to score higher on cognitive, reading, and math tests (Campbell et al. 2002).

- Program participants were also more likely to have attended a four-year college and to delay parenthood than were control children (Campbell et al. 2002).

Taken as a whole, these findings support the notion of implementing educational interventions before children enter school, because it may be more effective, and even more cost-effective, than initiating them later.

The Child-Parent Centers (CPC) and Expansion Program was initiated in 1967 for children in the Chicago public schools deemed at risk for low academic achievement and school failure because of poverty. It is the second oldest (after Head Start) federally funded preschool program in the United States (Reynolds 2000). Operating twenty-four centers in the Chicago public schools, the CPC offers center-based, comprehensive educational and family support services for children aged three to nine, for up to six years of continuous intervention. A main tenet is to encourage parents to participate in their child's preschool and primary grade education within the context of a stable and enriching environment. Children participate for a half-day in preschool, a full or half-day in kindergarten, and a full day in first and second grade or first to third grade in elementary school.

The Chicago Longitudinal Study of the CPC has tracked more than one thousand low-income children (primarily African-American) born in 1980 who participated in the program at age three and graduated from kindergarten in 1986 (see Reynolds 1998, 2000). Children have been followed to the end of high school and will be assessed again at age twenty-two. A group of more than three hundred children who participated in government-funded kindergarten programs in Chicago in 1986 served as a comparison group.

- In grades four to six, preschool group children had significantly better reading and math achievement test scores than control children had.
- Through grade six, preschool participants' parents were more involved in their schooling than were parents of controls.
- Lower rates of grade retention and special education placement continued through sixth grade for the preschool group.
- Children who attended the preschool program for one or two years had higher cognitive school readiness at school entry, were retained in grade less often, and had lower rates of special education placement through age thirteen compared to control children (Reynolds 2000).
- Children who participated in the program for five or six years had lower rates of grade retention and placement in special education than did children who participated for two to three years.
- When children's program participation extended into second and third grade, they did better in school by the end of sixth grade than did children who did not participate after kindergarten. A similar pattern of findings emerged

when the participants were fourteen to twenty years old (Reynolds 2000).

■ CPC participants had higher reading and math scores, were less likely to be retained during elementary grades, and were less likely to be placed in special education than were the comparison group. Participation for at least four years showed positive results for several outcomes, with five or six years of participation linked to the best school performance.

Beyond IQ: Other Benefits of Early Childhood Interventions

The controversy over the influence of early environments on young children's development must be shifted from a preoccupation with "boosting brainpower" and racking up IQ points to broader assessments of children's functioning. Some of the strongest and most unexpected changes have been demonstrated for both educational (for example, grade retention and special education placement) and behavioral (for example, arrests and welfare use) outcomes. Changes in these kinds of areas indicate savings to society through reduced spending on remedial education and decreases in crime-related and other social service costs.

Despite these important findings, critics of the effectiveness of early intervention programs dismiss benefits attained in areas other than intellectual functioning (see Bruer 1999). For example, John Bruer's *Myth of the First Three Years* finds fault with the Abecedarian program, arguing that changes in IQ scores have been interpreted as a reflection of changes in early brain development even though the program did not incorporate brain research. Overall, the Abecedarian study is considered to be one of the most intensive interventions in terms of duration and timing, producing some of the largest and most lasting effects, especially compared to less intensive programs (Karweit 1994). The preoccupation with changing IQ and early brain development should not be used to negate the clear benefits for children in a variety of other domains as demonstrated by several early intervention programs.

Recent evaluation studies show beneficial long-term outcomes beyond IQ scores in areas such as social behavior, self-sufficiency, family functioning, and maternal outcomes. Hirokazu Yoshikawa (1995) reviewed the effects of forty early education and family support programs on risk factors found to be associated with chronic delinquency (for example, early cognitive ability, early parenting factors, and life-course variables). Based on findings from four programs that directly measured antisocial behavior and delinquency, programs demonstrating long-term effects addressed multiple risk factors relevant to both children and their parents. Essentially, it was the combination of early childhood education and family support services that made a difference for children in terms of preventing early onset, chronic delinquency.

A report by the Fight Crime: Invest in Kids organization emphasizes several links between educational preschool or child care programs and reduced rates of later violence and crime (Newman et al. 2000). As previously discussed, the High/Scope Perry Preschool Program was developed primarily as a means to improve school-related outcomes, yet improvements were found for children's later delinquency, arrest rates, economic productivity, and commitment to marriage. Children who attended the program compared to those who did not attend were only one-fifth as likely to become chronic offenders (that is, 7 percent program group versus 35 percent control group with five or more arrests) by age twenty-seven (Schweinhart et al. 1993). In addition, a benefit-cost analysis revealed that for every dollar invested in the program, a $7.16 reduction in costs to the public (for example, welfare, schooling, crime, loss of tax revenues) was realized (Schweinhart et al. 1993). Similarly, Reynolds (2000) reported that CPC preschool participation was associated with lower rates of official juvenile arrests by age eighteen in comparison to controls. A benefit-cost analysis of the CPC preschool program demonstrated that for every dollar invested, society gained $4.71 in terms of reduced remedial education and justice system costs and increased earnings and tax revenues (Reynolds 2000).

The Syracuse University Family Development Program provided families with high-quality educational child care, weekly parenting-education home visits, and other services starting prenatally and lasting into the child's early school years. Among children who did not receive the program's services, nearly 20 percent had already been charged with offenses between the ages of thirteen and sixteen, and nearly 10 percent were deemed chronic offenders. Only 1.5 percent of program participants had records for delinquent activities by their early to mid-teens (Lally, Mangione, and Honig 1988).

David Olds and his colleagues (1998) conducted a randomized controlled trial of a nurse home-visitation program, also discussed in Chapter 5, and found evidence for long-term effects on children's criminal and antisocial behavior. Fifteen years after the program, adolescents whose mothers were most at risk (that is, unmarried and economically disadvantaged) and received nurse visits during pregnancy and the postnatal period reported fewer arrests, fewer convictions and violations of probation, fewer cigarettes smoked per day, and fewer days of alcohol consumption in the last six months than did their control group counterparts.

IQ Is Only One Measure of Intelligence

In early studies of early childhood interventions, the most commonly used outcome measure was the magnitude of change in IQ score to mark a program's effectiveness. Early interventions were thought to improve intellectual functioning, which would subsequently increase children's chances for academic and economic success. Based on the converging evidence reviewed above, enhanced IQ scores appear to be associated with participation in the short-term; in most cases, however, these gains fade over the long-term (with the exception of the Abecedarian program, see Campbell et al. 2001, 2002).

It is expectable that changes in IQ test scores associated with program participation tend to fade over time. Herman Spitz (1986) noted the difficulty of effecting true increases in IQ, largely because IQ measurements tend to be highly stable and thus difficult to change (Zigler 1988). Furthermore, many have argued that IQ test scores play a small role in explaining why some children succeed in school and others do not. In fact, studies have shown that IQ and school achievement are correlated at about .50, which means that intelligence can account for only part of the total variability in achievement (McCall 1977; Zigler 1970a).

Indeed, a number of researchers contend that intelligence tests do not capture all aspects of intellectual functioning or all mental abilities (Salovey and Mayer 1989–90; Sternberg 1999; Zigler and Butterfield 1968). Consider the student from a low-income family who may not be motivated to do well on a test or who may not want to take the test in the first place: Zigler and Butterfield (1968) demonstrated that a low IQ score did not necessarily indicate that child's low intelligence but rather the child's lack of interest and motivation to do well on the test. Zigler and Butterfield (1968) posited that performance on an intelligence test is best conceptualized by three separate factors: normal cognitive processes; achievement and experience-based knowledge; and motivation and emotion.

Given this conception, a primary aim of early intervention is therefore to help children develop and maintain social competence, of which intelligence is just one aspect. Social competence reflects four interrelated components of the individual as a whole, developing within his or her various contexts: physical and mental health and nutrition; cognitive ability; achievement in school subject matter; and social and psychological development (Zigler and Trickett 1978).

The stated goal of Head Start, for example, shifted from an earlier emphasis on changing children's intellectual abilities to enhancing children's social competence (Raver and Zigler 1997; Zigler and Styfco 1997). The achievement of good health for children has always been emphasized in Head Start programs through dental checkups, nutritious meals, and immunizations (Zigler, Piotrkowski, and Collins 1994). Another essential component of Head Start has been to encourage parental involvement in their child's Head Start center (for example, from policy decision-making to volunteering in the classroom) in acknowledgment of the critical role that parents play in their children's development (see *Head Start Program Performance Measures: Second Progress Report* [U.S. Department of Health and Human Services 1998] for an overview of the quality and effectiveness of Head Start).

Child Care

As we have noted earlier, early intervention program focus on children who, owing to their socioeconomic or other circumstances, are at risk for educational failure. However, an increasing number of preschool children are not in early intervention programs but in child care programs, the quality of which has a significant influence on their development. Our concern is that whereas child care is needed as a service and support for working parents, it is also an environment where children are spending many of their waking hours. It is therefore an environment at which we need to take a close look.

A fairly dismal picture emerged when the National Council of Jewish Women released its report *Windows on Day Care*, describing the inadequacies of child care in the United States (Keyserling 1972). Nearly three decades later, a 1999 follow-up report called *Opening a New Window on Child Care* indicated that little progress had been made. For example, the number of women with children under age six and who were employed outside the home doubled from 1972 to 1999, and the lack of federal standards in 1972 still persisted. These findings are especially relevant at a time when the number of children in child care is higher than ever and there is unprecedented national concern over the readiness of young children for school (National Center for Education Statistics 1996; National Education Goals Panel 1997). Despite this concern, the United States remains in the throes of a child care crisis that stems largely from a lack of high-quality, developmentally appropriate, affordable, and accessible supplemental child care.

In part, the child care crisis exists because the demand for high-quality child care has outpaced the supply, particularly given the changes in labor force demographics. Over the past decades the median family income level, adjusted for inflation, has dropped. This economic reality has brought many more women into the out-of-home workforce. An estimated 75 percent of mothers of school-age children and 60 percent of mothers of preschool-age children worked outside the home in 1997 (U.S. Bureau of the Census 1997). By 1998, 55 percent of mothers with infants aged one year and under were working; for mothers with a college education, this figure increased to 68 percent (Children's Defense Fund [CDF] 1998).

Despite the high need, it can be even harder to find accessible, affordable, flexible, and high-quality infant care because optimal care for babies differs from care for older children. For example, infants fare better when cared for by the same person or a few people most of the time, yet high rates of staff turnover predominate in the field of child care. Some parents may desire only part-time care for their infants, but many programs do not offer such flexibility.

The Personal Responsibility and Work Opportunity Reconciliation Act of 1996 also introduced new difficulties for working-class parents. Families receiving Temporary Assistance to Needy Families (TANF), many of them headed by single parents, face federally imposed work requirements. In order to work, however, parents must secure affordable, reliable, high-quality child care.

The Challenges of Child Care

The widely held view of child care as an individual family issue to be addressed by parents presents a major barrier toward improving the quality of child care in this country. There is little corporate support to help parents balance work and family. Whereas some corporations allow employees flexible schedules for child-rearing responsibilities, most do not (Friedman 1987). Although the federal government has taken some steps, such as with the passage of the Family Support Act and the Child Care and Development Block Grant to provide families in-need with financial assistance for child care (Finn-Stevenson and Zigler 1999; Zigler and Lang 1991), these and other pieces of legislation are not enough to meet families' needs. For instance, the Child and Dependent Care Tax Credit allows for a portion of a family's child care costs to be credited against taxes (for example, seven hundred dollars for one child and fourteen hundred dollars for two children), but this is nonrefundable and tends to benefit the affluent. The passage of the Family and Medical Leave Act in 1993 was revolutionary in that it was the first nondisability-based parental leave law in U.S. history (Frank and Zigler 1996). The FMLA provides individuals with twelve weeks of unpaid leave to care for a newborn, newly adopted, or seriously ill child, but this does not include employees at companies with fewer than fifty workers, who work part-time, or who have worked for less than a year, representing as much as 40 percent of the workforce (Wisensale 2000).

Another challenge is the lack of infrastructure for child care. No unified federal system of child care standards and regulations governs and guides the operation of child care facilities, so we are left with an unregulated hodge-podge of various types. In addition, since there is no federal leadership on the issue, each state (including the District of Columbia) has its own standards and regulations, leaving child care open to extreme variation both between and within states. Not all states even have regulations, and in those that do, enforcement is often poor (Phillips and Zigler 1987).

Attempts to regulate child care at the federal level have been made since 1941, when the Office of Education recommended specific staff-child ratios. In 1968, the first Federal Interagency Day Care Requirements (FIDCR) were proposed and revised in 1972 and 1980 (FIDCR 1968, 1972, 1980). The 1980 version recommended standards for health, safety, staff training, social services, and staff-child ratios (for example, 1:3 for infant care and 1:4 for toddlers). Another set of standards for center-based programs was developed in 1984 by the National Association for the Education of Young Children (NAEYC), a professional organization of early childhood educators and others dedicated to improving the quality of early childhood programs. Criteria for accreditation of child-care centers was provided, with the goal of improving the quality of life for young children (Hayes, Palmer, and Zaslow 1990). In the absence of a regulated system with adequate standards, such attributes as costs, staff-child ratios, caregiver training, and access to care are variables that affect quality, resulting in child care arrangements that run the gamut from stellar to deplorable (see box, "Child Care in the News: Just How Bad Is It?").

Kathryn Young and Edward Zigler (1986) reviewed the status of infant and toddler day-care regulations for all fifty states in terms of staff-child ratios and group sizes, staff qualifications and training, and whether there was a call for developmentally appropriate care. Not a single state met the FIDCR for staff-child ratios and group sizes. Only eight states required caregivers to have training in child care and development. In a follow-up study, Young, Katherine Marsland, and Zigler (1997) found that only seventeen states had regulations rated as "minimally acceptable," but thirty-seven states were rated as "poor" or "very poor." Almost all states received "poor" or "very poor" ratings for caregiver education, training, and in-service programs. The FIDCR have never been enforced, largely due to conflict between proponents of

Child Care in the News: Just How Bad Is It?

■ "Baby Jessica" became the nation's top story in October 1987 when she was discovered trapped in a twenty-two-foot hole in Midland, Texas. It was fifty-eight hours before she was rescued. Few people realize, however, that the incident occurred in the backyard of a family day care center.

■ As an example of the range of quality in child care options available to parents, during the 1995–1996 season of *PrimeTime Live,* Diane Sawyer conducted an investigation of home child care. She reported often finding poor-quality child care, too many children, and little supervision. In the week that followed her initial broadcast about home child care, Sawyer next reported on a stellar child care facility, located in none other than the U.S. Senate Office Building.

■ In November 1996, Sunil and Deborah Eappen of Newton, Massachusetts, hired nineteen-year-old Louise Woodward, an English au pair, to care for their two children. On 4 February 1997, Woodward called the police to report that the Eappens' eight-month-old son, Matthew, was having difficulty breathing. Four days later, Matthew died in the hospital of complications resulting from a fractured skull. Woodward was accused of first-degree murder for allegedly shaking Matthew to death when she became impatient with his crying. On 30 October 1997 at Middlesex Superior Court in Cambridge, Massachusetts, a jury convicted Woodward of second-degree murder in Matthew's death. Judge Hiller Zobel reduced this verdict to manslaughter on 7 November and sentenced Woodward to 279 days in prison. By 16 June 1998, Louise Woodward was allowed to return home to England after

the Supreme Judicial Court of Massachusetts upheld Judge
Zobel's sentence.

■ In Memphis, Tennessee, on a hundred-degree day in
July 1999, a twenty-two-month-old girl was left in a day
care van for hours until she died from heat exposure. On
the same day, a two-year-old boy suffered the same fate in
another van from a different day care center. Over the
past years, several children statewide have been left at
centers, wandered away, or been passengers in vehicles
with intoxicated drivers.

■ In 2000, a three-month-old infant was killed in a
child care center in Dubuque, Iowa. The stated cause of
death was the provider's having fallen on the child while
the child was seated in a car seat on the floor. The provider was never subjected to drug or alcohol tests.

low-cost care and advocates of high-quality care (Phillips and Zigler
1987). Consider what this means to parents: even if a center is licensed
by the state, they have no assurance that their child is in a safe setting.

Conditions are even worse regarding family child care. In a national study of family day care homes in Texas, North Carolina, and
California, only 12 percent of providers who were regulated by their
state, 3 percent of providers who were unregulated, and 1 percent of relative caregivers who were unregulated were judged to have homes of
"good" quality (Galinsky et al. 1994). Over half of the total family day
care homes were unregulated, and of those homes, 81 percent were ille-
gally regulated because they cared for more children than was legal.
This is especially worrisome because family day care homes tend to
serve families with very young children.

Another issue involving quality is whether child care is developmentally oriented. James Gallagher, Robin Rooney, and Susan Campbell (1999) analyzed the child care regulations pertaining to structure,

operations, personnel, and context of the four states involved in another national study called the Cost, Quality, and Child Outcomes (CQCO) Study (1995). Across every domain, these states were found to set higher standards for protecting children than for enhancing their development. Context (the facility and surrounding community) and personnel (staff qualifications) were rated the lowest, indicative of unacceptable standards for these domains of child care. The results of these and other studies of child care quality are frustrating, given that our society knows how to provide quality care for children of any age (for example, many good centers exist that are NAEYC-accredited based on FIDCR standards).

As an example of how better regulation can affect the health and well-being of children, consider the following. In 1996, the American Academy of Pediatrics published a recommendation that all healthy infants be placed in the supine position (on their backs) for sleep because placement in the prone or side positions was found to be associated with sudden infant death syndrome (SIDS). A review of SIDS cases revealed that of 1,900 examined, 20 percent had occurred in child care settings (Moon, Patel, and Shaefer 2000). About 12 percent of the SIDS deaths occurred in family day care homes, whereas only 3 percent happened in center-based care. The researchers attribute this finding in part to infants being placed in sleeping positions to which they were unaccustomed. They encourage parents to discuss infants' sleeping positions with any caretakers and to educate child care providers further about the importance of supine sleep for infants. This problem might have been a smaller one if family day care providers were better regulated: because they may not be licensed and are less regulated, they are unlikely to receive systematically important information such as these American Academy of Pediatrics recommendations.

The lack of standards and regulations guarantees a vast range of child care costs, staffing requirements, reliability, and accessibility. Costs of child care vary widely across geographical regions, types of care, and age groups, and at times can be prohibitively high. Yearly rates for preschool child care average from four to eight thousand dollars. High-quality infant day care can cost as much as ten thousand dollars or more per year.

Child care is expensive for parents of all social strata, but costs weigh more heavily on low- than on middle- or upper-income families. Low-income two-parent families spend almost a quarter of their annual earnings and low-income single mothers can spend up to half of their earnings on child care (Zigler and Hall 2000). Full-day child care for two children can easily cost a family twelve thousand dollars a year, well beyond the annual incomes of parents working full-time at minimum wage jobs (CDF 1998). In almost all states, such expenditures reach the cost of a year's tuition at a public university (CDF 1998).

A number of staffing issues are problematic as well. Centers are often understaffed, leaving too many children supervised by too few caretakers. According to the National Child Care Staffing Study (Whitebook, Howes, and Phillips 1998), 27 percent of child care teachers left their jobs in 1997. That there is a shortage in providers and high staff turnover is not surprising. Annual earnings for child-care providers typically fall below the poverty level, and benefits are rarely offered. In the study, child care teachers were found to make on average about seven dollars an hour and to earn between thirteen thousand and nineteen thousand dollars annually; less than one-fourth of providers offered paid health care coverage for their employees (Whitebook, Howes, and Phillips 1998).

Because state standards set only a basic minimum, poor-quality child care is almost guaranteed. Establishing standards and regulations and enforcing them stringently would lead to more manageable costs for families, more qualified and better compensated staff, greater accessibility, and care that enhances children's development. The problem is, however, that better regulations and standards as well as higher pay for caregivers would incur greater costs. Because parents bear the brunt of child care costs, they do not push for higher caregiver wages and improved standards and regulations. To procure change in quality, child care costs must be subsidized by the government at all levels, such as is done for education.

High-Quality Child Care and Children's Development

In spite of controversy over the extent to which child care affects children's development (see Scarr 1997), most experts agree that the most critical dimension is the *quality* of care (CQCO Study 1995; Galinsky et al. 1994; Howes, Phillips, and Whitebook 1992; Phillips 1987). National studies on child care quality indicate that the average child care experience is barely adequate; it does not appear to harm the child, but neither does it demonstrably promote growth and learning. Good-quality care is associated with school readiness and better social skills that persist into the school years (NICHD 1998). Poor-quality care is generally associated with negative behavior patterns that can persist into the early school years and beyond (Hayes, Palmer, and Zaslow 1990; NICHD 1998). Specific regulatory aspects of child care such as standards for caregiver qualifications (for instance, education and specialized training) have been linked to the delivery of more sensitive and appropriate caregiving (Whitebook, Howes, and Phillips 1998) and to improvements in children's cognitive development (NICHD 1998) and cooperative behavior (Deater-Deckard, Pinkerton, and Scarr 1996).

In the national Cost, Quality, and Child Outcomes Study (1995), the quality of 401 child care centers randomly selected from California, Colorado, Connecticut, and North Carolina was assessed. Although 14 percent of the centers were found to be of high quality, most provided child care of poor to mediocre quality, indicating that children's health and safety needs were not met some of the time, warmth or support from adults was not observed, and few learning experiences were provided (CQCO Study 1995). Almost half of the infant and toddler rooms were of poor quality, and 40 percent were found to actually endanger children's health and safety. Only one of out twelve infant and toddler rooms provided developmentally appropriate care. Infants in poor-quality settings are subjected to more opportunities for illness when conditions are not sanitary, miss out on important chances for learning, and lose out on supportive and warm interchanges with adults. In Galinsky and colleagues' (1994) study of family day care, over one-third of the settings were found to be inadequate, with quality poor enough to harm children's development. Only 9 percent of the homes were rated as being of good quality (enhancing children's growth and development). Moreover, low-income and minority children in family day care were more likely to be in lower-quality settings than were other children. Overall, safety may be viewed as the bare minimum, but the threshold for good quality must be set higher to ensure that children benefit from their experiences in care.

In 1991, the NICHD began a study of the effects of child care on children. Selecting ten sites, the study followed 1,364 children in child care settings for the first seven years of life. The study found that higher-quality child care was associated with better scores on measures of cognitive and language development; greater school readiness; better mother-child relationships; lower likelihood of insecure attachments for infants whose mothers were low in sensitivity to their children; and less incidence of behavior problems (NICHD 1997, 1998). Lower-quality care was linked with children having more behavior problems and less harmonious relationships with their mothers (NICHD 1997, 1998). These findings document that child care quality interacts with both the quality of the mother-child relationship and family characteristics at an individual level.

The CQCO Study (1995) also found that, regardless of children's gender and ethnicity and mothers' educational level, children in high-quality centers demonstrated better receptive language ability and pre-mathematics skills than did children who attended poor-quality centers. Children who attended high-quality centers also showed more advanced social skills, and positive self-perceptions and attitudes toward their child care.

Four years later, the children in the CQCO Study were assessed at the end of second grade (Peisner-Feinberg et al. 1999). From preschool into elementary school, children who attended child care with higher-quality classroom practices demonstrated better math and language abilities. When children had closer teacher-child relationships in child care, they had better classroom social and thinking skills, language ability, and math skills from preschool through second grade. Even stronger effects were found for children whose mothers had less education; better-quality child care practices were related to better math skills and fewer behavior problems through second grade among these children. In the second grade, children who attended higher-quality child care had better cognitive and social skills and peer relationships.

The need for high-quality child care does not end when children begin school. Concern over the child care arrangements available for school-age children has increased recently, particularly in light of the high numbers of children left to care for themselves after school (sometimes called latchkey children and children in self-care). One study found that an estimated four million six- to twelve-year-old children have employed mothers and that one in five of these children is left without adult supervision after school regularly, or in self-care (that is, an arrangement where a child regularly spends time caring for themselves or taking care of a sibling younger than thirteen during the school year; Capizzano, Tout, and Adams 2000). The rates of self-care were highest among ten- to twelve-year-old children, and particularly children from higher-income and white families, with mothers who work traditional hours. A study of suburban children left unsupervised after school (for example, allowed to "hang out") found that they were more susceptible to negative peer pressure and had more difficulties with school achievement, behavior problems, and experimentation with alcohol than did children who went home after school (Goyette-Ewing, in press; Steinberg 1986). Richardson and colleagues (1989) found that eighth-grade students who cared for themselves eleven or more hours per week were at twice the risk for substance abuse than children who did not care for themselves, regardless of socioeconomic status, extracurricular activities, sources of social influences, and stress.

Other research has examined the role of after-school program participation. Jill Posner and Deborah Vandell (1994) found that urban children who attended after-school programs demonstrated better academic achievement and social adjustment than children in other forms of after-school care. Children who spent time in unorganized neighborhood activities had worse adjustment and work habits. In a review of several studies linking after-school program participation and self-care on children's adjustment in elementary school, Deborah Vandell and Lee Shumow (1999) found benefits for many children, particularly in light of the risks associated with self-care. For instance, benefits were strongest for low-income children, children in urban or high-crime neighborhoods, younger children, and boys. Positive effects also depended on program features such as the emotional climate and opportunities for children to make choices. These kinds of features may be related to structural factors such as staff qualifications or child-staff ratios. It is important, of course, to consider the reasons behind families' reliance on self-care arrangements and to view these arrangements along a continuum. Some parents do stay in contact and have rules with their children during the after-school hours, and some children blossom with the increased responsibility that is associated with self-care (Belle 1997; Hofferth et al. 1991).

We believe that child care needs to be looked at in a different light. Overall, child care should be considered as more than just custodial care for children while their parents work. It is an environment where children spend much of their time. For example, in 1990, children under five with employed mothers were in child care an average of thirty-five to forty hours per week (Hofferth et al. 1991), illustrating an opportunity for society to make good use of the time to facilitate optimal development. Similarly, for older children, there is an increased risk for problems associated with unsupervised and unstructured time after school. For instance, among adolescents, the peak time for violence, crime, and sexual activity is after school between the hours of 3 and 6 P.M. when they are often unsupervised by an adult (Besharov 1999). These findings highlight the importance of using high-quality after-school programs as a means for reducing such major social problems as adolescent drug use and juvenile delinquency.

It is also important to use language about child care with care. For many people, the phrase "child care" brings to mind a safe, convenient, and affordable place for children to stay while their mothers are at work. Conceptually, however, child care and education go hand in hand. The term "educare," coined by Bettye Caldwell of the University of Arkansas, reflects this view. Likewise, the Benton Foundation (1998) has suggested that child care be reframed as "early education," where the goal is to focus on the needs of the child. Many advocates and researchers have adopted the term "early care and education," which encompasses both preschool education, and may include part-day programs as well as all-day, year-round child care. The term also conveys the notion that the time children spend in any form of care, at any age, should be capitalized on to provide appropriate educational and social experiences.

Policy Efforts
The Link Between Early Intervention and Child Care

Early intervention and child care are linked by a shared potential: to ensure that young children have appropriate experiences that enable them to enter school ready to learn and able to benefit from academic instruction. School readiness is, in fact, the first of eight goals in the Goals 2000 Plan (Goals 2000: Educate America Act 1994). By law, it is now the stated goal of Head Start (Zigler 1998), which is particularly salient, given reports from kindergarten teachers who estimate that one in three children enters the classroom unprepared to meet the challenges of school (Carnegie Corporation 1996). Prominent educator Ernest Boyer (1991) likewise reported that 35 percent of children are not ready for school owing to five years of poor child care and a lack of preschool. Close to 60 percent of children in inner cities are not ready for school, which is especially important because preschool attendance is tied to parental income (Boyer 1991). There is essentially no difference between good-quality child care and good-quality preschool programs and interventions except for the length of the day.

Caution must be taken so that the concept of school readiness is not entangled with past preoccupations with boosting brainpower or increasing IQ points. The term "school readiness" refers to a broad range of abilities that children need to develop for increased chances of success throughout school and life (Kagan and Neuman 1997; Peth-Pierce 2000), including physical health and motor development, social and emotional development, approaches toward learning, language usage, and cognition and general knowledge (Kagan, Moore, and Bredekamp 1995).

Comparable to social competence, as discussed earlier, school readiness reflects that a child is effective in dealing with his or her environment and able to meet age-appropriate social expectancies (Zigler 1998). Children who are not healthy, who cannot deal with their environments competently, and/or who do not demonstrate abilities that are reasonably expected of their age group are not ready for school.

Current Policy Recommendations and Initiatives

We now accept the premise that during the first few years of life, the brain lays down basic patterns required for language, reasoning, emotional, and social skills (Nelson 2000). These patterns provide a foundation that can make later learning and development easier or harder. Although the research on early brain development has been misrepresented and misused at times, as we have discussed in previous chapters, it has been an effective means for focusing the nation's attention on the fact that early education and care affect children's cognitive, emotional, and social development (Carnegie Corporation 1994; Shore 1997). This interest has been critical to the generation and expansion of greatly needed programming and policies for very young children (for example, the initiation of Early Head Start and the Early Learning Opportunities Act), particularly in the context of school readiness.

A driving force behind the policy interest was the Carnegie Corporation report *Starting Points* (1994). Among the four main goals it delineated for meeting the needs of infants and toddlers was the push for high-quality child care. To reach that goal, the report suggested a number of strategies, including: adopting family-friendly workplace policies, channeling federal funds into child care to ensure quality and affordability, providing greater incentives to states to adopt and monitor child care standards of quality, and improving salary and benefits of child care providers. Since *Starting Points,* new initiatives emerged across the nation and many efforts already in place were expanded to include families with younger children. New programs to help families from the prenatal period to age three have been secured as a result of this interest in and advocacy for the early years. Other efforts have emphasized the need to officially begin school at age three. Still, some argue that age three is not early enough and that our efforts must encompass the years from birth to eight (Reynolds et al. 1997; Zigler and Styfco 1993).

For the most part, the policy interest lies in school readiness and child care. For example, in 1999, several senators from both parties cosponsored a two-billion-dollar proposal to establish the Early Learning Trust Fund Act. This unique early childhood proposal would provide states with flexible matching funds to support the expansion of both prekindergarten programs and the Early Head Start and Head Start programs to full-day, full-year programs. In addition, funds would be allocated to support high-quality child care and programs for all children. These funds would also assist states' efforts to increase staff compensation and professional development for those who provide education and comprehensive support services to children.

Some advocates have argued that early childhood education is the best investment government can make. For example, James Heckman (2000), Nobel laureate in economics in 2000, contends that learning is made easier by teaching critical skills, such as social skills, to children early on. William Gale and Isabel Sawhill (1999) of the Brookings Institution suggest that federal budget surpluses should be invested, not in government debt or in tax cuts, but in educating our future workforce. The greatest return on such a surplus would come from investments in children's early education and care in the form of more productive and self-sufficient adults who are better trained to use society's latest technologies. Sawhill (1999) suggests that if we invest in children's early education and care, then we can increase the chances that children will be more ready for school, do better in school, and as a result become more productive citizens. Similarly, a report prepared by an expert panel convened by the anticrime group Fight Crime: Invest in Kids indicated that nine out of ten police chiefs believed that crime could be greatly reduced if educational child care programs and after-school programs were expanded (Newman et al. 2000). These police chiefs also declared that if investments in child care programs are not increased now, then expenditures toward crime and welfare systems will be even greater in the future.

The United States lags behind Denmark, France, and Italy, where the education and care of young children is publicly subsidized as children begin school at age three and the child's day during these early years lasts as long as a parent's work day (U.S. General Accounting Office 1995). The federal government supports three major initiatives in child care and early education: Head Start, the Child Care and Development Block Grant, and the Child and Dependent Care Tax Credit. Those programs are an excellent start, but what remains lacking is a strong educational component that focuses on school readiness and meets the needs of all eligible children. To address some of these issues, federal policies for universal preschool or prekindergarten programs have been proposed. In his bid for the presidency former Vice President Gore included a proposal to spend fifty billion dollars on making preschool available to every four-year-old in the country and to improve the quality of preschool programs. The overarching goal of Gore's plan was to promote school readiness by providing all children with early education and to help meet the child care needs of working families.

Forty-two states currently offer free or subsidized preschool programs for children who have not entered kindergarten (Blank et al. 1999). Many of these programs target children in poverty, but some states are making preschool available to all children. For example, Georgia created the Georgia Voluntary Pre-kindergarten Program in 1993, where all four-year-olds are eligible to participate in this free, statewide program geared toward ensuring school readiness. Children considered at risk receive additional free services, such as before- and after-school care and meals. More than sixty thousand children attended one of sixteen hundred sites in 1998, serving about 70 percent of the state's four-year-olds. Funding for the program comes for a state lottery system, which pays about $3,600 per child. In 1997, New York enacted legislation to provide free early childhood education to every four-year-old in the state. Almost $500 million was allocated, representing the largest investment New York has made in early education in many years. Connecticut enacted the Connecticut School Readiness bill with the long-term mission of readying all children for school by supporting child care and preschool programs for three- and four-year-olds. Building on the *Starting Points* report, California's Children and Families First Act of 1998 was proposed to implement a comprehensive, collaborative, and integrated system of information and services (such as health care and parent education) to promote and support child development from the prenatal period to age five.

Policy interest in after-school programs was also generated. For example, there is federal support for the 21st Century Community Learning Centers program to keep children safe, help them learn, and enhance their critical skills during the after-school hours and during the summer. Access to homework centers and tutors, and recreational and nutritional opportunities are also provided. In 1999, Congress appropriated $200 million for after-school programs, up from $40 million in 1998 (U.S. Department of Education 1999).

Every public elementary school in Hawaii now offers the A+ Program, which was established in 1990 to provide families with high-quality, affordable school-age child care (U.S. Department of Education, State of Hawaii 2000). During the 1999–2000 school year, more than twenty thousand students in kindergarten through sixth grade were served in a given month. The A+ Program is the nation's first statewide after-school care program and is directed at serving latchkey children whose parents cannot afford private after-school programs. Child care is provided until 5:30 P.M. during the school year. Children received homework assistance, enrichment activities, and supervised recreational activities with a focus on child-oriented development and an emphasis on community coordination and cooperation.

A New Generation of Model Programs: The Prenatal Period to Adolescence

Head Start historically has been available primarily to four-year-olds. Early Head Start (EHS) was initiated in 1995 to extend the model to include younger children, newborns to children age three. Early Head Start provides high-quality services to pregnant women and infants and toddlers in home-based, center-based, and mixed settings. The program operates under the same framework as Head Start, with an emphasis on parental involvement and service provision. At present, 635 EHS programs serve forty-five thousand low-income children and their families (U.S. Department of Health and Human Services 2000). Current funding, however, allows EHS to serve only about 50 percent of eligible infants and toddlers, leaving the needs of many impoverished children unmet.

Another promising program for promoting children's optimal development is the School of the 21st Century (21C). This program supports children's need for good health, a supportive family life, and high-quality child care from birth through age twelve via school-based and school-linked family support programs (Finn-Stevenson and Zigler 1999). Schools implementing the program are open from as early as 6 A.M. and stay open until 6 P.M. year-round, providing not only the regular school academic program but also all-day, year-round child care for preschool children ages three to five, similar to what is available to families in France and Italy. These schools also offer before- and after-school care and vacation care to children ages five to twelve. Some of the schools also provide programs for older children. Additional support services such as information and referrals, home visitation for families with children from birth to age three, and health and nutrition are also included in 21C. Hence 21C is noted for its comprehensive approach and the continuity of care and support from the birth of the child through age twelve and beyond. Equally important, 21C is a universal program; it is available to all children and families who want to participate.

The growth of 21C schools has been phenomenal, with schools implemented in more than thirteen hundred communities across twenty states. A national evaluation indicates that 21C schools provide good-quality child care services (Henrich et al. 2002) and that 21C is successfully providing an infrastructure for the four interrelated social systems that largely affect children's development: family, school, health care services, and child care environments. With its "whole child" philosophy, the 21C program reinforces the message that the first three years of life are just as important as the years that follow.

There is clearly no one magic period in a child's life. Each stage of development progresses naturally from the preceding period. Given this fact, our efforts should not be focused on providing societal supports at just one stage, as if intervening then absolves us from the need to be concerned with other ages. The task at hand is not to find the right age at which to intervene but to find the right intervention for each age to promote optimal development.

5

Home Visitation
and Parent Education

Today, in the early years of the twenty-first century, the lives of American citizens are cushioned by a fairly strong national economy, a thriving health care system reflecting rapid advances in the treatment and prevention of disease, and an education system in which a greater proportion of people than ever before in our nation's history are literate, have completed high school, and have had the opportunity to participate in some form of postsecondary education. And yet, in spite of these many advantages, far too many families still suffer the effects of poverty and the lack of important support services.

Children, of course, are among the most vulnerable of our citizens. Over thirteen million young children live in poverty in the United States, almost five million of them under the age of six (Children's Defense Fund 1998; National Center for Children in Poverty 2000). Not all of their parents are unemployed: one-fifth of children living below

We gratefully acknowledge the contributions of Mildred Winter, founding director of the Parents as Teachers program, for assisting in our writing about the program, Kathryn Taffe McLearn, who provided an overview of the Healthy Steps program, and Sarah Walzer, for her description of the Parent-Child Home program the poverty line have at least one parent who is employed full-time (Wertheimer 1999). Parents forced off welfare by the newly stringent eligibility requirements often encounter such obstacles as limited employment opportunities, lack of health care benefits, poor access to child care, and transportation problems. The family may also face other problems, including chronic illness or disability, adolescent parents, maternal depression, inadequate housing, and a history of poor parenting, which put children at heightened risk for child abuse, school failure, antisocial behavior, physical and mental health problems, and other developmental difficulties.

As psychologists, health care providers, and early education specialists have grown in their understanding of these problems, a number of different family support programs have been developed to address them, some more effective than others. Although many have improved life for families in need, others have been hastily conceived and implemented too quickly or don't succeed because they convey attitudes and pursue practices that are patronizing and offensive to the families being served. The most successful programs are characterized by two principles that are consistent among the most effective family support programs: they work with both children and their families ("two generation" programs), and they start as early in the life of the child as possible, ideally in the prenatal period.

Even given our understanding of the intricate relationship of nature and nurture, and our belief in the importance of interventions that target preschoolers, school-age children, and even adolescents and adults, it remains powerfully clear that the prenatal period and the first three postpartum years present a uniquely important opportunity for improving the lives of young children and for bettering their odds of avoiding or ameliorating the effects of the various social, cognitive, educational, and physical and mental health challenges many will face in the years to come.

Both traditional behavioral research and newer neurological findings support the long-held notion that early intervention (and the earlier the better) is the most effective form of intercession in the lives of families. The old saw, an ounce of prevention is worth a pound of cure, holds true: primary prevention is always more effective, efficient, and cost-effective than secondary or tertiary attempts to resolve problems that have already arisen. Clearing children's path of hurdles that might injure or impede them makes infinitely more sense than picking them up and bandaging them or offering them a crutch to use after they have tripped and fallen. Even more effective and humane is providing children's parents with the tools to smooth the way—not only for a particular child but for all children and indeed themselves.

Home Visitation

We frequently speak of "early intervention" without stopping to ask what it really means, but it's important to note that, since the 1960s, new ideas have emerged both about what it means to "intervene" in the lives of children and families and about what constitutes "early" (Frank Porter Graham Child Development Center 1998; Shonkoff and Meisels 1990). Although we have noted in previous chapters that human development (and therefore the opportunity for intervention that may make a positive difference in an individual's life) continues throughout every stage of the life span, there is no question that important occasions for intervention have already come and gone by the time a child reaches school age (Begley 1996). Indeed, critical efforts to optimize child health and development can begin before conception and are understood to be a vital, and now routine, part of prenatal and well-baby care.

A broad definition "early intervention" may include any number of approaches to problem solving or prevention in any area important to the lives of children and families, but the phrase generally refers to actions that may begin in the preconceptual period or during pregnancy and continue up to about age eight. Systematic and intentional manipulations of a family's or child's environment with the ultimate goal of enhancing school readiness, improving child health, minimizing the incidence or impact of child abuse, or supporting parents are commonly accepted today by theorists and practitioners of developmental and clinical psychology, psychiatry, pediatrics, social work, and education. Clearly, these goals are intertwined. Improvements in physical health are linked to helping children to attain their potential at cognitive and social tasks, and parent education has been associated both with higher levels of school readiness in young children and with attenuated rates of child abuse and neglect (Daro and Harding 1998; Olds 1992; Zigler and Styfco 1993).

Bringing such programs into the home makes sense. Working with parents and children in the familiar context of their environment is a logical manifestation of the need to intervene expeditiously, thoughtfully, and effectively with all children, but especially when children and their parents are at risk for social, educational, or medical problems.

The field of home visitation is built on several important principles. First, home visitation theory grows out of an ecological approach to child development. In other words, we assume that children are affected not only by their parents and other caregivers: other important influences might include their health and health care providers, the community in which they live, their parents' workplace, the environment in which they receive child care, the schools they attend, and so on.

Second, we take it as a given not only that the child is affected by each of these systems but that the child also has an impact on those who care for him or her, which in turn affects the way the child is cared for or treated. Indeed, every component within this ecology can influence—and mediate—virtually any other. Home visitation programs work with parents and children within this rich environment and help parents to deal with and take advantage of opportunities afforded by different parts of their world.

Third, we further assume that early childhood and the experiences that occur during that period have important implications for later child and adult development. Even taking into account the continuing debate over the relative importance of the early years, it seems clear that it is best to help a child get off to a good start as early in life as possible. No good child developmental specialist would hold that development or opportunities for developmental intervention or optimization ends after the first three years. Home visitation programs assume that genetic, biological, and environmental problems can be overcome or attenuated through efforts initiated early in the child's life.

That the solutions to the challenges facing families today must be as diverse and individualized as the problems and the families themselves is another tenet of home visitation programs. The most successful programs are those that eschew a one-size-fits-all approach, holding instead that each family has unique needs and, even more important, unique strengths upon which they can build to support and improve outcomes for their children. Home visitation programs are most effective when they seek not to supplant parental values and authority but to respect and build on the primacy of mothers and fathers as caregivers and to help these parents and all family members build on their strengths to create loving, supportive, healthy environments for their children. Involving parents in making decisions for their children is a critical component of home visitation, as is respect for cultural, ethnic, and linguistic diversity.

The Goals of Home Visitation Programs

Home visitation programs have many diverse, interconnected goals. Some programs, like the Nurse Home Visiting Program (NHVP), began with a specific goal—in this case, the lowering of child abuse rates in the New York county with the highest incidence of child maltreatment. This program was later replicated in other places and shown to have other positive effects as well. Other programs, such as Yale University's Child Welfare Research Program, began as a more broadly based outreach, offering services in a variety of areas ranging from health care provision to meal planning. In virtually every case, the benefits of effective programs spread well beyond their original goals, often reaching unexpected areas and family members well beyond those first targeted by the intervention.

The notion that such goals should be achievable through home-based early interventions is based on the commonly held belief that the mechanism behind the desired change or changes is parental behavior. A substantial body of literature supports the link between providing support and education as a means of changing parental behavior and producing enhanced outcomes related to child health, effective parenting, maternal employment and education, deliberately spaced childbearing, strengthened community ties, enhanced socioeconomic standing, improved child school readiness and educational attainment, and avoidance by the child of antisocial behaviors during the school or adolescent years (Zero to Three 1992).

School Readiness

In recent years there has been increasing concern about children who do not arrive for their first year of school with the repertoire of experiences that will prepare them to succeed. American kindergarten teachers report that nearly half of all students entering school are not ready to learn (National Center for Early Development and Learning 1998). These students lack the skills they need for even basic educational successes: they have trouble listening and following directions, taking turns, paying attention, demonstrating confidence, working independently, cooperating with others in the group, and communicating with teachers and peers. They often fail to meet criteria associated with school success, such as eagerness to learn, curiosity, and well-developed social and emotional skills, and do not have a home life that promotes learning and a commitment to education (S. L. Ramey and C. T. Ramey 1999).

Our failure to prepare children adequately for school takes both a personal and an economic toll. Educational and social deficits translate into calculable losses, in terms of lost wages and taxes, of more than $240 billion annually. This figure rises by billions of dollars when we factor in money spent on special services related to educational deficits, such as crime, welfare, and health care. The human costs associated with these figures—loss of opportunity, of self-esteem, of life satisfaction—are beyond reckoning.

David Hamburg (1987) has observed that the best school investment strategies include policies tailored to address the needs of the whole child, which means that the child must be considered within the framework of family, school, and community. To be most effective at promoting educational readiness in young children, home visitation programs should be implemented early in the child's life, possibly even targeting parents in the prenatal period. The best of these programs include such components as prenatal and postnatal care, developmental screening for infants and toddlers, parent education for mothers and fathers, and efforts that will help the family connect to other community services and supports. Such interventions have been linked not only with increased school readiness and thus with an enhanced likelihood of school success but also with attenuated rates of delinquency and criminality later in life (Yoshikawa 1995; Zigler, Taussig, and Black 1992).

No researchers, to our knowledge, have scanned the brains of children before and after involvement in an early intervention program or compared the neurological density of the brains of children who begin school ready or not ready to learn. A wealth of longitudinal behavioral and observational research, however, demonstrates a firm link between the richness and quality of the child's environment and relationships during the early years of life with increased success in a number of areas, including—but not limited to—school readiness. Wendy Williams (1994), for instance, cites a number of home-linked variables (among other categories) as likely mechanisms behind the overall rise in IQ scores during the last two-thirds of the twentieth century. Among the variables she connects to this phenomenon are the trend toward smaller families, an increase in average educational attainment of parents, changes in parental style (away from the authoritarian and toward the authoritative), changes in stress levels affecting women and their babies, and an overall improvement in health and nutrition. With respect to the importance of parenting style, for instance, she cites several studies (Bee et al. 1982; Estrada et al. 1987; Hess et al. 1984) that identify the "quality of mother-infant interaction" as the best predictor of IQ at every age tested and even of high school grades (Dornbusch et al. 1987).

Even areas we traditionally think of as cognitively oriented may have their basis in the early social skills we developed (or not) in the arms of nurturing parents. There is new evidence (Kotulak 1997) that school readiness has far less to do with the kinds of academically oriented interventions that have been proposed in past decades (teaching our infants to read, "enriching" their environments with educational toys and flash cards) than with simple maternal nurturing. Research by the U.S. Department of Health and Human Services (1997), released in a report entitled "A Good Beginning," indicates that risk factors linked to difficulties with school are not parents' failure to provide flash cards or the appropriate high-contrast baby toys but rather low birth weight, poor-quality day care, child abuse and neglect, and unresponsive parenting. Study findings emphasize that parents ought to foster in their infants and toddlers—through the provision of secure, loving, predictable environments—independence, curiosity, motivation, persistence, self-control, empathy, and the ability to communicate. These traits translate into the kinds of school readiness markers teachers look for in young children—not necessarily the ability to read early or identify all the historical figures on the flash cards but patience, kindness, the ability to delay gratification, share, take turns, listen, express their needs, and deal with frustration in age-appropriate ways (S. L. Ramey and C. T. Ramey 1999).

Other studies, too, have strongly suggested that nurturing may promote intelligence. One, for instance, followed 205 urban children for ten years, into early adolescence, and found that resilience unexpected in the face of the risk factors common to low socioeconomic areas was more likely to have been overcome by children with certain intellectual resources and at least one parent figure whose parenting was characterized by warmth, reasonable expectations, and the ability to structure the child's world (Marston et al. 1999).

Our parenting skills are shaped by many things: our own childhood experiences and the nature of our parents' skills and resources, the nature and number of stressors impinging on our lives, the unique challenges presented by each individual child, the supports available to us in the form of a spouse or coparent, community resources, and our knowledge of child rearing (Lerner and Dombro 2000). For those who come to parenting without a full complement of resources and information pertinent to the raising of children, home visitation programs provide a unique opportunity to address potential risk factors in a familiar, respectful context.

The Programs

For decades the traditional approach to early intervention focused on the child in isolation and out of the family context. Preschool programs and other educational enrichments provided in a school or laboratory setting were typical (Lazar and Darlington 1979). The developers of Head Start broke new ground both in implementing a more broadly based and comprehensive package of services to their clients and in involving parents directly in their intervention. Today it is standard operating procedure to intervene in the lives of young children in a family context that involves parents (typically mothers) and, at times, siblings and other family members. These two-generation programs work directly with parents and children together, effectively facilitating positive and long-lasting changes in the lives of children by improving parenting skills, education, and socioeconomic status.

Research on the child's brain during the first three years of life appears to demonstrate what behavioral studies have shown all along: that the quality of the parent-child relationship has an indelible and demonstrable effect on the both child's behavior and neural architecture (Gopnik and Meltzoff 1997; Gopnik, Meltzoff, and Kuhl 1999; Huttenlocher 1990, 1994). This interactive environment largely determines the extent to which a child's further social relationships and cognitive development will prove successful and rewarding (Pruett 2000a; Zigler, Hopper, and Hall 1993).

The parent's role in the development of the child's growing social self and sense of self-worth is paramount. Long before the preschool period the child has already begun to develop a sense of the degree to which she or he is valued by the family; reinforcement of the child's sense of being unique, important, and valued by the important people in his or her life results in the internalization of these ideas. The successful groundwork for feelings of genuine self-worth must be laid during the earliest years and by the child's first teachers, the family (Brazelton and Greenspan 2000; Greenspan 2002; Pruett 2000a; C. T. Ramey and S. L. Ramey 1999). Intelligence can neither fully develop nor manifest itself in any meaningful way without having done so in a context of appropriate social development. Social, as well as cognitive, development depends on and facilitates healthy brain development (Gopnik, Meltzoff, and Kuhl 1999).

No matter which type or target of intervention is involved, certain conditions need to be met by programs before growth and development can be optimized. Among the critical conditions for early growth are:

- Early and consistent prenatal care
- Protection of the fetus and child from parental substance abuse
- Access to health care
- A supportive, caring community
- Access to social services

- Responsive caregivers
- Caregivers who have a basic understanding of and reasonable expectations regarding child development
- Safe and protective environments

In what follows we describe programs whose approach and range of services, delivered in whole or in part in the context of home visitation, have proven to be effective means of changing outcomes for young children by enhancing parenting skills and understanding.

Healthy Start

Hawaii's Healthy Start program begun by Dr. Cal Sia as a demonstration program in 1985, aims to prevent child abuse and neglect by improving family coping skills and functioning, promoting positive parenting skills, and enhancing healthy child development. The program features home visitation by trained paraprofessionals, continuity of health care, and supportive services for families of newborns. The program's original design emphasized identification of families with newborns believed to be at risk for abuse and neglect through a review of medical records to identify potential risk factors. Families determined to be at risk were offered home visitation with a focus on improving parents' problem-solving skills and on increasing their ties to community services. In addition, parents received education about child development and modeling of appropriate parent-child interactions; home visitors also helped to make sure that each family had a source of primary pediatric care. Services were offered for three to five years.

Outcome evaluations have produced promising but mixed results. After its first three years of operation, not one case of child abuse had been reported among the 241 high-risk families served in the initial iteration (Breakey and Pratt 1991). In a larger study of several program sites, Healthy Start children were more likely, after two years of service, to have a primary care physician, and parents reported greater levels of parenting efficacy, less stress, greater use of nonviolent discipline, fewer injuries from partner violence. However, no overall program effects were found on adequacy of well-child care, maternal life skills, mental health, social support, substance use, or child abuse and neglect (Duggan et al. 1999). David Olds and colleagues (2000) have expressed concern about design issues that they feel may compromise the interpretation of findings.

Healthy Start has expanded its services and gained widespread acceptance and support. In 1992, the Hawaii state legislature appropriated seven million dollars in funding for the project to enable it to serve at-risk children from birth to three throughout the state (Sia 1992). The project has become the model for another program, Healthy Families America, now based in several cities across the nation, including Chicago and Washington, D.C.

Healthy Families America

Healthy Families America (HFA), an outgrowth of Hawaii's Healthy Start program, provides first-time parents with supports in the form of home visits, hands-on baby care information and child development education, and referrals to local parent support groups. The program started with 20 sites nationwide in 1992 and now boasts 345 sites in the United States and Canada, serving more than thirty-three thousand families every year. Support for the program comes from private donations (Ronald McDonald House Charities and the Freddie Mac Foundation are supporters) and through funding derived from federal and state block grants. Healthy Families America sites work closely with prenatal clinics and other agencies to identify families who could benefit from available support services. The program's principles emphasize the initiation of service provision at or before birth; a standardized needs assessment process; a level of service provision commensurate with family risk level; three to five years of service delivery; cultural sensitivity; and intensive, ongoing training of the paraprofessional staff (Healthy Families America 2002).

Outcome research is ongoing and includes a true randomized controlled study of HFA in San Diego. Some studies of the program have been troubled by subject attrition bias (families at greatest risk are most likely to drop out of the studies) and lack of blindness to group status by researchers (Olds et al. 2000), but so far the findings are encouraging and indicate significant decreases in parental stress and the child abuse linked to it. In Indiana, for instance, less than 1 percent of high-risk families served reported instances of child abuse while in the program. In addition, 90 percent of children whose parents are served by the program are up-to-date on immunizations (contrasted with 77.5 percent of all children and 70 percent of those below the poverty line); at least 90 percent keep regular appointments for well-child care, and over 94 percent have a stable source of medical care for their child (Kirkpatrick 1999).

The summary of findings from randomized controlled and quasi-experimental studies indicate some likely benefits, including reductions in abuse and neglect. None of these studies have been published (and thus subject to peer review).

Parents as Teachers

Investing in good beginnings for children diminishes the probability of later spending on social costs such as child abuse and neglect, remedial education, juvenile detainment, and welfare dependency. Parents who themselves have difficulty negotiating the educational and social systems often don't know how to best prepare their children for school and society. Thus, in 1981, the Missouri Department of Elementary and Secondary Education launched the Parents as Teachers (PAT) program to assist and support parents in their teaching role from the onset of learning, with the goal of reducing the number of children entering kindergarten in need of special help.

From the pilot program, launched in four schools in 1981 and serving 380 families expecting their first child, Parents as Teachers has grown to more than 2,550 programs in forty-nine U.S. states, Australia, Canada, Great Britain, New Zealand, Puerto Rico, the South Pacific islands, and the West Indies. The Parents as Teachers National Center (PATNC) was established in 1987 to provide training and leadership for the program and to ensure that PAT remained on the cutting edge of scholarship and research in early child development and family support.

From the outset, PAT was designed as a partnership with families to give children the best possible start in life. It was intended for the voluntary participation of families of all configurations, cultural backgrounds, and life circumstances. The philosophy underlying PAT is that parents are a child's first and most influential teachers and that the role of schools is to assist families in giving their children a solid educational foundation. The program's guiding principles include universal, voluntary access to the program; family-centered programming in the child's home; a reliance on the unique strengths of parent participants; the optimization of child development and learning through individualized programming; the formation of mutually trusting, equal partnerships among PAT staff and parents; and collaboration with other agencies and community resources.

Parents as Teachers offers all families regularly scheduled personal visits by certified parent educators, group meetings with other parents, and monitoring of children's progress by both parents and professional educators to detect and treat any emerging problems as early as possible. Those who are facing the greatest challenges can receive additional visits and help in connecting to other support services. Personal visits with families, which can begin before birth, are scheduled monthly, biweekly, or weekly, according to family preference and need. Parent educators certified by PAT and trained in child development and home visiting help parents understand and have appropriate expectations for each stage of their child's development. They model and involve parents in activities with their children that encourage learning and promote strong parent-child relations. Book sharing is an integral part of every visit, beginning in the prenatal period. All resource materials for parents are written on two reading levels in English and Spanish. Group meetings serve three major purposes: first, to provide a vehicle for additional inputs from the staff as well as from outside speakers; second, to create opportunities for families to share successes and common concerns about their children's behavior and development; and third, to help parents build support networks. Parent-child activities, sometimes combined with social events, are provided during many group meetings to reinforce the importance of family interaction. A final means of input of information for families and staff is developmental screening, which has a twofold purpose: to reassure parents that the child is developing on target and to identify problems early so as to assist parents with appropriate interventions.

Adaptability is key to the success of Parents as Teachers. Although it is a national model with cutting-edge curricula and a professional training program, it is truly a local program. As shown in the findings of PAT evaluation studies and lessons learned in the field, the program is adaptable to the needs of broadly diverse families and cultures. Program adaptations include those for working with teen parents, parents of children with special needs, families living on Native American reservations, homeless and formerly homeless families, families living on military bases, and families in prison and in probation and parole systems. The program is also available in an adaptation tailored to the needs of both center-based and family child care providers.

True success is measured in terms of changed lives, and PAT programs are themselves evaluated frequently. Independent evaluation studies vary extensively in their sample sizes, types of outcome indicators, and use of comparison groups. Some have investigated PAT as a stand-alone program, whereas others have looked at it as part of a more comprehensive initiative. Recent findings appear to demonstrate its effectiveness. An independent evaluation of the PAT pilot project showed that participating children, at age three, were significantly advanced over their peers in language, social development, problem solving, and other intellectual abilities. Parents who participated in PAT were more knowledgeable about child-rearing practices and child development (Pfannenstiel and Seltzer 1989).

In addition, a follow-up study of the pilot project showed that PAT children scored significantly higher than comparison group children on standardized measures of reading and math achievement in first grade. A significantly higher proportion of PAT parents initiated contacts with teachers and took an active role in their child's schooling (Pfannenstiel 1989). A 1991 study of how effective PAT would be if administered statewide demonstrated benefits for both parents and children. At age three, PAT children performed significantly above national norms on measures of intellectual and language abilities, even though this sample was overrepresented on all traditional characteristics of risk. More than half of the children with observed developmental delays overcame them by age three. Parent knowledge of child development and appropriate parenting practices increased for all types of families, and only two cases of child abuse were documented among the four hundred study families during the three-year period (Pfannenstiel, Lambson, and Yarnell 1991). A longitudinal study by the Parkway School District in St. Louis County, Missouri, reported that

Born to Learn

The Parents as Teachers home visitation curriculum, Born to Learn (1999), integrates information gathered from brain development research with what has long been known about optimizing parent-child relationships and early child development. Handouts like this promote a realistic understanding of each developmental stage and what parents can do to support social and cognitive growth.

third-graders who received PAT with screening services from birth to age three scored significantly higher on the Stanford Achievement Test than nonparticipating counterparts. Parents as Teachers graduates were less likely to receive remedial reading assistance or to be retained in grade. Fourth-grader PAT graduates also significantly outperformed non-PAT children on the Stanford Achievement Test (Coates 1996).

The wealth of information from the scientific community on the development of the brain and its link to behavior—and the controversy surrounding this link—led PAT developers to seek a partnership with a team of prominent neuroscientists at Washington University in St. Louis interested in helping program administrators to translate neuroscience findings into concrete information and guidance for parents. The result, the Born to Learn neuroscience project, is a curriculum aimed at translating our growing understanding of early brain development into hands-on information for parents (see box, "Born to Learn"). A sixteen-segment video series contains short presentations, in easy-to-understand language, on specific ways parents can foster healthy social and cognitive development in their young children. In addition, entertaining and accessible lesson plans centering on parent-child interaction, brain development, stage-by-stage child development, nutrition, discipline, and other topics are provided and are supplemented by detailed home visit plans, child development and neuroscience information for parents written at two reading levels, and resource materials for parent educators.

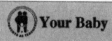 **Your Baby**

5-1/2 to 8 Months

Social-Emotional Development

Look for your baby to

Be happy much of the time.

Enjoy playing with people.

Reach out for your face.

Want you to pay attention to her.

Be shy or afraid around new people.

Be upset when you leave the room.

Ways you can help

Rock and cuddle your baby. Tell her how happy she makes you feel.

Play peek-a-boo and pat-a-cake.

Let your baby touch your face. Look at her when you talk to her.

Play with her. Talk to her. Show her you are there for her.

Hold your baby when she is afraid of new people.

Tell her you will come back soon. Peek around the corner and call to her to show her you are near.

Your baby's brain .

- Makes new connections when your child explores, touches, sees, and hears.

Healthy Steps

Like Parents as Teachers, Healthy Steps is a home visiting–based intervention targeting new parents. The program received its initial support from the Commonwealth Fund, and program materials were developed by the Brown University School of Medicine, with the American Academy of Pediatrics as a cosponsor. The Commonwealth Fund's 1996 "Survey of Parents with Young Children" revealed that parents surveyed were uniformly eager for expert advice on child rearing, discipline, and problem management, but only about half of the respondents felt that their child's physician gave adequate guidance in these areas (parents expressed high levels of satisfaction with those pediatricians who *did* provide information of this sort). Healthy Steps was designed to remedy this situation by delivering sound information about child development (emphasizing the first three years) to new parents through a combination of home visits, regularly scheduled pediatric office visits, a telephone hotline, and newsletters ("LINKletter") that precede each office visit by about two weeks.

In Healthy Steps' two-generation model, parents and their newborns are initially seen in the hospital following delivery or at the initial pediatric visit, within a few days of the child's birth. The first home visit takes place between three and five days after the child is born. Home visitors who are specialists in child development—either early childhood educators or pediatric nurses—give parents information during these home visits and at extended office visits. Parents can also get answers to pressing questions or advice about how to handle a crisis or concern by using a special telephone hotline.

The child development specialist acts as a parenting coach, helping parents by providing nonjudgmental support and information. Home visitors may educate parents with respect to age-appropriate behavior and discipline, answer their questions about sleep, eating, and elimination, or help parents with their medical and developmental concerns. Mothers are encouraged, but not pressured, to try breast-feeding, and many find that the gentle support helps them breast-feed successfully for extended periods. One home visitor notes, "I work with mothers who did not breastfeed or were not successful in breast feeding their first Healthy Steps baby, but because of Healthy Steps, seek out help and are more determined to breastfeed a subsequent baby" (Healthy Steps 2001). Participation in the program continues for three years.

Healthy Steps was implemented in 1995. Since then, partnerships between funders (the Commonwealth Fund, along with a variety of managed care systems, hospitals, and foundations operating at the community, state, and local levels) and health care delivery systems like Kaiser Permanente, Advocate Health Care System, the University of North Carolina at Chapel Hill's Pediatric Clinic, and others have made it possible for the program to expand into sixteen states. In the initial three-year period, nearly 4,500 families were served, and the Commonwealth Fund is currently finding ways to continue to fund Healthy Steps and to increase the number of participating clinics and pediatric practices.

The initial evaluation of the Healthy Steps program is not yet complete. Anecdotal evidence strongly suggests that the program enhances thoughtful, informed parenting and decreases stresses related to child rearing, promotes breast-feeding and literacy (parents are encouraged to read to their children, starting early in the first year), helps parents to appreciate the young child's ability to learn and to interact meaningfully with caregivers, and supports parents as they build a healthy cognitive and emotional foundation for their child's future. The effects appear to continue with second children as well as firstborns. The ongoing, fifteen-site national evaluation of Healthy Steps will examine whether the program improves outcomes for children, their parents, and/or their pediatricians and to what extent the program saves money over time by preventing health problems.

The Home Instruction Program for Preschool Youngsters

The Home Instruction Program for Preschool Youngsters (HIPPY) targets parents of three-, four-, and five-year-old children with the goal of increasing continuity between home and school by using paraprofessionals from the child's community to help parents enhance the home's learning environment during the preschool period (Baker, Piotrkowski, and Brooks-Gunn 1998). The curriculum revolves around the use of developmentally appropriate storybooks and related materials to challenge children's language, sensory and perceptual discrimination, visual motor, and problem-solving skills. Weekly visits take place during a thirty-week period coinciding with the school year.

Findings of one outcome study (HIPPY 2002) indicate a modestly positive impact on school suspensions, use of Title I services (remedial or compensatory education programs funded under the Elementary and Secondary Education Act of 1965), child behavior, and achievement test scores in third and sixth grades. A quasi-experimental study (Baker et al. 1998) matched HIPPY recipients to two other groups of children, one with no preschool experience and one with experience from a different preschool program. Program findings within one study site varied by cohort, with one group achieving positive outcomes relative to cognitive skills and classroom adaptation in kindergarten and first grade, and another group demonstrating no such outcomes. In his review of home visitation programs, Olds (Olds et al. 2000) cautions that this makes findings difficult to interpret. HIPPY has undergone recent modifications and expansions, evaluations of which may be easier to interpret.

The Parent-Child Home Program

Parent-Child Home Program (PCHP) is a home-based literacy and parenting program offered to parents challenged by low socioeconomic status, a low level of education, or language barriers. In place for more than thirty years, PCHP targets families of two- and three-year-olds, offering them twice-weekly home visits by trained paraprofessionals with the goals of increasing the families' language and literacy skills and the child's school readiness, and fostering the development of parenting skills with a focus on verbal interaction and age-appropriate behavioral expectations.

Home visitors interact with the child around books and toys, and model behavior and language, emphasizing the parents' role as the child's most important teachers. This national program, developed in Freeport, New York, by educator Phyllis Levenstein, is based on the philosophy that early use of language is critical for building the cognitive skills necessary for academic success. Parents from low-income homes, for instance, have been found to use fewer words with their child; the number of words per hour that a parent addresses to a child is directly related to the child's vocabulary growth rate, use of words, and IQ scores (Hart and Risley 1995). Similarly, students who make successful transitions to kindergarten are likely to have parents who are involved with their education at home, reading, talking, and playing with them (National Education Goals Report 1994).

Ongoing short- and long-term studies (that appear to be conducted by program developers) indicate successes at increasing parent-child verbal interaction and positive cognitive outcomes. According to one study, participants perform at or above national norms on standardized reading and math achievement tests throughout elementary school. Participants graduate from high school at rates equal to those of middle-class students, significantly better than children from similar low-income backgrounds (Levenstein et al. 1998).

In first grade, PCHP children demonstrate significant correlation between increased verbal interaction and academic skills (Levenstein, O'Hara, and Madden 1983), and the average seventeen-point IQ gain by children over two years in the program was sustained to age ten (Lazar et al. 1982). The program has also been shown to effect significant improvement in mothers' positive interactions with their children in at least one study (McLaren 1988). Other research has shown that the program can be successfully replicated in other communities, and PCHP is currently being replicated in communities throughout the United States and in Bermuda, Canada, and the Netherlands.

The Nurse Home Visitor Program

The Nurse Home Visitor Program (NHVP) began by recruiting young, poor, first-time parents (see box, "Fathers Need Intervention, Too") from an area plagued by New York State's highest child abuse rates (Kitzman et al. 1997; Olds et al. 1999). Its goals focus on improving pregnancy outcomes by helping women to improve their health-related behaviors; improving the health and development of the child by helping parents provide more responsible and competent care; and improving parents' economic self-sufficiency by helping women plan future pregnancies, complete their education, and find employment.

Fathers Need Intervention, Too

Children at risk for social and educational failure are disproportionately likely to be living apart from their fathers. Evidence indicates that fathers bring unique characteristics to parenting which benefit children both directly and indirectly. It is of growing concern, therefore, that over 50 percent of all American children are expected to spend some portion of their childhoods living without their fathers present in the home. A child from a fatherless home is five times more likely to live below the poverty level than are children whose fathers reside with them, and the rate of fatherless families has doubled in the past fifteen years and is still increasing (Hernandez 1993). The absence of the father has also been associated with increased rates of arrest, school failure, sex-role and gender identity dysfunction, and displays of aggression (Federal Interagency Forum on Child and Family Statistics 1998; Hetherington and Stanley-Hagan 1986).

Positive father involvement, in sharp contrast, has been associated with improved outcomes for children relative to their cognitive development, educational performance, delinquency, social competence, and psychological functioning (Cabrera and Peters 2000; Greene and Moore 1999; Harris, Furstenburg, and Marmer 1998; Lamb 1997; LeMenestrel 2000; Pruett 1987).

Few intervention programs, and no home visitation programs of which we are aware, specifically target fathers. Social scientists like N. J. Cabrera and colleagues (2000) describe how a father's absence may negatively affect children: through the lack of a coparent; through economic loss; through social isolation and societal disapproval of single-parent families; through psychological distress in the child stemming from a sense of abandonment; and through conflict between the parents over the father's lack of presence in the home. In an era when father involvement in intact families is increasing significantly (Yeung et al. 1998) and greater involvement in day-to-day parenting activities is increasingly expected of fathers (Pruett 1987; Wilkie 1993), we find it likely that fathers will soon be offered a greater level of services comparable to those now available to many women through home visitation and other parent support programs.

When this time arrives, we hope that policy makers will seek to avoid many of the pitfalls and shortcomings that plague research about fathering in general. Studies of the roles of fathers in child-rearing and of the effects of the quality of father-child relationships have been hampered by a number of factors. First among these is that fathers have often been studied simply in terms of whether they are physically present in their children's lives (Cabrera and Peters 2000). Even this variable is problematic, for at least one study has demonstrated that many allegedly absent fathers (as many as two-thirds, in some populations) are regularly in contact with their children and are likely to provide informal economic support as well as participating in child-rearing activities (Greene and Moore 2000). In addition, longitudinal data on father-child relationships are scarce, and there are no prospective studies of fathering that begin before birth or early in the life of the child; in some cases, data that do exist are actually obtained from mothers (Coplin and Houts 1991).

In 1995, President Bill Clinton asked federal agencies to review programs and policies with the goal of strengthening and supporting fathers in families and studying the unique contributions they make to their children and families. This request to improve data collection on fathers, fathering behavior, and the outcomes of father involvement in children's lives is the responsibility of the Federal Interagency Forum on Child and Family Statistics, which sponsored the Fatherhood Initiative 1996–1997. The forum's report emphasizes the contributions of fathers across racial, ethnic, and economic subgroups. It recommends that policy makers and program developers take into account the needs and perspectives of both fathers and mothers, that the role of fathers be studied across the life course, and that the motivations and effects of fathers' behavior be examined. Other recent research efforts have focused on the impact of welfare reform legislation on fathers and fathering (Coley and Case-Lansdale 2000; Roy 2000). We hope that data like these will soon form the foundation of home visitation programs for fathers as well as mothers.

The program's philosophy is grounded firmly in epidemiology, child development research, and human attachment theory. Biweekly visits by nurses take place during the prenatal period and up to the child's second birthday. Parents are offered regular prenatal and well-child care, pre- and postnatal home visits by a nurse, and developmental education, including advice on how to involve other family members and friends in the pregnancy and later care of the child. Nurse visitors also help mothers connect with other social service agencies as needed.

The results of these studies offer some of the most compelling findings to date supporting the use of prenatal and follow-up home visits as a means of fostering better child cognitive development, as well as improved maternal perceptions of child behavior, mother-child interactions, and child medical care and a reduction in the occurrence of child abuse, at least for the duration of the intervention (Wolfe 1993). In a typical program evaluation, only 4 percent of program mothers, in contrast to nearly 20 percent comparison group mothers, had abused their children (Olds and Kitzman 1993). Olds and Henderson (1989) note that for programs to have a sustained impact, parent education services must be coupled with equal emphasis on improving conditions in the home.

Fifteen-year follow-up studies indicate that during pregnancy, women visited by nurses made greater use of community services, reported better social support, made better improvements to their diet, and had fewer kidney infections. Women who were smokers were more likely to reduce their use of tobacco. Mothers under age seventeen when they entered the program had newborns averaging 395 grams heavier than those of control groups members of the same age. Olds emphasizes in the most recent reports of the studies that program effects are significant for several variables (abuse rates, for instance) only for mothers at greater risk by dint of marital status or age, suggesting that a targeted program is more likely to be effective than one casting a wider net.

Yale Child Welfare Research Program

Begun in the late 1960s, the Yale Child Welfare Research Program, conceived and implemented by Sally Provence of the Yale Child Study

Center, followed eighteen children from seventeen families since birth (Seitz and Apfel 1994). All of the children were firstborns, except for one sibling born during the study. Mothers were chosen during pregnancy from hospital obstetric records based on these criteria: inner-city residence, income below the federal poverty guideline, no serious complications of pregnancy, and no mental retardation or marked psychosis. Twelve of the children were black, two were white, two were of mixed-race parentage, and two were Puerto Rican. A comparison group of eighteen children matched for sex and ethnicity was chosen for follow-up purposes a year after the program ended.

The program provided broad-based, family-oriented services tailored to meet the needs of each family. For slightly over two years (until program funding ended), participants received services that included pediatric care and developmental screenings; home visits (by social workers, psychologists, and a nurse) to provide budget planning, nutritional counseling, and help in establishing links to other community services and support agencies; and, for families who desired it, high-quality, university-based day care (Provence and Naylor 1983).

The program has been regularly evaluated since its ending. Immediate effects included better health care for program children and the mobilization of parents to obtain needed services. When program children were thirteen and comparison group children were eleven, a follow-up study revealed a number of positive effects of the children and their families. Program children were less likely to have been retained a grade or more in school and less likely to need remedial educational services. Teachers reported that program children got along better with teachers and peers and had fewer behavioral problems than comparison group children. The behavior of program boys was rated significantly more positively by their teachers than that of comparison group boys, who had higher rates of truancy and other problem behaviors, including cheating, lying, and chronic disobedience. Parents, too, had more problems with comparison group children than with program children. Mothers of comparison group children were more likely to report that, at age eleven, their children were stealing, staying out overnight without permission, fighting, and in general engaging in or being at higher risk for involvement in juvenile delinquency (Rescorla, Provence, and Naylor 1982).

Family effects at the ten-year follow-up also reflected positive outcomes for program participants. Families of program children had fewer children and spaced their births at greater intervals than comparison group families. There was also a slight positive difference in the number of two-parent families (more likely in the program group) and in the number of program families who were working rather than receiving public assistance. For mothers, program participation was associated with having achieved a higher level of education (Seitz, Rosenbaum, and Apfel 1985). No overt drug-related variables have been reviewed to date by program evaluators, but many of the resiliency factors (such as ties to family and commitment to education) are clearly stronger in program families.

The Yale program has also been shown to be cost-effective. Money spent on services to each family has been matched more than by money saved by the school system on grade repetitions and provision of special services. Furthermore, fewer program families were receiving public assistance at follow-up, increasing the cost-effectiveness of program participation (Seitz, Rosenbaum, and Apfel 1985).

Far from finding child-oriented home visits intrusive or patronizing, three-fourths of American parents surveyed indicate a wish to receive assistance in taking care of newborns, and more than two-thirds believe that child abuse is strongly linked to lack of parenting experience or skill. The availability of such support, however, scarcely keeps up with demand. Only 14 percent of families receive home visitation support. Of those who do, the vast majority welcome them as useful and supportive. More than three-fourths of Americans would support the allocation of public funds for home visiting services to new parents (Kirkpatrick 1999).

In order to keep such services welcome and useful to families, however, we must continue to observe certain principles of intervention:

First, except where mandated by a court, services must be accepted voluntarily. Creative, persistent, but respectful outreach efforts can be used to help keep parents in the program for as long as services are available. Frequent contacts (that is, at least weekly) are critical for continuity of support and availability to help parents cope with problems as they arise.

Second, services, materials, and supports offered should be culturally sensitive, acknowledging and respecting ethnic, racial, linguistic, and regional diversity.

Third, home visitors' loads must permit them to spend adequate time with each family they are assigned and to be available to those families as needed.

Last, all home visitation programs must be based on the tenet that, though the parents may be able to benefit from education and services, they are the child's primary caregiver and most important teacher, and because of this, their wishes must be observed and respected whenever possible. Even families at risk for parenting problems love and care about their children and want to do their best for them.

A good home visitation program can best accomplish its goals by making the parents the primary partners in their child's care. Not all home visitation programs are created equal. Because of the diversity among existing programs concerning their goals, the nature of their interventions, their research designs, and the methods of assessing their outcome, it is hard to draw conclusions about the overall worth of home visitation programs (Gomby, Culross, and Behrman 1999; Olds et al. 2000; C. T. Ramey and S. L. Ramey 1998). Careful analysis by Olds and his colleagues, in several studies of both his and other home visitation programs, also reveals that many programs that are found not to have positive outcomes for all participants may in fact be highly beneficial for those with specific risk factors (Olds et al. 2000). Finally, inconsistent findings within one program, even at one study site, may indicate problems related to quality control and continuity of service delivery.

These caveats notwithstanding, the question of the efficacy of home visitation programs has been answered positively by years of longitudinal research on the consequences of participation in an early intervention effort. New research on brain development during the early years of life have simply confirmed—in some cases dramatically— what we have long known about the worth of such interventions. Specialized evaluation research reveals that comprehensive intervention programs can dramatically improve parenting skills and parents' understanding of child development to reduce the risk of child abuse and neglect, to strengthen social competence, physical and mental health, and overall family functioning, and to enhance educational readiness.

In the face of shrinking federal, state, and local budgets, however, early intervention programs will survive and continue to succeed only if we seek creative solutions to problems and funding needs, and if we clearly and realistically define their goals and demonstrate their effectiveness through ongoing evaluations.

In most cases early family interventions have traditionally been aimed not at enriching what would be thought of, as the influential psychoanalyst D. W. Winnicott would call "good enough" parenting, but rather at raising to that threshold parenting skills and environments that are so far below "good enough" that they hinder development. Far too many children in America today start off two steps behind their more fortunate peers. It behooves all of us not only from a humanitarian standpoint but also from an economic and national security position to provide early intervention services such as home visitation to those who can benefit from them. By doing so, we can hope to decrease both the human and economic costs inherent in the waste of potentially productive and fully functional individuals, the very people who will become workers and the parents for the next generation of Americans.

We must at the same time, however, bear in mind two factors that would argue in favor of a more universal application of home visitation and other early intervention services. First, there is the potential that negative effects will accrue from the stigmatization associated with targeting families for intervention services. The denigrating specter of the deficit-model attitudes of many program developers in the 1960s and 1970s still clings to attempts to target families based on the label "at risk." The notion that certain families or demographic groups are *lacking* in qualities commonly perceived as necessary for social and cognitive success has largely been replaced with the idea that each family brings unique attributes, needs, and strengths to bear on situations both quotidian and challenging. Second, we believe that what is good for some children in America is good for all children. Parents as Teachers has demonstrated that it is not only possible but highly beneficial to provide home-based, early enrichment programs to all children in a given state. Given what we know of the cost-effectiveness of such programs (Shonkoff and Phillips 2000), we believe that extending proven, high-quality programs of this nature to all children will, in the not-very-long run, more than pay for itself.

6

Child Abuse and the Brain

In each chapter in this book we have pointed out that findings emerging from neurological research confirm and strengthen our belief that the experiences of early childhood have long-lasting effects and powerful implications for later development. Sadly and importantly, nowhere has this been truer than in the study of child maltreatment. Our tools for detecting abuse and studying its consequences have evolved over the decades, and will no doubt continue to do so, but the resources available to us at present demonstrate irrefutably that, directly and indirectly, abusive experiences in early childhood trigger a cascade of changes in the ways children grow to think, learn, and interact with others. Only by putting this information in a context that includes an understanding of both the history of child maltreatment and multidisciplinary contributions to our understanding of the outcomes of maltreatment can we best shape our service and policy responses to this profound and endemic problem.

What Is Child Abuse?

Child abuse is surprisingly difficult to define. Most people would agree that beating or starving a child is abusive, but many others feel that it is possible to draw a line between child abuse and "nonabusive" corporal punishment. A Zero to Three poll (2000) found that 61 percent of American parents agree that spanking is acceptable "as a regular form of punishment." Even parents who profess to be opposed to spanking apparently engage in the practice: only 50 percent of parents taking part in a Gallup Organization poll (1997) supported spanking, but fully 94 percent reported having spanked their own child. Most American parents condone and practice corporal punishment and believe physical discipline is not only necessary but desirable to shape their child's behavior and character. Over two-thirds of parents oppose the enactment of a federal law prohibiting parents from spanking their children; less than one-fifth would actively support such a law (Zero to Three 2000).

These practices continue in the United States (see box, "Corporal Punishment in Schools and Child Care," for an overview of nations that have outlawed corporal punishment in the home) in spite of the steadfast insistence of most child health and development experts that corporal punishment is not only an ineffective form of discipline (Maurer and Wallerstein 1987) but also inhumane and a violation of the child's civil liberties. Many studies describe a connection between corporal punishment and increased—rather than decreased—anger and resentment in children (American Academy of Pediatrics 2000; Lerner 1998; Weininger 1998).

Corporal punishment, moreover, is strongly associated with injury to children. At least 60 percent of physical child abuse is associated with a parental attempt to discipline or punish the child (Zigler and Hall 2000). Spanking or "paddling" not infrequently results in muscular and skeletal damage, central nervous system hemorrhage, spine and sciatic nerve damage, blood clots, and other injuries (S. L. Ramey and C. T. Ramey 1998). Even so, spanking and even more extreme forms of punishment, which are often administered by parents who do not set out to inflict lasting harm, are so deeply rooted in American society that it is hard to draw a clear line between discipline and child abuse.

The 1974 Child Abuse Prevention and Treatment Act (CAPTA) and its 1996 revision (PL 104-235) have attempted to provide some guidelines for the definition of abuse. Abuse is currently defined in CAPTA as any action (or lack thereof), "resulting in imminent risk of serious harm, death, serious physical or emotional harm, sexual abuse, or exploitation . . . Of a child . . . under 18 . . . by a parent or caretaker (including any employee of a residential facility or any staff person providing out-of-home care) who is responsible for the child's welfare."

These actions need not have been intentional or meant to cause harm in order to constitute abuse, so that overly vigorous discipline may easily fall into this category. Neglect, sexual abuse, and emotional abuse are similarly defined by CAPTA. These guidelines have gone a long way toward establishing the legal limits of abuse, but difficulties have nonetheless arisen over the disparate definitions employed by individual states. The policy implications of such definitions provide somewhat more rigor but may also exclude more children and families from eligibility for support services intended to prevent child abuse or remedy its outcomes.

Practical issues in describing child abuse also abound. Not all cases of suspected abuse are reported. Further, in the face of increasing belt-tightening on the part of agencies feeling the pinch from state and federal budget cuts, available services may not be sufficient to compensate for disruptions in investigation and service provision.

Compared to the plight of children in centuries past, children in the United States today fare far better. Widespread infanticide does not make the front pages of the *New York Times;* the airwaves do not daily broadcast tales of American children found chained in their homes. Even so, grim statistics tell a story of children as much at risk at the hands of parents, and, in some states, school personnel, as many children from centuries past (see box, "Child Maltreatment in History").

Statistics compiled by the U.S. Department of Health and Human Services in 1999 (the most recent year for which figures are available) indicate that nearly 3 million referrals were made to child protective agencies alleging child abuse; over 60 percent of these were investigated and referred for assessment. Contrast this with the 669,000 reports of child abuse and neglect a quarter of a century ago—though there is controversy over whether the contemporary rise in cases is due to an actual rise in child maltreatment or to heightened awareness and a consequent increase in reporting. Ultimately, the 3 million reported alleged instances of child maltreatment resulted in the identification of 826,000 victims of child abuse in the United States in 1999. This figure represents 11.8 cases per 1,000 U.S. children, a decrease from the previ-

Corporal Punishment in Schools
and Child Care

Many Americans take for granted parents' right to spank their children. After all, the use of corporal punishment within families boasts a
high approval rating: more American parents approve, rather than dis-
approve, of parental spanking. In fact, however, the United States stands
distinctly apart from most of its economic peers, and even from many
developing nations, in permitting corporal punishment to remain legal.
Nations that have prohibited the corporal punishment of children include (arranged in the order in which they enacted anti-spanking legislation, beginning with Norway in the early 1800s): Netherlands, Italy,
Belgium, Austria, Luxembourg, Finland, France, Russia, Turkey, Norway,
Japan, China, Portugal, Sweden, Denmark, Cyprus, Germany, Switzerland, Ireland, Greece, United Kingdom, New Zealand, Namibia, South
Africa, American Samoa, Zimbabwe, Zambia, Thailand, and Trinidad
and Tobago.

In the absence of a federal mandate, corporal punishment of a child
in a school by a member of the faculty or school administration is still
legal in twenty-three U.S. states. This is in spite of strong recommendations from the American Academy of Pediatrics (AAP) that corporal
punishment in schools be prohibited in all states. The AAP estimates
that corporal punishment in schools is administered between one and
two million times a year (AAP 2000; U.S. Department of Education
1987). Its member physicians stand behind research indicating that
such treatment is not only deleterious to a child's self-image but is
counterproductive in the long run, contributing to *more* disruptive and
violent behavior on the part of the student (Hyman and Wise 1979;
Poole, Ushkov, and Nader 1991). Of more pressing concern is that
corporal punishment is often associated with a range of childhood injuries (Dolins and Christoffel 1994).

The U.S. Supreme Court has upheld the right of public school au-
thorities to administer physical punishment, even when, as in the case

of *Baker v. Owen* (1975), this violates a parent's specific written instructions to the contrary. In *Ingraham v. Wright* (1977), not even the two-foot-long wooden paddle used by two teachers to beat a junior high school boy (who was injured by the treatment) was found to constitute cruel and unusual punishment. On the other side of the issue, many specialists believe that laws permitting corporal punishment send parents the wrong message by giving the schools' carte blanche to the use of physical violence as discipline (Feshbach 1980). In many states, children are the only citizens whom it is legal to hit.

Organizations like the National Committee to Prevent Child Abuse, the National Center for the Study of Corporal Punishment and Alternatives, and the Committee to End Violence Against the Next Generation gather information about the uses and outcomes of corporal punishment and lobby against its continued use in both homes and schools.

Ironically, even as many parents and legislators continue to champion the use of physical discipline in schools, there is widespread criticism and occasional hysteria over possible instances of child abuse in day care facilities. As the 1999 National Child Abuse and Neglect Reporting System findings clearly demonstrate, the vast majority of instances of child abuse—physical, sexual, and emotional—take place at the hands of family members. Conditions vary tremendously in child care settings in the United States, and many legitimate concerns about the quality of child care, the training and continuity of child care staff, and the potential outcomes of early child care exist. In spite of the clear need for legislative action to remedy poor-quality and unsafe conditions in many child care facilities, it seems likely that the potential for child abuse in these settings has been grossly exaggerated. The National Child Protection Act, signed into law in 1993, mandates that states report child abuse crimes perpetrated by child care providers to a national background check system. The act does not address private child care providers or nannies, nor does it address the overall substandard nature of much of the child care in the United States.

Child Maltreatment in History

Child abuse in America has been called "a swatch from the fabric of a violent society" (Hobbes, in Zigler and Hall 1989, 41). Child maltreatment is not, of course, a new phenomenon. Only since the mid-twentieth century has it been a major focus of public concern and scientific study (Ariès 1962; Boswell 1988; Greenleaf 1978; Zigler and Hall 1989), but throughout history, children have suffered many forms of maltreatment at adult hands. Infanticide was once commonly practiced in regions as diverse as ancient Greece and Rome, China, and the Middle East, among others. Biblical accounts of the calculated slaughters of infant boys at the foretelling of the births of Moses and Jesus describe common practices of that time. The classical conception of Hell as a burning pit, in fact, derives from descriptions of Hinnom, the burning valley in which Old Testament kings like Solomon and Manasseh sacrificed children to the god Moloch; King Ahaz, we read, "burnt incense in the valley of the son of Hinnom and burnt his children in the fire" (2 Chron. 28.3). The biblically described practice of interring live newborns in the foundations of buildings continued, in some places, into the twentieth century; the foundations of London Bridge and the dikes of Oldenberg in Germany have been found to contain infant remains (Stern 1948).

Poverty has always exacerbated the likelihood that children who had become an economic liability would be abandoned, sold, or mutilated (to make them more pitiable beggars). During the Middle Ages, even children whose families were affluent enough to provide schooling fared poorly: corporal punishment in schools was framed either as a sort of monastic self-abnegation or as a tool to enhance moral development and educational prowess. During the Industrial Revolution in Western Europe and the United States, even very young children of the working classes labored long hours under harsh and hazardous conditions, subject to occupational injuries, diseases, and deformities (Cahn and Cahn 1972; Hanway 1785).

In the United States, the case of Mary Ellen Wilson in the 1870s marked the beginning of public outcry against the maltreatment of children. Eight-year-old Mary Ellen was discovered in the home of her adoptive parents, chained to a bedpost, starved, beaten, and deprived of contact with the outside world. Because no agency then existed to take responsibility for this case, Henry Berg, founder and president of the Society for the Prevention of Cruelty to Animals, intervened and saw the case brought to trial. The newspapers widely publicized the proceedings. Eventually, her adoptive mother was briefly jailed, and Mary Ellen was placed in an orphanage. In 1875, one year after the case came to trial, the Society for the Prevention of Cruelty was founded, and other child protective organizations were soon established in the same mold.

In the 1940s, important advances in pediatric radiology provided the first images of bone and soft-tissue injuries, which often led to suspicion of child maltreatment (Caffey 1946). Not until the 1960s, however, was the term "child abuse" coined (Helfer and Kempe 1968). The field of child abuse study as we know it today is relatively new and remains very much in a state of growth, often accented by controversy. Today, recently developed imaging techniques—CT scanning, fMRI, and other diagnostic tools—give us new awareness not only of what is happening in a child's bones and soft tissues when abuse takes place but opens a window into how the child's brain develops in response to long-term abuse.

ous year's rate of 12.6. Most of these children were age three or under. In almost 90 percent of all cases, the perpetrator of abuse was a parent.

During 1999, approximately 1,100 children died as a result of abuse and neglect, a rate representing roughly 1.62 deaths for each 100,000 children in the general population. Almost 43 percent of these children died in their first year of life; 86.1 percent were younger than six (Child Welfare League of America 2001).

Parents list many causes as factors in their abusive behavior: economic stress, substance abuse, parental history of abuse, and others.

Second only to substance abuse as the most often listed reason for child abuse is "lack of parenting experience or skills," cited by 67 percent of parents surveyed (Kirkpatrick 1999). Notes the director of a child abuse prevention agency, A. Sidney Johnson: "As a society, we're good at helping parents make sure the baby dresses well and is fed properly. But when it comes to helping them learn how to become good parents, they're on their own" (Kirkpatrick 1999, 1).

Child Abuse in Context

The long-term effects of abuse are well demonstrated. Research points decisively to the disturbing outcomes associated with child abuse and neglect that go well beyond the immediate—and far from inconsequential—harms of the abuse itself. Social withdrawal or antisocial behavior, learning deficits, post-traumatic stress syndrome, major depressive disorder, substance abuse, and other mental health problems have long been linked to a history of child abuse (Cicchetti and Carlson 1989; Glaser 2000; Kaufman and Charney 2000). The mechanisms underlying these phenomena, however, have been less well understood. In light of recent advances in brain imaging technology, neurobiologists have turned their attention to examining the neurological mechanisms by which the abusive experience affects the child's psychological functioning and behavior. These findings have taken their place within the broader context represented by the developmental and ecological framework that developmental psychologists employ to help them make sense of the behaviors and needs of the young child and his or her family. Assembling the pieces in this way—developmental, social, and neurological—can shed more light on just how damaging child maltreatment can become and why it is so vital that we implement and support policies that fund and foster child-protection prevention and treatment efforts.

While taking a multidisciplinary approach to the problems associated with child maltreatment has yielded new insights, prevention strategies, and treatment options, it has also enriched, and sometimes complicated, our understanding of these problems. Our view of the child as changing, responding to, and interacting within a variety of spheres guides the way we view and propose to treat child abuse. These spheres, which can be envisioned as a series of concentric circles with the child at their center, range from the most intimate dyadic relationships (mother-child, father-child) to broader influences exercised by schools, communities, child care arrangements, even public policy.

The young child's relationship with the world and its inhabitants and the way in which the child receives and acts on physical, cognitive, and social stimuli are affected by developmental changes. That child is more than just a passive recipient of a caregiver's actions; instead, he or she interacts with the caregiver in (in the best of all possible worlds) a fully mutual relationship.

Imagine a baby girl of six months in an infant seat being fed by her father, for instance. She takes in the bites of baby food as he offers them but also signals her reactions—delight at peaches, disgust at spinach, refusal of more food when full or interested in something else—through her body language and vocalizations. She screws up her face if the food is distasteful, opens her mouth wide for her favorites, and babbles in response to his description of her gourmet meal or her big-girl appetite. Similarly, a responsive dad takes a break or ends the meal when she begins to turn away from the proffered spoonful, or looks for the source of her distress—a wet diaper, a bubble of gas—if she cries. In turn, she rewards his responsiveness to her with displays of happy affection and with a willingness to interact and to explore her environment.

Now imagine a similar but less happy scenario. Perhaps the mother feeding her son is young and inexperienced, or she is tired from working a double shift. Perhaps her child is ill, was born prematurely, suffered from drug or alcohol exposure in utero, or is simply of a more reactive temperament: he hesitates to try new foods or cannot clearly signal that he is ready to take a break from eating strained carrots so that he can play with the spoon she's wielding. Frustrated by what she may perceive as a deliberate lack of cooperation, she may chase him with the food as he turns away or become impatient with his agenda and take his rejection personally. Whereas the first scenario ended with a well-fed baby and a dad and daughter both ready to play, this scene ends with mom angry and her son frustrated and in tears. A parent unaware of what constitutes normal infant behavior (as this boy's does) may respond punitively.

Each stage in a child's life makes unique demands on the caregiver, and each stage brings with it a set of specific developmental needs and vulnerabilities. This illustration of how a parent and child affect each other and engage in mutual interactions is the ecological perspective on an intimate scale. Because children are a part of a changing and developing system that includes their parents, caregivers, community members, extended families, and so on, they get into increasingly complex experiential realms as they grow and mature, and each of their reactions to a new experience is informed by those that have come before. For a young child whose attachments to significant adults are in a crucial stage of development, an abusive experience will have far different effects on him or her, and on the family, than will a similar incident when the child is ten or a teenager or a young adult.

Brain Research and Child Abuse

The tools we now have access to, such as PET scans and fMRI technology, which give us glimpses into the workings of the brain, are having as significant an impact on our understanding of child abuse and its aftereffects as early radiologic studies of children in the 1940s, which provided the first concrete diagnostic evidence of child maltreatment (Caffey 1946). Using these and other techniques, neurobiologists and neurochemists working on issues related to the brain and child abuse have uncovered findings far more fascinating—and shocking—than the long-bone fractures first viewed in the context of acknowledged child abuse more than fifty years ago.

The findings of these studies have been startling, providing profound affirmation of the notion that a child's experiences and interactions with others actually change the very architecture of the brain in ways that, in turn, affect behavior and future cognitive and social development. Both human and animal studies confirm our belief that experience and neurological development are inextricably linked (Cicchetti, in press; Verrengia 2000). As Bruce Perry and his colleagues assert, "The brain organizes and develops as a reflection of developmental experience. When a stressful event is severe enough and of a sufficient duration, an increase in neurotransmitter activity causes abnormal development in the central nervous system of the traumatized child. . . . Affective or emotional memories are indelibly implanted into the brain stem and midbrain and result in alterations in basic physiological functioning" (Perry and Pate 1994, 147).

Sufficient empirical evidence exists to substantiate this assertion, and increasingly sophisticated brain research on precisely how the experience of maltreatment changes young children is yielding fresh insights into the long-term implications of abuse and neglect (Cicchetti and Rogosch, unpubl. ms, 1997; Cicchetti and Toth 2000). Research on the outcomes of abuse formerly focused almost entirely on psychological and behavioral consequences of maltreatment. Today, however, our growing ability to examine the neurobiological correlates of abuse is shedding light on the mechanisms that both contribute to and protect children from poor outcomes associated with abuse. Early emotional traumas or stresses, for example, have been shown to raise concentrations of stress hormones like cortisol to levels that are actually toxic to brain cells, thus reducing the density of connections among cells (Gunnar 1992; Gunnar et al. 1992; Gunnar and Nelson 1994). And in a review of brain research related to child maltreatment (Glaser 2000), child abuse is demonstrably associated with biochemical, structural, and functional modifications to the brain. Early and chronic abuse can be assumed to have more severe effects than episodic or less frequent or later-occurring events. Statistical analyses of large data sets on individuals with a history of child abuse can reliably distinguish the neurological aftereffects of maltreatment from those associated merely with the same stressors that might have precipitated the abuse in the first place (Mullen et al. 1996).

Both trauma and deprivation (abuse and neglect) have been found to have perceivable deleterious effects on the human brain (DeBellis and Putnam 1994). PET scan studies of the brains of adults with a history of post-traumatic stress disorder, for instance, showed changes in areas of the brain associated with memory and a dampening of the effectiveness of language-producing areas (Rauch et al. 1996). Several studies of abused children (such as DeBellis et al. 1999) have confirmed an association between maltreatment and overall reduction in brain size, with the length of exposure to abuse associated with the degree of reduction in brain volume. Kaufman and Charney (2000) also describe persistent changes in the structure of the brains of children with a history of child abuse. These changes are linked to an increased vulnerability to the development of the types of depressive disorders seen at disproportionately high levels in abused children. Reductions in hippocampal volume are also associated with a history of physical and sexual abuse during childhood (Perry and Marcellus 1998; Perry et al. 1995). Studies of this type have clear implications for cognitive development in children with a history of abuse, as well as for the development (and prevention) of socially maladaptive behaviors associated with abuse (Emens et al. 1996; Kaufman and Zigler 1996).

Child Abuse and Social Policy

The child abuse research described in brief here, particularly when viewed in a context incorporating decades of behavioral research, bears directly and positively on the notion of brain changes that occur in direct response to environmental influences and that, further, have a lasting impact on an individual's behavior. The message from such research is clear: as we have long suspected, based on the findings of observational and behavioral research, the impact of child abuse—particularly during the early years—has the potential to be profound and long-lasting, and may be much more severe and persistent than had previously been thought.

Programs and policies designed to prevent child abuse and to improve outcomes for children and families whose lives are touched by child maltreatment are not only humane but cost-effective. One study finds that the economic costs of child abuse and neglect in the United States are staggering, an estimated $285 million *per day*, the equivalent of nearly $1,500 per day per U.S. family (Levine 2000). These costs include not only direct costs, such as for emergency and chronic medical care, mental health care, and the administration of the child welfare system and judicial system, but indirect costs related to law enforcement, juvenile delinquency, lost productivity to society, and adult criminality (Lewis, Mallouh, and Webb 1989; Olweus 1980; Widom 1989).

Policies and action plans are critically needed in at least three areas: addressing the adequacy of child abuse investigation and service delivery planning and funding, working with parents to prevent child maltreatment, and continuing to fund and mount studies about the neurological aspects of child abuse to increase our understanding of the mechanisms at play and to help us develop techniques to mediate and ameliorate these outcomes.

Child Protective Services

The Administration for Children and Families (2001), a division of the U.S. Department of Health and Human Services, keeps track of services typically provided to families of children who have been neglected or abused. In 1999, some 1.5 million children, or 2.2 percent of the child population, received services that might have included one or more of the following: respite care, parenting education, housing assistance, substance abuse treatment, child care, home visiting (discussed in Chapter 5), individual and family counseling, transportation, and domestic violence services, among others (Administration for Children and Families 2001). Funding for such services is provided through a variety of programs at federal, state, and local levels, pursuant to legislation including subsections of the Social Security Act and amendments to the Child Abuse Prevention and Treatment Act of 1974.

In addition to families that received preventive services, nearly half a million children received postinvestigative services after they were identified as victims of abuse (some families receive both types of services). In most cases, however, families receive no services, even when the state finds reasonable support for allegations of maltreatment. Reasons for the lack of services to families identified as being most at risk for child abuse are complex. They include lack of funding for appropriate service provision and adherence to a uniquely American philosophy that gives primacy to the rights of parents (over and above those of their children) to determine how their children will be treated.

Caseworker overloads play a major role in the lack of adequate service provision. A recent study of caseworkers for state child welfare agencies across the nation revealed that these agencies lose roughly 20 percent of their staffs in a given year, a statistic linked directly to the pressures associated with unreasonably heavy caseloads, low pay, and the pressures of administrative responsibilities related to monitoring cases (Child Welfare League of America 2001). Budget cuts at state and federal levels have slashed both human and material resources from child protective agencies. Catastrophic cuts from welfare rolls nation-wide have been made as a result of the passage of the Personal Respon-sibility and Work Opportunity Reconciliation Act of 1996. Social ser-vices caseworkers tend to be overburdened and under-trained (Gelles 1996). They report feeling stressed by the life-or-death decision mak-ing that characterizes their daily work lives, underappreciated when their actions save lives, and guilty when they do not.

Caseworkers are also caught between conflicting philosophical underpinnings of child protection. In theory, caseworkers are there to protect and serve the needs of young children, but as we stated above, this drive often conflicts with a strong tendency in the United States to promote family preservation. Keeping biological families together as a priority often overrides the needs of children to be protected from those very families. Statistics from the 1999 National Child Abuse and Neglect Reporting System (Administration for Children and Families 2001) indicate that 12.5 percent of the families of children who died as a result of abuse and neglect in the nation during that year had received family preservation services during the five years preceding the child's death. Child abuse expert Richard Gelles (1996) blames such deaths on heavy casework loads and an overemphasis on the philosophy of fam-ily preservation, which emphasizes the rights of biological parents over those of their children. The welfare of the child should always be the foremost concern of those who mount, fund, and evaluate interven-tions in cases or suspected cases of child abuse and neglect. Certainly many families can improve their functioning with the aid of support-ive services, but strong evidence indicates that not all families will be able to provide optimal or even adequate care to these children.

Working with Parents

Stopping child abuse before it starts would be the strategy of choice in the best of all possible worlds. It is perhaps surprising that as of this writing, parents in the United States, on average, appear to be *more* rather than less willing to accept corporal punishment as a routine part of child raising (Alexander 2001), reversing an earlier trend. High-pro-file child guidance gurus have achieved strong media visibility by pro-moting a parent's "right" or even "responsibility" to employ corporal punishment (Ezzo and Ezzo 1998; Rosemond 1994). In spite of such a trend, experts continue to warn that the negative outcomes of corporal punishment far outweigh any benefit parents might feel they derive from spanking their children. One study, for instance, notes that it takes an average of eight spankings triggered by a particular behavior to prompt a child to change that behavior in the desired direction. But the same number of time-outs will have the same effect, without the negative outcomes and potential for harm (Straus and Mathner 1996). Respected groups like the American Academy of Pediatrics and Zero to Three remain staunchly opposed to the use of physical punishment by parents and committed to parent education campaigns that may help to reverse the most recent trend back toward widespread acceptance of spanking and other forms of corporal punishment.

Even when secondary prevention efforts—those that keep identified child abusers from repeating their actions—are effective, the devastation that can affect a family in which abuse has taken place and protective (but often invasive) services have been applied often cannot be healed completely. The physical affects of child abuse are likely to fade long before the emotional, cognitive, and legal outcomes have been resolved. Reliable research indicates that a domino effect may also be associated with child abuse, such that, even if stopped early, related, delayed effects may be manifested later in life (Aber and Cicchetti 1984; Cicchetti and Carlson 1989). Primary prevention of child abuse —that is, providing the services families need to avoid abusive behavior in the first place—are the answer.

Parent education—helping parents to understand their child's behavior, to anticipate developmental crises (such as increased crying in the first three months or the negativity common in the second year of life), and to maintain a realistic set of beliefs about developmentally appropriate behaviors (Zigler and Hall 1989)—is typically at the core of such preventive efforts. As the previous chapter discussed, home visitation programs are one effective means to address this goal, especially when intervention is implemented early, even, when possible, in the prenatal period.

In keeping with a developmental-ecological framework, we propose that broad-based, comprehensive family support programs offer the most promising means to both prevent and—where necessary—

treat child abuse (Daro 1993; Zigler and Gilman 1993). The School of the 21st Century program, which includes in its components a child care program and outreach efforts to assist, support, and educate parents, and the Illinois-based Ounce of Prevention fund, whose family-based program has been highly successful in controlling child abuse and decreasing the influence of negative outcomes, are two examples of such programs. Parent-education programs, particularly those that target young people *before* they become parents, have also been shown to be effective at preventing child abuse, both by encouraging delayed childbearing and by giving new and prospective parents a realistic sense of developmentally appropriate behaviors in infancy and early childhood (Pfannenstiel, Lambson, and Yarnell 1991).

Parent education can also be provided through media outlets. The use of brief public service announcements such as the nationally promoted Don't Shake the Baby campaign, can inform parents about the dangers of corporal punishment, anger management, stress reduction, and where and how to seek help for abusive impulses or behaviors.

Last, the need for more research on child abuse and all its aspects —social, cognitive, and neurological—is profound. Further information on how abusive experiences affect the structure of the brain and its ability to mediate stress, learning, and depression can help us both to promote appropriate parenting and to find ways to alleviate or buffer the effects of child maltreatment. A commitment to effective policies based on sound research is the least we owe to children and families.

7

The Mozart Effect
Not Learning from History

In earlier chapters we have described how news reports on the impact of early experience on the developing brain are being used to influence social policies and interventions for young children. One compelling example is the so-called Mozart effect—the widely publicized yet empirically unsupported link between listening to Mozart piano sonatas and increases in cognitive abilities. In this chapter we will look at how the Mozart effect and other similar studies have been used in the service of misguided, quick-fix solutions to issues that are, in truth, far more complicated. Contrasted with these false solutions are the substantive contributions by high-quality, intensive, multi-domain interventions to early cognitive and social development.

Early Experience and the Development of the Human Brain

One way of measuring the relation between early experience and cognitive development is to study language acquisition. Language is a cognitive function that is highly dependent on experience and relatively easy to quantify. In *Meaningful Differences in the Everyday Experience of Young American Children* (1995), Betty Hart and Todd Risley describe a study of this type. The authors examined the language development of children raised in professional, working-class, and welfare families, and they found significant differences in the number and quality of parental verbalizations directed toward the child among these three groups. Observations of the children when they were between thirteen and thirty-six months old revealed that the children heard an average of 487 parental utterances per hour in the professional families, 301 in the working-class families, and 178 in the families receiving public aid. Furthermore, the quality (use of nouns, modifiers, past-tense verbs, declarative sentences, and so on) of the utterances was highest in the professional group. Most significant, these differences in the amount and quality of parental language were related to the child's vocabulary growth, vocabulary use, and IQ at age three, as well as to scores on tests of verbal intelligence at ages nine to ten. Interestingly, within the working-class group, differences in the parents' language were not related to whether the families were middle or low income, but these speech differences accounted for much of the variation in children's vocabulary and IQ at age three. This finding suggests that the verbal environment of the home has greater bearing on a child's language development than a parent's economic resources (and the things that money can buy).

Hart and Risley's findings are not without precedent. In another study (Huttenlocher et al. 1991), researchers found that the amount of parents' speech when children were sixteen months old was related to the children's vocabulary growth over the period of study. Having established that individual experiences affect children's later observed abilities, the next set of questions becomes more focused on process: How are social experiences, such as the amount and quality of parental language early in life, translated into concrete and measurable differences in young children's development?

Research with animals and new brain imaging, scanning, and electrical recording technology (Chugani 1996; Nelson and Bloom 1997) have advanced our understanding of the impact of early experience on the developing brain. Such investigations are beginning to give us some tentative answers about the mechanisms behind findings like those reported by Hart and Risley, Janellen Huttenlocher and col-

leagues, and others (for example, Fox, Calkins, and Bell 1994). The biological work suggests that early experience influences the brain in two
primary ways: first, by affecting the normal developmental growth
process, and second, by affecting stress circuits in the brain due to repeated exposure to glucocorticoid hormones, also known as cortisol.
In discussing these processes, we should note that much of this work
has been conducted with animals and that the new technology being
used is still new and imprecise.

Normal Developmental Growth and Synaptogenesis

The first years of life are characterized by dramatic growth in synapse
formation and dendritic density in the developing brain. (Recall that a
synapse is a junction of two nerve cells; through dendrites, signals from
nerve cells branch out to other cells.) As we discussed in the earlier
chapter on brain development, growth rates in many areas of the brain
peak between two and three years of age and subsequently decrease,
leveling off at adult levels during adolescence (Bourgeois, Goldman-
Rakic, and Rakic 1995; Huttenlocher 1994; Huttenlocher and Dabholkar 1997). Continued activation of new synapses, formed primarily
through experiences during these early years, drives a pruning or selective retention process in which both the density and the structure of
synapses are altered and reduced (Greenough, Black, and Wallace 1987;
Hockfield and Lombroso 1998a; Huttenlocher 1994). This reduction
appears to be necessary for the development of higher-level skills
(Bruer 1999). Further, even though synaptic connections are being reduced even faster after age three, there is still opportunity for the
growth of new connections in response to experience (Gunnar and
Barr 1998). From this process researchers have derived the notion of
plasticity, which refers to the malleability of the system and its ability
to respond to environmental changes (Huttenlocher 1994). William
Greenough and his colleagues (Greenough and Black 1992; Greenough
et al. 1987) break this process down further, differentiating environment-
expectant and environment-dependent processes and tagging the former specifically to critical or sensitive periods in synapse formation.

Environment-expectant processes happen early in development
and are characterized by the overproduction of synapses in expectation

that a particular sensory stimulus will occur. The stimuli are those expected to be present in the average environment of the young of a particular species. After repeated exposure to the stimulus, the activated synapses are strengthened, while those that remain unactivated are pruned away. The overproduction of synapses in expectation of a particular environmental or sensory event has been described by Greenough and colleagues (1987) as "readiness for experience." The process allows for the potential range of stimuli within the global category of the species' natural surroundings.

An example is the universal responsiveness of infants to phonemes regardless of the caregiver's language (Werker and Tees 1984). A related finding is that infant babbling before nine months of age is indistinguishable across languages (Blake and de Boysson-Bardies 1992). After a period of exposure to a single language, the infant becomes responsive only to its phonemes and begins to babble in sounds characteristic of that language (Kuhl 2000). These findings suggest that the infant is becoming "ready" for the development of native language through an overproduction of synapses. Those that are needed will be selectively preserved based on the infant's linguistic exposure.

Extensive research on animals supports the notion of environment-expectant processes and, more generally, of critical or sensitive periods for sensory development. In a classic study, described more fully earlier in Chapter 2, researchers showed that if a kitten has visual input in only one eye during a brief period early in the kitten's development, the majority of synapses formed between neurons in the visual cortex will be devoted to the stimulated eye. As a result, one eye takes control of the visual cortex, and the other eye becomes disconnected (Wiesel 1982; Wiesel and Hubel 1963). Additional studies suggest that such outcomes cannot be reversed by stimulation in both eyes later in development (Crabtree and Riesen 1979). In research with human infants, Fox, Calkins, and Bell (1994) also support the notion of experience-expectant processes. Using EEG technology, these researchers found that just before the onset of crawling, infants were higher on measures of electrical activity between two distinct locations of the brain, indicating an overproduction of synaptic connections. Children who had begun crawling or had been crawling for several months had significantly lower levels of electrical activity between these sites, indicating a process of synaptic pruning.

The second component of Greenough's model is the concept of experience-dependent processes, or processes that occur in response to experiences unique to the individual. This component is based on the premise that much of the information necessary for successful development is specific to each person (Greenough et al. 1987). The neural activity thought to underlie this process is that new events trigger the creation of synaptic connections and an expansion in dendritic complexity. By contrast, low exposure to novel experiences results in low generation of synaptic connections and less dendritic complexity.

Research supporting the experience-dependent process has focused primarily on the effects of either enriched or deprived environments on development. Work with rats and mice has revealed that being reared in what is described as an enriched environment (in a cage with multiple objects and other animals in contrast to an empty, isolated cage) results in a heavier and thicker cerebral cortex. This greater mass is largely due to a greater number of synaptic connections and dendritic branchings (Greenough 1975; Hockfield and Lombroso 1998b; Rosenzweig, Bennett, and Diamond 1972). For example, researchers (Kempermann, Kuhn, and Gage 1997) found significantly more neurons in the hippocampus as well as greater hippocampal volume in mice reared in an enriched environment compared to those reared in a "standard" cage (empty of objects and with few companions). One observed effect of these increases was that the enriched group showed greater speed in learning a task involving a water maze.

Glucocorticoids and Stress

Another area in which experience-dependent processes are at work is in the production of glucocorticoid hormones in response to specific environmental events and, in particular, to events that cause stress (see Glaser 2000 for a review). Persistent exposure to glucocorticoids (cortisol) has been found to result in dendritic atrophy in the hippocampus and, under conditions of excessive exposure, in neuron death (Lombroso and Sapolsky 1998). Thus, an abundance of glucocorticoid hormones can reduce the number of glucocorticoid receptors in the brain, affecting the brain's ability to modulate and respond to future exposure (Benes 1994; Gunnar and Barr 1998). The result is a future inability to regulate responses to stress (Clark and Schneider 1993). In other words, "full-blown response patterns (e.g., hyperarousal or dissociation) can be elicited by apparently minor stressors" (Perry et al. 1995, 275).

High levels of stress and subsequent high levels of cortisol have implications for the healthy development of young children. For example, Joan Kaufman and colleagues (1997; see also Kaufman and Charney 2000) reported increased cortisol secretion in a group of depressed, abused children who were experiencing ongoing familial and environmental stressors as compared to depressed, nonabused children and a control group. Other researchers have found higher cortisol levels to be related to poor attentional focus and self-control in preschoolers (Gunnar et al. 1997); the ability to remember new information (Gunnar and Nelson 1994); the use of a disorganized or avoidant attachment strategy in infancy and toddlerhood (Nachmias et al. 1996; Spangler and Grossman 1993); and increased likelihood of aggressive and violent behavior in boys later in development (Perry 1997). Very high levels of neurotransmitters (due to prolonged stress) in the prefrontal cortex have also been found to affect working memory (Arnsten 1999). These findings hint that a stressful environment can harm the brain and permanently affect social and emotional behavior.

Reactions to Early Brain Development Research

Taken together, the research described above suggests that the infant is born with a basic genetic blueprint for development that guides the overproduction of synapses in expectation of "normal" environmental stimuli. The effect of stimuli unique to the individual is to structure both the pruning of unused synapses and the further production and strengthening of existing synapses. Although much more work needs to be done, these findings have captured a great deal of political, media, and research attention. In spite of the tremendous interest shown by the general public, policy makers, program operators, and educators in the new brain research and its potential applications, some scientists have called for caution in interpreting and especially in acting on the findings. One well-known critic of the media and policy hype surrounding the brain research is John Bruer, whose book *The Myth of the First Three Years* we have discussed in previous chapters. Despite the misleading overstatement of his title and the resulting misguided media and political questions about the value of early intervention for young children, we agree with Bruer's suggestion that the brain findings be interpreted with several important caveats. In this regard, two important points need to be underscored.

First, the majority of the evidence supporting synaptogenesis, critical periods, and the relative benefits of enriched environments has been conducted with animal populations. The studies done thus far with humans have been primarily indirect (Fox et al. 1994), where the impact of particular environments on the brain is inferred. Although new PET and fMRI technology has enabled researchers to examine directly and noninvasively the brains of young children, this work is very recent and has been conducted primarily with small numbers of children who have medical difficulties (such as epilepsy) or have suffered extreme deprivation and trauma. It is not appropriate to generalize findings from studies with such select populations to our understanding of the normal development of the human brain.

Second, evidence that is being cited to show the benefits of "enriched" environments actually proves no more than the harmful effects of deprived environments. For example, many studies have compared animals residing in groups in cages with lots of objects and toys with animals reared alone (or in smaller groups) in cages with no objects. Some researchers have explained that the environments that include a variety of stimuli are less "enriched" than they are a gross approximation of the natural environment—that they are, in other words, normative. Greenough, too, suggests that these environments might better be described as "complex" environments (Greenough and Black 1992; Kempermann et al. 1997). Consequently, findings from such studies suggest less about the increased capacities resulting from enrichment than they do about the reduced capacities resulting from deprivation. Furthermore, although the results tell us much about biological development under differing environmental conditions, they tell us very little about the power of interventions to change behavior and promote positive developmental outcomes within deprived environments.

The results from the animal experiments tell us even less about the power of the environment to affect human development. In the state of nature, there is actually little variation, in, say, rats' behavior. A mother rat instinctively cares for her pups in a way that is conducive to their growth and development. In human beings, there is wide range of possible maternal and paternal behaviors—some more and some less beneficial to the child. Further, rats are nurtured during a very brief childhood, whereas human babies are under their parents' influence for a relatively long period of time. What this all means is that rodents are rarely deprived of good caregiving during their period of growth. Humans may receive good, neutral, or poor caregiving at various times over their different stages of development. And human environments do not come in the two flavors, "standard" and "enriched," like those provided to laboratory animals. People are born into environments ranging from very deprived to very enriched with every possibility in between. This is why many fields of human biology and psychology treat the environment as a continuum and refer to what is called the "threshold effect." This means that a certain level of environmental nutrients, be they adequate food or verbal stimulation, is required for normal development to occur. Below this level, development will be harmed. At or above the threshold, development will proceed as it should. Note that here again, scientists are only sure about what will happen in deprived conditions, not what value is added by enrichment.

Neither the lack of ability to generalize from animals to humans nor the true meaning of environmental variation studies has deterred American capitalists seeking profits or politicians seeking votes. Some professionals have used the brain research to promote very early interventions, not just for disadvantaged children but for all American babies. Some ideas are simple and free, like advice to sing or read to newborns. Others have evolved to a variety of misguided "quick-fix" solutions and commercial promises that this or that gadget will provide the experiences necessary to grow a baby's brain. Among such quick fixes, perhaps none are so recently prominent as those based upon what is popularly termed the Mozart effect.

The Mozart Effect and IQ Change

In 1998 Georgia's governor Zell Miller proposed a bill to spend $105,000 to give each newborn child in the state a cassette or compact disc of classical music. Governor Miller's enthusiasm and policy proposal were inspired by the highly touted Mozart effect, first reported in 1993 by re-searchers at the University of California at Irvine. In a study published in the journal *Nature*, Francis Rauscher, Gordon Shaw, and Katherine Ky (1993) found that college students who had spent ten minutes lis-tening to Mozart's Sonata for Two Pianos in D Major had Stanford-Binet spatial subtest IQ scores (measuring abilities in visual-spatial thinking and the simultaneous processing of information) that were eight to nine points higher than students who had listened to either a relaxation tape or nothing. The IQ effects did not persist beyond the ten-to-fifteen-minute testing session. In a follow-up study, Rauscher, Shaw, and Ky (1995) attempted to replicate their findings with a new sample of seventy-nine college students. Over the course of five testing days, they examined differences in visual-spatial abilities and visual-motor coordination skills using the paper cutting and folding task of the Stanford-Binet among students who had listened for ten minutes to Mozart's Sonata K. 448 and those who had heard nothing or had lis-tened to a variety of nonclassical musical selections. The Mozart group had significantly higher scores by day two, but their scores were not significantly different from the other two groups on days three, four, and five. Interestingly, the effect of listening to Mozart in this study was not immediate, as it had been in the first study. In both experi-ments, however, the effect did not persist.

Most relevant to our topic are findings with preschool children. In one study, children between the ages of three and five who had pri-vate piano keyboard lessons ten minutes a day for six months were compared to those who had computer lessons, singing lessons, or no lessons. The piano group had higher post-test scores on the object as-sembly task of the Weschler Preschool and Primary School Test of In-telligence (WPPSI), which requires spatial-temporal reasoning skills (Rauscher et al. 1997). The researchers described these changes inspatial-temporal reasoning as "long-term" because they were equally evident for children who were tested less than a day after their final lesson and those tested more than a day later. The authors concluded that "music training, unlike listening, produces long-term modifications in neural circuitry . . . in regions not primarily concerned with music" and that the improvement for the piano group was equivalent to "an increase

from the 50th percentile on the WPPSI-R standardized test to above
the 85th percentile" (Rauscher et al. 1997, 7).

In their studies of both preschoolers and college students, Rauscher
and her colleagues (1995, 1997) conjecture about the mechanism underlying the findings. They suggest that exposure to music (Mozart in
particular) primes the portion of the cortex responsible for spatial-
temporal reasoning skills, or the ability to envision and rotate images
in the mind. This "priming," if it occurs over a period of time, pre-
sumably strengthens those neural circuits and results in "long-term"
change. Yet the exceptionally limited definition of "long-term" in this
context (ten minutes and a day or two) makes this conclusion purely
speculative.

Other researchers who have attempted to replicate the Mozart effect have had little success. Efforts to discern music-induced superior-
ity on mental tasks have failed (Kenealy and Monseth 1994; Steele,
Ball, and Runk 1997; Steele, Bass, and Crook 1999; Newman et al.
1995; Stough et al. 1994; Wilson and Brown 1997). As of this writing,
the work with preschoolers has not been replicated. Finally, scientists
have levied serious criticisms of the original work on methodological
grounds, some of which may account for the lack of replication (Chabris
1998; Newman et al. 1995).

In spite of its scientifically weak base, the Mozart effect has gained
a durable reputation with the public. The original research has given
rise to claims about the power of short-term "enrichment" experiences
to alter neural structure. Entrepreneurs, not surprisingly, have capitalized on the phenomenon, and the Mozart effect has quickly found its
way into a variety of products for families with infants and young children. Among these are videotapes shown in maternity wards, a variety
of CDs with names like "Beethoven for Babies," and a popular book
and CD package by Don Campbell entitled *The Mozart Effect: Tap-
ping the Power of Music to Heal the Body, Strengthen the Mind, and Un-
lock the Creative Spirit.* Governor Miller's well-meaning efforts, as well
as similar programs supported by the governors of both Tennessee and
Florida, have surely spiked the sales of certain types of classical music.
And although we have nothing against music in the nursery, these
leaders' proposals could have the effect of turning attention, as well as
critical state money, away from more substantive (if more expensive)

programs that are proven to have positive and genuinely long-lasting effects on young children growing up under deprived conditions.

Déjà Vu

The tendency to embrace easy ways to induce fast learning is not new; history provides plenty of illustrations of our previous steps down this path. During the early 1960s a profusion of "educational" toys and gimmicks, such as crib mobiles and talking typewriters, enjoyed the same high status as Mozart sonatas in the 1990s, marketed as sure-fire tools to raise children's intelligence. The popularity of crib mobiles, for example, was based on a study (White and Held 1966) that found that psychomotor abilities called "fisted swiping" and "top-level reaching" appeared moderately sooner when infants had a visual stabile in their cribs. In reviewing results from such short-term projects, J. O. Miller (1970) concluded, "Where limited intervention objectives in the psychomotor or cognitive areas are clearly delineated and intervention techniques are specifically designed to accomplish those objectives, significant gains can be obtained over a short intervention period." He cautioned, however, that "little evidence is available concerning the longevity of obtained effects nor the effect of specific gains on more complex skills" (1970, 468). Such cautions clearly apply to the current supply of gimmicks inspired by brain research.

Claims about the susceptibility of intelligence to environmental enhancers, both in the 1960s and today, are rooted in the long-standing, mostly American, infatuation with IQ. This interest was foreshadowed by Donald Hebb's (1949) early findings on the superior learning ability of rats reared as pets compared to those reared in the laboratory. Over time, American psychologists gradually abandoned their long-held belief that intelligence is fixed and began to emphasize the primacy of environment in shaping cognitive development (Spitz 1986; Zigler and Styfco 1997). This "environmental mystique," as Zigler described it in 1970, "holds that intelligence is essentially trainable: that the intellect (that collection of cognitive processes—memory, concept formation, the formal structure of cognition and intelligence) is essentially the result of environmental input and, in essence, that intelligence is an environmental product" (1970a, 403–404). Zigler noted that this "viewpoint, this environmental mystique," was "sweeping the country" (404). It seems, some thirty years later, that the environmental mystique is alive and well and finding support from poor-quality, poorly replicated research such as that describing the Mozart effect.

Jump back a generation or so from the California researchers who discovered the supposed power of Mozart. In the 1960s two early proponents of the potential of early environmental conditions to raise IQ were Benjamin Bloom and J. McVicker Hunt. Bloom estimated, for example, that "in terms of intelligence measured at age 17, about 50% of the development takes place between conception and age four," and that "the effect of extreme environments on intelligence is about 20 IQ points" (1964, 88–89). Bloom's contentions not only invoke the notion of a critical period for the development of intelligence but also suggest specifically that environmental conditions during these periods can seriously influence IQ. Hunt, in his seminal work *Intelligence and Experience,* also critiqued the notion of fixed intelligence and concluded that scientists need to investigate ways to "govern the encounters that children have with their environments, especially during the early years of their development, to achieve a faster rate of intellectual development and a substantially higher adult level of intellectual capacity" (1961, 363). In later work he reported IQ changes as great as fifty to seventy points with appropriate intervention (Hunt 1971).

In a backlash to this naive environmentalism, some later theorists contended that intelligence is a stable, predominantly heritable characteristic. The backlash was inevitable, given the lofty promises being made that could not possibly be kept. A telling illustration comes from the story of Head Start, the comprehensive intervention program for economically disadvantaged preschoolers and their families. Head Start began in 1965, at the height of fervent environmentalism. The project's goal was to help poor children prepare for elementary school. To achieve this end, it provided physical and mental health care, preschool education, parent and community involvement, and social support services for children and their families. For reasons that included the widespread infatuation with IQ and the lack of standardized measures of some of the program's objectives, early evaluations focused narrowly on cognition. Initial reports showed that children's IQ scores increased by ten or more points after spending only six to eight weeks in Head Start.

On common sense grounds alone, Zigler, a member of the Head Start's original planning committee and one of the founders of the program, knew there was no magical environmental wand that would raise preschoolers' IQs by almost a full standard deviation in a mere six weeks. In a series of empirical studies, he demonstrated that the surprisingly large increase in IQ reported in the first summer of Head Start was due to changes in motivational factors that influenced the children's test-taking behavior rather than to real changes in the children's intellectual status (Seitz et al. 1975; Zigler et al. 1982; Zigler and Butterfield 1968). But IQ scores make better headlines than traits like self-confidence and willingness to try. The IQ findings propelled Head Start to instant popularity with lawmakers and the public—that is, until findings began to trickle in that the IQ gains disappeared within a few years (the famous fade-out effect). The nation's love affair with Head Start came to an abrupt end, and plans were drawn to phase it out. The disappointment led to a prolonged period when many believed that little could be done to help poor children succeed in school. Head Start survived only because of its broad base of grassroots support, devoted parent constituency, and the efforts of Elliot Richardson, secretary of the Department of Health, Education, and Welfare, the government agency where Head Start was housed in the early 1970s.

One can go back even further in history to see the same pendulum swing between hope and hopelessness over the malleability of IQ. In the mid-nineteenth century, there was a great deal of optimism among workers that individuals with mental retardation could be "reawakened" and taught to become intellectually "normal" (see Zigler 1987). Around the country, "training schools" were built where people with mental retardation could come to live and receive care and education. By the early twentieth century, when it became evident that training did not "cure" mental retardation, hope turned to despair. The training schools turned into human warehouses where these individuals were locked away, neglected, sterilized, feared, and forgotten. It was not until the 1960s and 1970s, after exposés of the horrid conditions in these institutions and the passage of what is now called the Individuals with Disabilities Education Act, that persons with mental retardation again began to secure some public compassion.

The lesson from these examples is that one extreme preordains the other. When we naively come to believe that IQ can be raised substantially by intervention—whether in the form of a training school or crib mobile or Head Start—we set ourselves up for failure. When that failure becomes apparent, as it inevitably will, dashed hopes lead us to quit—to abandon those we had believed we could help. History repeats itself, and this will happen to the Mozart craze. The wild claims being made for the brain-stimulation products are simply too grand to be achieved. When the pendulum completes its swing, early intervention will fall from grace. And although this may not harm babies who have healthy environments, those who do not and who could benefit the most from intervention will suffer.

A bright spot from history comes from those times when the debate over IQ floated to middle ground, moving from the extreme positions of heritability versus environment toward a compromise: heredity *and* environment. Interest also shifts sometimes from intelligence to the "whole child"—in other words, the physical, cognitive, *and* socioemotional domains of development (Zigler and Styfco 1993). Each domain affects the others. For example, positive changes in the social environment can have a powerful impact on the child's emotional development, affecting a child's motivation to be successful. Heightened motivation in turn affects cognitive growth and achievement (Greenspan and Benderly 1997; Zero to Three, 1992; Zigler and Muenchow 1992; Zigler and Trickett 1978). This broader view acknowledges the contributions of both heredity and the environment, but importantly, it also forces us to recognize that intellectual development is not independent of the rest of the child. As Edward Zigler and Sally Styfco have observed, "The physical and socioemotional aspects of development are more strongly controlled by the environment and, therefore, more effectively targeted by intervention. Indeed, improvements in these aspects are suspected to underlie the initial gains in IQ following preschool experience" (1997, 293).

It is worth noting that the value of social competence as opposed to IQ change as an indicator of the success of early interventions has been well established (Raver and Zigler 1997; Zigler and Trickett 1978). After thirty-five years of confusion, the 1998 Head Start reauthorization explicitly stated that improvement in school readiness is the ultimate goal of the program. A close analysis of the school readiness and social competence constructs indicates that they are one and the same.

Obviously the debate over the malleability of intelligence and the appropriate development of policies and interventions for young children has been played out before. The difference is that this time the debate has moved to the world of new and exciting neuroscience research on the developing brain. But again, interest is focused on the brain's cognitive functions. Overlooked is the fact that the brain also controls emotions and the accompanying motivational system. We submit that a child's sense of security, self-image, curiosity, willingness to try, and a host of other psychological features—all based somewhere in the brain—strongly influence how well that child applies his or her intelligence to learning tasks. By focusing on raw intelligence and ignoring the processes that drive its use, even the most sophisticated brain research will not help children do better in school.

What Have We Learned from Early Intervention Research?

Can brain development research inform a meaningful intervention policy? Not yet, at least not in the manner suggested by the Mozart effect (Shonkoff and Phillips 2000). One lesson we can draw from Greenough's research on environment-dependent processes is the potential negative impact of environmental factors on brain development. Certainly one cannot equate negative environmental conditions such as those described in the studies of mice with such complex conditions as poverty, family and community disorganization, and violence. However, such complex factors are known to place children at risk for poor cognitive and socioemotional outcomes, and brain research may offer a preliminary understanding of the physiological processes involved (Nelson and Bloom 1997).

At this stage then, brain research is not the most valuable information we have to help at-risk children develop their capabilities. That information comes from years of early intervention research and experience. (For reviews see Barnett 1995; Consortium for Longitudinal Studies 1983; Guralnick 1997; Karoly et al. 1998; Reynolds 2000; and Shonkoff and Meisels 2000.)

This work clearly shows that we can help children who live in poverty do better in school and later in life. The formula has nothing to do with Mozart's music or any other sort of magic inoculations. We have learned that successful interventions take time and effort. Specifically, programs that work must be comprehensive, of high quality, and of sufficient duration and intensity (Bronfenbrenner 1975; C. T. Ramey and S. L. Ramey 1998; Schorr 1988; Seitz 1990; Zigler and Styfco 1997). These ingredients are briefly described below.

Comprehensiveness is built on Urie Bronfenbrenner's (1979) ecological model of human development. In this model development is seen as unfolding within a nested and interactive set of systems, extending from the child, to the family, to the community and beyond. Research has shown that programs that address needs at multiple levels of this model by providing a broad spectrum of services both to parents (such as parenting education and job training) and to children (such as nutrition and health in addition to education) have the most potential for success (Zigler and Styfco 1997). For example, Yoshikawa (1995) reported that programs that provide both family support and child education are more likely to be successful in reducing future problem behaviors and perhaps delinquency than programs that focus on one or the other.

High-quality interventions are those that, in addition to maintaining minimum standards in basic features (such as staff-child ratios and teacher training), also target outcomes appropriate to the child's stage of development. Targeting such "stage-salient" developmental tasks (Sroufe 1979; Waters and Sroufe 1983) ensures that the program will supply the appropriate developmental "nutrients" the child needs at the time. For example, one important task of the early school-age child is to learn to negotiate and resolve conflicts with peers. Efforts to maximize school achievement at this age should include interpersonal problem-solving skills; the idea is that when children know how to solve social problems, they have more time to focus on schoolwork (Aber and Jones 1997). Developmental appropriateness also means that children are not pushed to achieve skills they are not developmentally ready to accomplish.

Last, interventions must be of sufficient duration and intensity to be effective. Child development is not over by age three, and certainly not by the time a few musical compositions are heard. Human development extends from the time of first breath to the last. Growth is, of course, fastest during childhood, so emerging abilities need to be encouraged throughout this time.

It is foolish to believe that one sonata or a year of one program or another will protect children who spend their entire youth in poverty-stricken and hazardous environments. Longer efforts may not guarantee positive outcomes, but their track record is certainly better than that of the quick fixes. The literature that has been built over forty years of intervention research contains no evidence that children grow up better off after some high-speed experience. It does, however, contain proof that high-quality, intensive, and coordinated efforts can and do have a positive impact on the health and development of children and families (Campbell and Ramey 1994; Reynolds 2000; Schweinhart, Barnes, and Weikart 1993).

Recent brain research is of value in elucidating the physiological processes of brain development and relating that development to basic environmental conditions. Moreover, in its clear support of the idea that deprivation early in life can have a strong and lasting negative effect on the life chances of young children, such research helps justify the development of intervention programs. But the use of brain data to support such phenomena as the Mozart effect or the creative efforts of the quick-buck community can do more harm than good. Further, they generate false hopes that must inevitably result in failure. The promotion of colorful but simplistic solutions creates false impressions about child development and draws attention and resources away from programs, policies, and ideas that have already been proven to be effective.

8

The Brain, Prenatal Development, and Nutrition

The brain may be the seat of human intellect and emotion, but it is also an organ. For it to grow and develop properly, the brain's physical needs must be met. Throughout our lives, the brain grows, develops, and adapts, becoming increasingly specialized in response to various experiences.

Still, there is no question that the first few years of life, from conception through the first three years, are a time of rapid brain development and, as such, of vital importance. During the prenatal period in particular, the brain is dependent on various needs and nutrients as well as on protection from adverse influence. The potential adverse effects of either the absence of essential needs and protective factors or the presence of toxic substances or both, during the nine months in utero are critical, not only for brain development but for the optimal growth and development of other organs as well. For this reason the prenatal period is termed a critical developmental period.

As we noted in Chapter 2, there is a distinction between a critical period and a sensitive period. With a sensitive period, adverse environmental influences can still be overcome; the door is not completely shut. The critical period is less forgiving: adverse outcomes associated with environmental influences during a critical period often cannot be healed or reversed. The impact of adverse effects before or after the critical period may vary, having less impact or no impact at all on development. During the nine-month prenatal period, various organs develop at different times and rates, so the critical period for each differs. There are also variations in how different factors influence development. Some adverse influences—maternal alcohol consumption, for example—when present at any time during the prenatal period, or throughout the period, can have various detrimental effects on the newborn. For other environmental factors, such as the rubella virus, the time frame for influence may be more limited: rubella early in pregnancy may cause miscarriage, deafness, blindness, or other birth defects, while the same disease later in the pregnancy is not harmful (see box, "Maternal Factors That May Influence Fetal Development").

Other environmental factors influence development—positively as well as adversely—not only during the prenatal period but later in life. One of these is nutrition. The need for and positive role of nutrients from food is obvious. Yet nutrition problems are attracting increasing attention among researchers and policymakers in the United States. The issue with nutrition is twofold. On one hand, some people in this country lack sufficient food. While food scarcity is not as enormous a problem in the United States as it is in developing countries, there is concern that many pregnant women and young children are not getting enough calories and that they experience periods of hunger, which can have a negative impact on development in general and brain development in particular. At the other end of the continuum, there is obesity and malnutrition; researchers are finding that increasing numbers of people may not necessarily be hungry but are malnourished and not getting appropriate nutrients. Malnutrition among pregnant women and young children may result in potential assaults to the developing brain as well as health problems that can become exacerbated over time.

In this chapter we highlight the importance and vulnerability of the prenatal period and we look in-depth at the impact of undernutrition and malnutrition. Our discussion on nutrition extends beyond pregnancy to include the early years of postnatal development. The research on nutrition during the prenatal and postnatal periods is only

Maternal Factors That May Affect Fetal Development

Maternal factors	Effect on the fetus
Drugs	
Alcohol	Small head size, defective joints, congenital heart defects, mental retardation
Nicotine	Low birth weight, premature birth, stillbirth, spontaneous abortion, nicotine dependence at birth; associated with sudden infant death syndrome (SIDS), hyperactivity, and increased respiratory infections during first year of life
Aspirin (moderate use)	Relatively safe until third trimester; use then may prolong labor and lengthen clotting time for both mother and baby, increasing risk of hemorrhage
Tetracycline	Liver, bone, and teeth damage, discolored teeth, abnormally short arms or legs, webbed hands
Thalidomide	Stunted limb growth
Tranquilizers	In first trimester, cleft palate and other birth defects, neonatal jaundice
Heroin	Low birth weight, maternal toxemia, postpartum maternal hemorrhaging (including risk of neonatal death), altered neonatal sleep patterns, fetal addiction and withdrawal, respiratory depression
Methadone	Low birth weight, hyperirritability, respiratory depression
Caffeine	Low birth weight
Marijuana	In animals: reduced growth rate, spontaneous abortion, low birth weight

| LSD | Poorly understood; stillbirth, spontaneous abortion (in animals: neonatal death, temporary chromosomal damage) |

Diseases and medical conditions

Rubella virus	First trimester miscarriage, deafness, blindness, cataracts, heart malformations, various other defects
Diabetes	Maternal toxemia, abnormally large fetus, stillbirth, spontaneous abortion
Syphilis	Malformations, mental retardation, syphilitic infant, deafness, blindness, spontaneous abortion, stillbirth
Influenza	In first trimester, malformations
Gonorrhea	Blindness, gonococcal arthritis, increased risk of ectopic pregnancy
Anemia	Neonatal anemia
Herpes, type II	Neonatal death

Hormones

Androgens	In females, masculinization of internal and/or external genitals
Estrogens	In males, less aggression and athletic skill compared to age-matched controls
Progesterone	Masculinization of female fetus
DES (diethylstilbestrol)	In males, semen and testicular abnormalities, reduced fertility; in females, abnormal vaginal or cervical growth or cancer, miscarriage later in life

Other

Oral contraceptives	Congenital abnormalities
Radiation	Massive dosages can result in fetal death; lesser dosages in mental and physical abnormalities
Maternal stress and nutrition	See discussion in this chapter

one aspect of the overall health and well-being of the child. But it is instructive not only because of the huge influence of nutrition but also because the research underscores several points regarding the role of environmental influence on development. We will show, for example, that the scope of damage or delay depends on the *timing, nature,* and *extent* of undernutrition; if a nutrient deficiency coincides with the growth spurt of a particular organ, irreversible damage may occur. Yet, in some cases, negative effects can be reversed with dietary supplements and other supports, highlighting the fact that although our priority should always be to prevent problems, intervention programs are important as well. Another point evident in the research is that in the case of undernutrition after birth, the effects can be damaging whether or not they are permanent or severe. A child who is hungry, for example, may lose motivation to explore his or her environment. This may result in a delay in the child's acquiring cognitive and social skills, regardless of whether brain damage has occurred, and this in turn may have a long-lasting impact on the child's ability to learn and eventually benefit from school experience. Although we make these points with the example of nutrition, they are applicable to other aspects of environmental influence, some of which we also discuss in this chapter.

The Prenatal Period
Early Brain Development

You will recall from previous chapters that during the period from conception through the early years, there is intense activity in brain development. One of the major tasks before birth, beginning in the embryonic period (third to eighth week after conception) is cell division and the development of brain cells and their migration to where they belong within the central nervous system and where they eventually perform their given function. This occurs rapidly; by birth, most of the billions of brain cells that form the mature brain are already in existence. Other tasks, which may begin but extend beyond the prenatal period include the sprouting of axons and dendrites for sending and receiving signals, the development of synapses, or connections, between nerve cells, and the development of protective myelin, which is important in our discussion here because it is affected by environmental factors, including nutrition. The process in its entirety is lengthy, but it is useful to think of the prenatal period as the time during which the brain's structure and its functioning are established. Master control genes, growth factors, and other signaling proteins guide the process, but from the earliest stages of development, environmental factors play a critical role and have the potential to disrupt as well as enhance the developmental process.

Neurotoxins. Normal development can be thrown off course by intrinsic factors and events (for example, genetic diseases or errors that may occur during neural migration) over which we may not have much control, and also by various prenatal conditions (maternal stress, for example) or exposure to neurotoxins. Neurotoxins are substances that have an adverse effect on the structural or functional components of the central nervous system (U.S. Congress, Office of Technology Assessment 1990). Knowledge of neurotoxins and an understanding of how they affect development are important if we are to prevent problems and enhance the outcome of pregnancies.

In the accompanying box, "Maternal Factors That May Influence Fetal Development," we list some of the factors known to have an adverse influence on the development of the brain and other organs. We cannot look in depth at all neurotoxins here, but some examples will illustrate their adverse influence. One example is alcohol; mothers who drink during pregnancy run the risk that their infants will be born with fetal alcohol syndrome (FAS) and other neurological problems. Alcohol is important to mention in part because it is commonly used and not considered by many as a drug, let alone one with enormous consequences for the developing fetus. We mention it here for two other reasons: first, knowledge about its effects can lead to simple steps to the prevention of developmental problems and disabilities, and second, unlike some factors such as aspirin (relatively safe, in moderation, until the third trimester of pregnancy) or rubella (with its impact noted in the first trimester), alcohol's influence extends throughout pregnancy.

The damage caused by alcohol depends on when, during pregnancy, the woman drinks; as we noted earlier, timing is an important contributing factor in the environmental impact of many neurotoxins on development. When consumed in the first trimester, alcohol affects the bones and other organs that develop early, resulting in various facial abnormalities, one of these being cleft palate. When taken during the last trimester, alcohol can retard fetal growth, resulting in low birth weight (discussed below). Because the brain grows throughout pregnancy, it is especially vulnerable to the effects of alcohol. Of significance is alcohol's effect on cell division, an important prenatal task in brain development.

Fetal alcohol syndrome is the most serious consequence of prenatal exposure to alcohol (Jones and Smith 1973), but it is not as prevalent as other consequences, such as neurological damage (National Research Council 1982). Neurological damage associated with prenatal alcohol exposure varies and could include severe brain dysfunction or numerous other problems that are at times not easily detected until later in childhood, such poor motor coordination or problems with attention and problem solving. Although some women who drink infrequently may not pay attention to warnings about the impact of alcohol on the developing fetus, occasional bouts of drinking actually have more serious consequences than regular drinking in moderation (Shonkoff and Phillips 2000).

Another commonly used substance with serious adverse influence on the developing fetus is nicotine. When a pregnant woman smokes, nicotine, along with other chemicals contained in the smoke, pass through the placental barrier (U.S. Department of Health, Education, and Welfare 1979). The smoke creates a dangerous environment in utero, increasing the level of carbon monoxide. This deprives the unborn child of oxygen, one of the vital needs for normal brain development (National Research Council 1982). For some unborn children, the consequences of maternal smoking are severe. A study in Great Britain found that mothers who smoked during pregnancy were 28 percent more likely than nonsmokers to deliver stillborn babies (Bolton 1983). In other cases, smoking has been shown to lead to premature birth and low birth weight (Butler, Goldstein, and Ross 1972). Not all children are affected to the same degree, however, and some may appear to escape the consequences altogether. A pregnant woman who doesn't wish to heed the warnings about smoking may point to a normally developing child whose mother smoked during pregnancy. Indeed, the adverse effects of nicotine—and other factors—are not inevitable; some unborn children may be more or less sensitive to a particular influence than others and some may have a genetic predisposition that makes them especially vulnerable to some environmental hazards. This also occurs with substances other than nicotine and alcohol. Another issue enters the picture with alcohol in particular; with successive pregnancies, the effects of prenatal alcohol exposure become more severe. Researchers speculate that this is because of changes over time in the way pregnant women metabolize alcohol. You can begin to see how complicated environmental effects can be (see box, "The Continuum of Reproductive and Caregiving Casualty").

Examples of how the developing brain and the very viability of the fetus are affected during pregnancy are numerous. Even seemingly good factors can be a problem (for example, tuna may contain high levels of mercury, which can have an adverse impact during prenatal development). Research in this area is important, not only for its contribution to the store of knowledge about the interplay of nature and nurture in the course of development, but also because the knowledge presents opportunities for prevention and intervention. For these reasons, all women are advised to seek regular prenatal care (see box, "Prenatal and Child Health Care").

Essential needs and protective factors. The news is not all bad. The developing fetus, and in particular the brain, is also receptive to positive influences. Indeed, for development to proceed normally, there is a need, beyond basic genetic makeup, for certain environmental conditions to be met. Regular prenatal care can ensure not only the absence of damaging factors but the presence of protective factors and essential needs.

One primary need is an adequate period of gestation. As we discuss later in the chapter, increasing numbers of infants born prematurely now survive and some eventually develop normally, owing to medical advances in neonatal intensive care and other interventions. Nevertheless, in premature birth there is a disruption in normal brain development, and this has the potential to affect later developmental function.

Besides adequate gestation, for the brain to develop normally in pregnancy, it needs oxygen. When oxygen supply is disrupted, by, for example, maternal smoking, the fetal heart rate increases rapidly (Quigley et al. 1979), and continued oxygen deprivation can lead to

The Continuum of Reproductive and Caregiving Casualty

The notion that damage to brain development during the prenatal and postnatal periods is not inevitable may be better understood within the context of a continuum of reproductive casualty (see Sameroff and Chandler 1975). In other words, how much influence specific factors have in the culmination of abnormalities varies. The variations occur on a continuum from relatively minor problems that may not be noticeable at birth (such as slightly retarded growth or learning difficulties) to major problems such as mental retardation. In part, the variations are due to the genetic sensitivity of the individual to a potentially damaging factor. Timely intervention may play a role as well (for example, getting the mother to stop smoking during pregnancy). Also important are experiences after birth that may determine the extent that an adverse influence may be manifest. This is referred to as the continuum of caregiving casualty, which ranges from a supportive and stable family environment to an unstable or dysfunctional family life that tends to exacerbate problems.

stillbirths. Also needed during the prenatal period are protein and energy and specific micronutrients, which are important not only during pregnancy but after birth as well. Regular prenatal health care enables physicians to monitor the pregnancy and assess pregnant women's needs for specific nutrients that may be missing from their diets and are essential for optimal fetal development. For example, iodine deficiency in early pregnancy (and associated thyroxine deficiency) can impair the central nervous system of the fetus, resulting in severe mental disabilities and serious neuromotor and hearing impairments in the infant (Hetzel 2000). The World Health Organization considers iodine deficiency as the most common preventable cause of brain damage in the world today, although international measures taken to iodize salt have stemmed the growth of this problem. Since noniodized salt is

Prenatal and Child Health Care

Knowledge about what environmental influences may harm the developing fetus, as well as what protective factors are essential for normal fetal development, provides opportunities for the prevention of problems or timely intervention to minimize their impact. For this reason, many programs include outreach for parents-to-be during the prenatal period. Several programs discussed in other chapters—the School of the 21st Century (see Chapter 4) and Parents as Teachers and Healthy Steps (Chapter 5)—strive to involve parents and provide information beginning during pregnancy. All prospective parents, not necessarily those from low-income or other high-risk families, can benefit from research on prenatal development as well as from regular prenatal care. It is during regularly scheduled visits that physicians not only can monitor fetal progress but also can prescribe essential vitamins for the mother and give her information about potential hazards she should avoid.

After the infant's birth, continued health care is important for several reasons, among them the need for immunizations. Regular health care can prevent potential problems such as ear infections, which, if untreated, can result in permanent hearing loss. Children who have access to regular health care can also be screened for visual, auditory, and motor delays, some of which may have resulted from prenatal exposure to environmental hazards but are not noticeable until later in life. If detected early and followed up with appropriate referral to specific services, these problems can be addressed before they take their toll on the child's development. Increased access to health care as well as to various home visitation and early childhood programs presents opportunities to screen children, detect potential developmental problems, and provide appropriate interventions.

as available in the markets as iodized salt, emphasis on the importance of iodized salt in the diet is critical.

Zinc, which is found in milk, red meat, and whole grains, is another important nutrient. The lack of zinc has been associated with growth deficiencies. Although for many years less has been known about zinc than about iodine, recent intervention studies have established a link between zinc deficiency and growth delay, illness, neurological problems, and abnormalities in fetal development, although lack of suitable indicators has impeded direct measurement (Hambidge 2000).

Vitamins are also essential. Most healthy pregnant women take a multiple vitamin supplement. Certain vitamins and nutrients such as folic acid are especially important in the early stages of pregnancy for the development of part of the central nervous system called the neural tube. In a landmark study (Milunsky et al. 1989) it was found that women who take multivitamins that include folic acid early in pregnancy sharply reduce the odds of having baby with neural tube defects. Such defects occur in the first six weeks of pregnancy and can cause devastating neurological disorders, paralysis, and even death.

Nutrition During the Prenatal Period and Early Years

Not only specific nutrients but sufficient food in general is a basic necessity of life. Although we are all familiar with the feeling of being hungry, it is less commonly understood that periods of undernutrition (not having enough food) and malnutrition (not having the right type of food to facilitate growth and development) can have long-lasting, devastating effects (see box, "Approaches to Studying the Effects of Nutrition").

Undernutrition in the Prenatal Period

Some pregnant women do not eat enough to sustain optimal fetal growth during the prenatal period. Referred to as undernutrition during pregnancy and measured by low maternal weight-for-height and low weight-gain during pregnancy, this has been linked with poor birth outcomes, including smaller head circumference and brain weight than healthy newborns (Meyers and Chawla 2000). Studies have also identified a relationship between these birth outcomes and later cognitive delays.

During the prenatal period, brain growth can be disrupted by chemical imbalance caused by undernutrition. As with other factors we have discussed, timing comes into play: undernutrition in the second trimester, for example, can result in too few neurons, whereas in the third trimester, it is associated with too few glial cells. Recall that neurons receive and send impulses or signals, whereas glial cells, or neuroglia, feed and support the neurons, among other important roles. In general, the earlier the nutritional deprivation occurs, the greater the reduction in brain size, and the longer nutritional deprivation continues, the greater the effect on the brain (Morgan and Winick 1985).

Prematurity and low birth weight. One result of maternal undernutrition is an increased risk for premature birth, defined as birth before the thirty-seventh week of gestation. Premature babies are highly vulnerable to health complications because they are unable independently to perform such basic biological functions as breathing and sucking. Medical advances have helped premature babies survive, even those born at twenty-four to twenty-eight weeks of gestation. Still, premature birth is the leading cause of death among African-American infants and the second leading cause of death among white infants (Centers for Disease Control and Prevention 2000). In addition, studies show that even though some premature infants survive, they process information more slowly and have lower intelligence and more learning problems at school than full-term infants (Friedman and Sigman 1992; Sigman and Parmelee 1974). However, the quality of experiences after birth is an important factor in the development of premature infants. Some premature infants, when raised in nurturing environments, grow normally, whereas others who live in stressful life conditions associated with poverty continue to lag behind (Sameroff and Chandler 1975).

Maternal undernutrition during pregnancy is also correlated with low birth weight. Low birth weight, meaning that the baby is born on time but is nevertheless small, is potentially more serious than premature birth since with premature delivery, intensive care can simulate

Approaches to Studying the Effects of Nutrition

Researchers have used various tools to examine the effects of under-nutrition and malnutrition in humans. These conditions, in particular undernutrition, do not occur in isolation but rather tend to be one of several factors, such as poor health care, associated with poverty. For this reason, research in this area is fraught with challenges; it is hard to disentangle the effect of malnutrition from the effects of other environmental assaults. Experimental studies would be important in this regard but present ethical issues; we cannot, for the sake of an experimental study, compromise the life and health of children by withholding food from them.

Various types of studies, however, do highlight the important role of nutrition and the potential for adverse impact owing to undernutrition or malnutrition. The approaches include experimental studies conducted with animals. The results, though not always directly applicable to humans, have played an important role in generating theories about the effects of undernutrition on humans, allowing researchers to isolate the effects of specific types of malnutrition. Studies of rodents in the 1970s, for example, showed that malnutrition impaired mental performance, not through direct damage to the brain, but through lack of energy associated with malnutrition: the malnourished rodents were less mobile and more withdrawn than their peers and less eager to explore their environment, an activity that is important in the development of cognitive skills (Levitsky and Barnes 1972).

Correlational studies conducted in low-income countries have also been used to study the effects of undernutrition. Such studies do not show cause and effect but rather a strong association between malnutrition and physical growth delays in children. More recently, researchers have explored associations between nutritional factors and cognitive delays. In countries where malnutrition is endemic, children who are taller and heavier (meaning that they are not suffering from hunger) are more likely to score well on tests of cognitive achievement than their shorter and lighter peers, who may not have received enough food or appropriate nutrients (Wachs 1995). Correlational studies, however, cannot rule out the influence of other factors that may account for these delays, such as poor health, and they are limited in their applicability to populations in developed countries.

Supplementation or intervention studies provide a more sophisticated approach to the study of nutrition's role in development. A body of research has accumulated using this method in which groups of people at risk for malnutrition are randomly assigned either to an experimental group, where they receive a supplement containing a particular nutrient, or to a control group receiving a different supplement or placebo (Idjradinata and Pollitt 1993; Pollitt et al. 1996; Wachs 1995). Although these studies have been undertaken largely in developing countries, the identification of a causal link between specific nutrients and areas of development has guided national supplementation programs in the United States. With notable exceptions, however (Rush et al. 1988a), the experimental supplementation design has not been the favored approach in the United States. Instead, American researchers have compared people who participate in federal programs that provide supplemental food with nonparticipants to identify the effects of undernutrition. We discuss the primary limitation of this approach, the possibility of selection bias, later in the chapter.

the uterine environment to an extent, allowing for continued growth of the infant, whereas with full-term delivery, this growth is completed. Low birth weight is a significant problem in the United States (see box, "Childhood Health Indicators") and an important indicator of concurrent and later health complications (National Academy of Science 1990). Low birth weight babies (defined as under 2.5 kilograms [5.5 pounds] for full-term babies) are biologically vulnerable and have an elevated risk of permanent neurological impairment; they also have difficulty regulating emotions and responding to parents and other adults. Parents often find low birth weight infants difficult to care for: they may be hard to calm, lethargic, and unresponsive to playful overtures on the part of the parents, which can lead to disappointment and frustration. For babies who are born premature *and* small for their gestational age, these problems are exacerbated.

Researchers have studied the effects of prenatal undernutrition by comparing the cognitive outcomes of children born to low-income women who received nutritional supplementation with a matched control group not receiving supplementation. An opportunity to conduct such studies exists with the federal food program popularly known as WIC, also referred to as the Special Supplemental Nutrition Program for Women, Infants, and Children. In addition to enabling low-income pregnant women and mothers of young children to buy dairy products and other nutritional foods, WIC provides nutrition education and health referrals. Although WIC studies have been criticized on methodological grounds (Besharov and Germanis 2001; see also box, "Approaches to Studying the Effects of Nutrition"), they enhance our understanding on the role of nutrition on development.

In a well-controlled study of WIC birth outcome effects (Devaney, Bilheimer and Schore 1991), researchers used Medicaid records to compare WIC participants and nonparticipants who had given birth between 1987 and 1988. Because Medicaid participants are automatically eligible for WIC services, attempts were made to control for selection bias, ensuring that the outcomes were attributable to WIC and not to inherent characteristics of mothers who chose to seek services. The study found that WIC participation was associated with increased birth weight, especially for premature infants (ranging from 138 to 259 grams between states), and with a reduced number of babies born with very low birth weights (under 1.5 kilograms). Similar results were documented in a study using the 1988 National Maternal and Infant Health Survey, which collected data from a national random sample of births recorded in 1988 (Gordon and Nelson 1995). This analysis found birth weight to be 68 grams higher for WIC participants compared to WIC-eligible nonparticipants.

Such marked differences in birth outcomes between infants who received adequate nutrition during pregnancy indicate the short-term impact of prenatal undernutrition. But WIC studies have also shown

Childhood Health Indicators

By most measures, life has improved for American children. In a report published by the Annie E. Casey Foundation (2001), infant mortality—that is, death during the first year of life—fell by 22 percent between 1990 and 1998. Childhood deaths from injuries were also reduced by 23 percent during that time, high school drop-out rates were reduced by 10 percent, and births to teenage parents fell by 19 percent. But one indicator, low birth weight, showed a negative trend: an increasing number of babies are being born dangerously small. Although this may in part represent an increase in the use of fertility drugs and a resultant increase in multiple births, where each of the babies is born smaller, it may also be an indication of inadequate prenatal nutrition and care.

that the detrimental effects of prenatal undernutrition have a long-term impact that may not be overcome. In one study, twenty-one pairs of siblings in Louisiana were tracked from birth to age six (Hicks and Langham 1985). In each case, the mother had participated in the WIC prenatal program with the younger but not the older child, creating conditions for a natural experiment: both siblings participated in the WIC infant program, meaning that they had adequate nutrition in infancy and toddlerhood, but only the younger one also had a nutritionally favorable prenatal experience. That younger child performed better on cognitive tests than the older child, suggesting that prenatal nutritional supplementation has long-lasting effects regardless of adequate nutrition in early childhood. This study, however, has been criticized for weaknesses in design (Rossi 1998); family circumstances, for example, may have differed for the two siblings.

Studies from developing countries have also found a relationship between prenatal nutrition supplements and later cognitive function. In Guatemala, more than two thousand pregnant women and children participated in a supplementation study between 1969 and 1977 in which they were randomly assigned to one of two groups. The first re-

ceived a high-protein supplement called Atole, and the second received a sweet drink called Fresco that contained calories but no protein. When more than 70 percent of the original participants were followed up in 1988 and 1989, the children who had received Atole either
prenatally or during the first two years of life performed better on cognitive tests than those who had taken Fresco (Pollitt et al. 1993), suggesting here not only that damage can occur but also that there is a potential for recovery through some intervention (in this case, dietary
supplements).

Although intervention studies such as these demonstrate both
the risks of prenatal undernutrition and the potential for prevention
and recovery, other studies also suggest that other aspects of the postnatal environment besides nutrition have an impact and can reduce or
eliminate cognitive delays for premature and low birth weight infants.
For example, studies of neonatal intensive care units have found that
premature infants respond better when they have frequent physical
contact, when they have the same caregivers over time, and when parents are involved in their treatment. Attention to environmental details such as lighting, noise levels, and sleep cycles also contribute to
improved brain function (Als and Gilkerson 1995; Shore 1997). In another study, infants born small and premature who received "touch intervention" (gentle stroking and moving of the limbs) had greater
weight gain, orientation, and alertness than low birth weight infants
who did not receive touch intervention. Moreover, these effects were
sustained when measured a year later (Field et al. 1986).

Breast-feeding. The beneficial effects of breast-feeding for the
cognitive development of premature and low birth weight infants are
significant. Breast milk contains specific nutrients and fatty acids that
cannot be found in formula milk. Randomized clinical trials confirm
the importance of these nutrients for vulnerable infants. In one study,
researchers compared premature infants (with birth weights less than
1.8 kg) who were fed with breast milk with those who received infant
formula (Lucas et al. 1990, 1992). When followed up eight years later,
the IQ scores of children who had received breast milk were 8.3 points
higher on average than those who had been fed with formula milk
only. Scores also varied according to the quantity of breast milk consumed. In this study, both groups of infants were tube-fed, isolating

the nutritional impact of breast milk from the emotional aspect of breast-feeding. It is widely agreed, however, that the overall advantages of breast-feeding derive from a combination of the nutrients and the experience of nursing (Meyers and Chawla 2000).

Undernutrition in the Infant and Toddler Years

As we know, brain development during the first few years of postnatal life focuses on synaptogenesis and myelination. Recall that beginning in the third trimester and continuing for the first two or three years of life, the brain is "wired" through the formation and pruning of synaptic connections. Although pruning occurs in normal development, environmental stimulation is important during this period because some synapses are eliminated selectively according to whether connections have been made. Also important is that poor nutrition affects behavioral and neurological function through its adverse impact on myelination: if children are severely malnourished during this period, brain development will be compromised, and even milder undernutrition can have serious consequences (Nelson 2000).

Infants and toddlers can be undernourished for a host of reasons relating to the infant, parent, and wider family and social context. These reasons include underfeeding due to food scarcity or the consumption of inappropriate foods; lack of particular nutrients, especially in the absence of breast-feeding; and food refusal arising from complex emotional or biological processes. The term "failure to thrive" (FTT, or "pediatric undernutrition" as it is sometimes called) tries to capture this meaning of undernutrition for infants. Marked by growth failure, FTT affects 5 to 10 percent of children under age three in the United States, the majority from low-income backgrounds (Sherry 1999). The disruption of feeding practices triggers an array of medical and social problems including reduced resistance to infection, diminished physical activity, and cognitive and emotional impairments (Kessler 1999). Although studies disagree about the long-term outcomes of FTT, this may result from problems of definition and sampling rather than indicating no effect, since studies of early childhood undernutrition in general have identified negative cognitive, social, and behavioral outcomes (Meyers and Chawla 2000).

Impact on social and emotional development. Standardized tests of cognitive achievement have been the primary measure of undernutrition in young children, overshadowing the effects on children's social and emotional development (Pollitt et al. 1996). Yet, as animal studies indicate, emotional well-being is sensitive to undernutrition and may serve as the primary cause of learning problems. Observing the activity level of infants is one way to study this interaction. In one of the few supplementation studies that included measures of activity, the effects of undernutrition on Mexican infants were observed (Chavez et al. 1975). The diet of one group was supplemented with powdered milk, vitamins, and minerals, while the diet of the other group consisted of prolonged breast-feeding. (Although breast-feeding is the recommended approach to feeding infants, in this community it had been resulting in malnutrition owing to the mothers' extremely poor diets.) From the time they were about six months old, the supplemented infants were sleeping less, playing more, and refusing to be carried in a baby sling. Such behaviors elicited greater interest from their parents and, therefore, opportunities for social interactions, which are essential for optimal growth and development and the acquisition of cognitive, social, and emotional skills. By nine months, the supplemented children were receiving more praise, stimulation, and rewards from both parents, again, providing opportunity for optimal development. At eighteen months, the mothers of the supplemented infants initiated more complex interactions with their offspring than the nonsupplemented mothers. That is to say, the infants' activity levels influenced the behavioral patterns within the family, the more active children eliciting greater stimulation from their parents.

This reciprocity in parent-child interactions is evident when infants are growing up in environments conducive to healthy development and is an important point to underscore. Many ingredients for early brain growth are obtained through the infant's relationships with parents and others. Parents and caregivers give the baby not only appropriate nutrition but also the social experiences necessary for brain growth. As one researcher notes, "People are toys for early brain growth, providing a rich variety of stimulation . . . that are integrated and enlivened through the emotional arousal that social interaction create in infants" (Thompson 1998, 75).

Impact on the development of motor skills. The negative effects of undernutrition on the development of motor skills—important in and of itself and also as a prerequisite for cognitive development—has been one of the most consistent findings of supplementation studies (Bertenthal and Campos 1990; Simeon and Grantham-McGregor 1990). An analysis of information collected in several studies found that infants in supplemented groups had better-developed motor skills across the age range tested from eight to twenty-four months (Pollitt and Oh 1994). In one of these studies conducted in Indonesia, infants randomly assigned to a three-month dietary supplementation group scored higher on the psychomotor development index of the Bayley Scales of Infant Development than controls (Husaini et al. 1991).

Impact on cognitive development. Almost all supplementation studies have incorporated some measure of cognitive development, and many have found at least modest gains as a result of improved nutrition. In the Guatemalan study described above, cognitive gains from improved nutrition in early childhood were sustained after considerable time had passed (Pollitt et al. 1993). In the United States, a national evaluation of WIC found positive effects of improved nutrition on vocabulary scores at ages four and five (Rush et al. 1988a). The evidence suggests that the effects of undernutrition on cognitive development are indirect rather than direct, mediated by emotional, social, and self-locomotion skills.

Micronutrient Deficiency

Beyond general undernutrition, some infants and young children are malnourished. Through the use of several study methods, researchers have identified developmental risks for young children associated with the lack of specific micronutrients. The findings are important given that the diets of more than half of children under three years lack the recommended amounts of essential nutrients (Alaimo et al. 1994). Poor eating habits, acquired at a young age, continue throughout childhood. Along with lack of sufficient exercise, generally sedentary lifestyle, and practices in some schools (see box, "Schools' Role in Nutrition"), poor eating habits are leading to increasing numbers of overweight and obese children in the United States. This is a serious matter; obesity contributes to the onset of disease that is usually associated with adults but is increasingly documented in young children (Brownell 2001).

Protein-energy malnutrition (PEM). Protein-energy malnutrition poses multiple risks to development (Ricci and Becker 1996). Protein is important for brain function because, when ingested, it breaks down into amino acids that contribute to the synthesis and balance of neurotransmitters (chemicals in the brain that enable the information to travel between neurons). Protein deficiency increases the risk of neurological and psychiatric disorders as well as delays in physical growth. The brain, which is highly active metabolically, requires energy, measured in calories. If energy is lacking, the body draws on amino acids, diverting them from their intended functions.

Children with PEM are typically lethargic, emotionally unresponsive, withdrawn, and passive. This is because the body uses energy supplies first for physical growth, leaving insufficient energy for motivation, attention, and curiosity, which are necessary components for such critical developmental processes as attachment, play, and learning (Galler et al. 1983). Such characteristics have been associated with cognitive deficits and poor school performance in later childhood as well as concurrent difficulties (Grantham-McGregor 1995). In supplementation studies, the most consistent impact of protein-energy supplements has been on infant motor skills, which importantly are known to be predictive of later cognitive ability (Pollitt et al. 1993).

Iron deficiency. Among the other important micronutrients, most is known about iron, which is found in breast milk, iron-fortified formula, iron-fortified cereals, beans, vegetables, and meat. Iron is necessary for normal red blood cell synthesis and is an essential constituent of brain tissue, including the system of neurotransmitters involved in information processing. It also helps the body fight off infection. Iron deficiency anemia affects as many as one-fourth of low-income children in the United States and is a significant cause of cognitive delays in young children (Center on Hunger, Poverty and Nutrition Policy 1998). Specifically, it can cause permanent damage to neurotransmission, affecting attention span, memory, and behavior (Yehuda and Youdim 1989).

The effects of iron have been discovered through the use of correlational and supplementation studies and through biochemical indi-

The Role of Schools in Nutrition

Over 90 percent of the nation's schools participate in the federal school meals program. But many schools also adopt practices that actually promote, rather than prevent, malnutrition, overweight, and obesity. When scheduling classes, academic subjects take priority, and health and fitness—even, in some cases, recess—take a back seat and are often cut entirely. Some schools bring in fast-food vendors, and many have installed vending machines filled with soft drinks, candy, and other junk food. Once a novelty in schools, vending machines have become a major way for many schools to raise money for extracurricular activities (Winter 2001). Although most schools are indeed financially strapped, with policies like these they are being fiscally short-sighted and irresponsible. The weight gain and malnutrition among children is taking its toll in deteriorating health and may contribute to the inability of children to succeed academically. On the positive side, however, Congress is considering measures to ban such practices from schools, and some states are already insisting that schools "expel" fast-food vendors and vending machines from the school (Egan 2002).

cators (Metallinos-Katsaras and Gorman 1999). In a study of one-year-olds in Costa Rica, moderate iron deficiency anemia was correlated with lower scores on the mental and psychomotor indexes of the Bayley Scales of Infant Development (Lozoff et al. 1987). In a follow-up study conducted more than ten years later, those who had been iron-deficient as young children performed less well on cognitive tests than the control group even though they had sufficient iron at the time of testing (Lozoff et al. 2000). Similarly, in Indonesia, infants and toddlers who were iron-deficient consistently underperformed on motor and mental development tests compared to their peers who had sufficient iron (Idjradinata and Pollitt 1993).

In terms of the potential for recovery, studies of iron therapy have yielded mixed results in improved test scores among infants (Idjradinata and Pollitt 1993; Lozoff et al. 1987). Also, in instances where iron-deficient infants have been followed into adolescence, cognitive and behavioral deficits have persisted (Lozoff et al. 2000). Milder deficiencies of iron and such other micronutrients as iodine can be reversed with dietary alterations, however. For example, a study of WIC detected a decline in anemia among children aged six to sixty months from 7.8 percent in 1975 to 2.9 percent in 1985 (Yip 1989). Some researchers have pointed to the study's methodological problems, however, noting that although WIC is effective during the prenatal period in addressing the need for nutrients, its impact on young children's overall nutrition and, especially, their nutritional habits is less impressive and needs to be addressed (it is suggested, for example, that more emphasis be placed on the nutrition education aspect of WIC; Besharov and Germanis 2001).

The role of food programs. There are other federal food programs besides WIC, but they are less focused than WIC, providing vouchers exchangeable for unspecified foods or subsidies for organizations such as schools to provide meals. The largest of these programs, the Food Stamp Program, is successful in increasing food availability and expenditure for low-income families but does not necessarily increase nutrient intake (Devaney, Ellwood, and Love 1997; Fraker 1990). Another initiative is federal support for school meals programs. Here the overall aim is to provide nutritious meals during the summer months as well as nutritious breakfasts and lunches to elementary and secondary schoolchildren by subsidizing the costs on a sliding scale for low-income families. The initiative achieves its basic objective of providing children with a significant proportion of the recommended dietary allowance of nutrients, but levels of energy derived from fat in such meals have been found to be excessively high. Moreover, although the participation rate among elementary and secondary schools is high, consumption rates are significantly lower, because many children choose not to eat the meals provided (Besharov 1999; Burghardt and Devaney 1995). Some schools, rather than direct their efforts toward educating children about nutrition, actually promote bad eating habits by contracting with fast-food chains to provide meal services and having machines that dispense soft drinks, candy, and other foods of low nutritional value (Brownell 2001). However, some school districts and some states, such as California and Texas, are taking steps to ban the sale of such foods in schools (Egan 2002).

Policy Implications

Although children in the United States do not experience food scarcity to the same degree as children in developing countries, surveys show that increasing numbers of children do indeed experience hunger and are at high risk for poor nutritional status. The evidence comes from annual surveys of hunger and food insecurity conducted by the U.S. Bureau of the Census in collaboration with the U.S. Department of Agriculture. In the surveys, "hunger" was defined as a recurrent and involuntary access to food, and "food insecurity" was defined as "lack of access to enough food to fully meet basic needs at all times" (Andrews et al. 2000). In 1999, the latest year for which data are available, 10 percent of households, representing 31 million Americans of whom 12 million were children, were food insecure. Five million adults and 2.7 million children experienced food scarcity to the extent of hunger. It is important to note, too, that the extent and severity of hunger and food insecurity are not modulated by economic cycles; even when the economy is robust and unemployment is low, many individuals experience hunger (Sullivan 2000). Given the research evidence of detrimental outcomes associated with undernutrition, these figures are a cause for grave concern.

What can be done at a policy level to improve the nutritional status and life outcomes of the nation's children? We suggest three approaches: increasing access to and participation in federal food programs to minimize hunger and food insecurity; promoting breast-feeding to improve the nutritional status of infants; and taking steps to address the issue of child poverty, since the research shows that life circumstances associated with poverty exacerbate the effects of undernutrition.

Increasing Access to and Participation in Federal Food Programs

As we have noted, several different food services are available through federal funds to address hunger and food insecurity. These include

WIC, as well as subsidizing the cost of school breakfast and lunch for low-income children. The combined federal food programs increase the availability of food for one in six low-income Americans. However, a large number of young children remain food insecure or poorly nourished. Among school-age children, one approach to improve the situation would be not only to increase the number of schools participating in the food programs during the year but also to encourage schools to take advantage of the summer school food program. Among an increasing number of schools, year-round services for children is becoming the norm (Finn-Stevenson and Zigler 1999), presenting opportunities for inclusion in the summer food program. But this is only a partial solution. One of the problems with the school meals and summer food programs is that even though children participate, they often do not eat the food. To address the fact that even in schools participating in the school food program many children simply do not eat what they are given, a leading nutrition policy expert suggests that teachers make available fortified cereals and milk in single-serving packages that need no refrigeration. Children may then eat cereal and milk when they arrive at school (Brown 1998). It is not a costly effort, nor one that would require national policy, but it could well alleviate the hunger that many children experience and help them concentrate on their schoolwork.

As we have shown, WIC is an effective program. But it serves only a portion of eligible women and children. That is due in part to cutbacks in services following welfare reform in 1996 and in part to families that either are unaware of their eligibility or choose not to participate. Lack of awareness may account for the gap between the numbers eligible for services and the numbers receiving services, which is highest among families with children age one to four. Since WIC is especially effective as a preventive effort in making food during prenatal development, this means that it is not being used to its full extent (Besharov and Germanis 2001). Increasing public awareness as well as encouraging and enabling eligible women to apply would be very beneficial for young children, since WIC provides important nutrition as well as other services during a critical developmental period. In addition to monthly food packages, WIC offers nutrition education, including breast-feeding support, and provides access to prenatal and well-baby care, immunizations, and medical services through its referral system. We recommend a review of outreach services associated with WIC to ascertain how to improve public knowledge of the importance of WIC. This review should also identify the reasons for failure to participate during the prenatal period and use this as the basis for changes in the program that would encourage families to participate.

Other services, such as the Child and Adult Care Food Program (CACFP), also suffer from low participation rates. Low participation in CACFP may be caused by stringent eligibility criteria and misconceptions about eligibility. Through CACFP, for example, child care centers and family child care homes and other organizations providing services can be reimbursed for up to two meals and one snack a day for low-income preschool children. Yet many child care facilities do not realize that they are eligible. Another issue is that procedures for participating are a burden for small organizations and, in particular, for family child care providers. In the case of family child care, where a woman takes care of several children in her home, it is often difficult to get widespread participation. In addition, the implementation of a means-test system has reduced reimbursements for family child care homes (Parker 2000). Because child care facilities need to be licensed to apply for CACFP, licensing should be encouraged as a step toward addressing, at least in part, the issue of food security among preschoolers.

Addressing Issues Related to Child Poverty

As in developing countries, undernutrition in the United States is strongly associated with poverty, a condition affecting one in five children, according to the National Center for Children in Poverty (NCCP 2000). Poverty not only limits access to nutritious foods but exacerbates the effects of undernutrition through poor-quality environments. The ill effect of lead is a prime example. Poor children in the United States often live in areas where lead is prevalent, and because they are more likely to have iron deficiency, poor children are also more likely to absorb lead (Brody et al. 1994; Yip 1989). High levels of lead, or lead poisoning, can disrupt the development of the central nervous system, leading ultimately to coma and death, but even low levels of lead exposure can have serious consequences such as learning and behavioral problems, stunted growth, and hearing problems (NCEH 2001).

Another issue is that children in low-income families are less likely to be immunized against potentially dangerous but preventable diseases, the risk for which is increased with poor nutrition (Children's Defense Fund 1998). Low rates of immunization are particularly prevalent among African-American and Hispanic children (Pollitt 1994), who generally lack access to regular health care. Beyond the need for immunizations, breast milk helps to protect infants from infections, and yet low-income mothers are less likely to breast-feed (Lazarov and Evans 2000).

If socioeconomic factors can lessen or exacerbate the impact of undernutrition, it is essential that policies address poverty reduction and health care access (through such efforts as CHIP, the child health insurance program) in tandem with improving nutrition for children. Although in recent years child poverty rates have dropped slightly, additional efforts in this regard are warranted. Admittedly, reducing child poverty rates is a difficult and complex approach that cannot be fully explored within the confines of this discussion. But, as the National Center for Children in Poverty (2000) suggests, there are some small steps that can be taken. First, help parents to earn enough to keep their children out of poverty through the provision by employers of increased wages. Second, expand the earned income tax credit, child care, health insurance, and public transport, thereby enabling families to obtain and keep employment. And third, expand cost-effective prevention programs such as WIC, preschool education, and family support programs (NCCP 2000).

We should also take note of a relatively recent trend in poverty distribution. Poverty has historically been regarded as an urban problem, with most of the poor concentrated in parts of large cities. However, in the past twenty years suburban and rural areas have experienced the highest growth rate in poverty (Cook and Brown 1994; Hernandez 1997). The reasons for this trend need to be explored and associated issues (such as lack of services and transportation in rural and suburban communities) considered for antipoverty strategies to succeed.

Promoting Breast-feeding

Breast-feeding, as we have noted, has considerably greater benefits for infants than feeding with formula milk. The breast milk of all women (apart from those in extremely poor nutritional health) carries all the nutrients an infant needs in the correct quantity and most easily digested form. Breast milk also contains essential fatty acids and more than fifty known immunological factors to protect infants against infectious and noninfectious illnesses, and the experience of breast-feeding is also beneficial in many ways (Lazarov and Evans 2000; Lucas et al. 1992). There are clear economic advantages to breast-feeding, since a year's supply of infant formula for a newborn costs more than nine hundred dollars, not to mention the savings in health costs associated with the benefits of breast milk.

Yet low-income mothers, for whose babies the benefits are likely to be greatest, are the least likely to breast-feed. Identified barriers include social and cultural attitudes and norms, lack of knowledge and support from health care providers, and extensive advertising by the formula industry (Lazarov and Evans 2000). Policies need to address these obstacles in order to maximize the nutritional status of young children. The contradictions within WIC policy also need to be addressed. At present, WIC is the largest distributor of free infant formula, although it also provides the means for educating and supporting women in breast-feeding.

With work requirements for low-income mothers and a lack of mandated paid parental leave, it is no surprise that the majority of women choose to feed their infants formula. Although federal law provides for unpaid parental leave, many parents cannot afford to take advantage of this.

In this chapter we have shown the critical role of the prenatal period and the potential of adequate prenatal care to prevent neurological problems. The role of nutrition on the developing brain, as well as on general growth and development, is significant. It is clear that hunger, food insecurity, and lack of appropriate nutrients are often part of the picture of deprivation in the environment of many children growing up in the United States. Yet there are opportunities for prevention and intervention through state and federal policy as well as local action. Some policy directions, such as taking steps to reduce child poverty rates, are difficult to execute—not only are they complex and tied to forces such as the economy over which many of us have no control, but they require long-term strategies to overcome. Yet other directions are available, focusing primarily on modifications of existing food programs. We have discussed some of these strategies. They are simple to implement but can have significant impact on the health and well-being of our nation's children.

9

The Brain Campaign
Brain Development and the Media

In its journey from the laboratory to the daily newspaper, information about brain development research and its implications for parents, educators, and policy makers has traveled a controversial course. Like other policy-related research findings, what we know about brain development has passed through the transforming—often distorting—lens of the popular press. The outcomes of this journey have at times been beneficial for the public and at other times have done parents and child advocates a disservice. At virtually all times, however, this translation of research that is based in an esoteric and often theoretical language into words that are more accessible to the general public has been affected by the tensions inherent in what one analysis has called the "uneasy partnership" that exists between social scientists and journalists (Thompson and Nelson 2001).

Media coverage of brain research plays an important role in bringing profoundly important information about brain development to public attention. The popular press has also played a critical role in bringing brain research to the consideration of child advocates and policy makers. No other group could arguably have conferred the benefits of bringing brain research findings to the attention of these players in the policy process. And yet, as we discussed in Chapter 7, this has also resulted in simplistic interpretations of what we know, fabrications of material to substitute for what we *don't* yet know, and misunderstandings about what all of this might mean for how we raise, educate, and care for our children. These oversimplifications and misunderstandings have distracted our attention from the most salient problems in child development, have wasted time, effort, and resources, and in some cases have tarnished the public perception of social sciences already too often viewed as imprecise or "soft." But in other cases overstatements of research findings have led to the development of programs and interventions that have actually provided valuable services to children at risk for educational and social failure (Grimes 1998; Resner 1997).

The excitement engendered among the public by recent neuroscience research has given journalists who write about child development a new forum for discussing traditional social science topics under the guise of "hard" science. This has brought a previously unanticipated level of public interest, but also problems: "Not only have developmental scientists witnessed unprecedented public attention to important questions of early childhood development, but they also have seen developmental research applied inappropriately, such as when critical-period formulations are used to conclude that Head Start begins too late to stimulate the developing brain or in reports that classical music instruction stimulates early intellectual growth" (Thompson and Nelson 2001, 1).

Significant changes in policy at any level do not happen by accident. Whether the subject of the policy in question concerns increases in military appropriations, penalty mandates for repeat offenders brought to juvenile court, or whether to cut down hundred-year-old oaks to widen the main road of a small town, certain features of the policy process remain constant. Several prerequisites are necessary for the successful development of social policies. First, a constituency must have a sense of the immediacy of the problem in question. This often results from the cumulative impact of a perennial problem (outdated military technology, chronic traffic tie-ups on Main Street) that the public perceives as worsening. At other times, a crisis or tragedy that befalls an individual (such as the 1994 murder of the seven-year-old New Jersey child that ultimately led to the passage of a set of sex-offender registration statutes known collectively as "Megan's laws") or a community (the 2000 mass shooting at Columbine High School in Littleton, Colorado, for example) can be a powerful political motivator.

In still other cases, a scientific breakthrough or the impact of an accumulated body of scholarly research—on cumulative damage to the earth's ozone layer, for instance—can trigger demands for legislative change. No matter which of these characterize how public opinion is galvanized for or against a measure, and regardless of whether the issue in question is tree preservation, gun control, regulation of auto emissions, or some other topic of concern to the public, nothing will change and no policy shift will come to pass without enhanced public awareness. The most pivotal role in disseminating information about the topic in general, and of the specific aspects of the problem and any proposed solutions, is played by print, broadcast, and digital media—newspapers, books, and magazines, television and radio, and the Internet. We can only reach a full understanding of the infant brain development controversy—how there came to be controversy in the first place, and what its implications have been and may continue to be—by understanding the media's role. And to do this, we need to look at the relationship between social science and the media.

The Growing Media Coverage of Children's Issues

The media's coverage of children's issues escalated in the 1990s. Formerly hidden in the features and women's sections of newspapers and a handful of magazines devoted to children, articles about child development, parenting, and child policy have become front-page fodder for newspapers and leading stories in televised news digests. The number of major newspapers that have added child and family beats to their news coverage has increased dramatically, and these assignments are now coveted by journalists who might previously have resented being relegated to covering children's stories (Lakshmi 1996).

The nature of the coverage of children's issues is not, however, always of the quality that will best serve children's needs over the long run. Much of the media coverage has been spurred by social crises and negative events related to substance abuse and by tragedies resulting from school and community violence. A little girl who dies of hyperthermia after being left unattended in a hot car at her day care center (Goldstein 2001; West 2001) generates a flurry of news stories; information about the ongoing national crisis in the quality of child care does not. Random accidental deaths to children with access to handguns in private homes generate little national interest, but a school shooting on the scale of the Columbine massacre stimulates round-the-clock news coverage for weeks (Dickinson 2001; Reaves 2001). Quiet crises in family life that have the potential to do incalculable harm to large numbers of children do find their way into the news (see Boo 2001 for one excellent example of this genre) in stories about the effects of divorce, child abuse, the failure of our health care system, and other issues, but these command far less journalistic attention than more dramatic, event-based stories. Too much coverage of child and family stories still follows the old newspaper dictum: "If it bleeds, it leads."

Yet not all such media coverage is negative or sensationalist in nature. Responsible reporting of scientific studies and the opinions of reputable policy makers and institutions has also taken a more prominent place in recent decades. For example, when the Carnegie Corporation of New York released *Starting Points: Meeting the Needs of Our Youngest Children* in 1994, the story appeared on the front page of the *New York Times* and received appropriate coverage in news weeklies and on talk radio and television.

The publication of *Starting Points* was a watershed moment for young children in the United States and for media responsive to the public's interest in the needs and problems of families. The quality of the environments in which young children are raised, in terms of parenting, health care, child care, and educational opportunities, became a focal point for national discussions that shaped child welfare initiatives at the local, state, and national levels. The critical importance of the first three years of life to the developing brain first came to national attention through a relatively brief mention in *Starting Points* that was intended to underscore the importance of providing nurturing, responsive, safe, and stimulating environments for children in the early years.

The needs of young children had by no means been ignored before the publication of *Starting Points,* but the discussion it sparked on early brain development galvanized forces for significant policy efforts.

Coming at a time when most working parents in the United States were struggling to find affordable, safe, reliable child care, a report that stressed the developmental needs of young children and the long-lasting dangers of poor-quality child care and health care found a receptive audience. Adding to its impact was the fact that many families were already uneasy about their children's safety in child care settings, after viewing a 1992 *PrimeTime Live* report by television journalist Diane Sawyer that highlighted child care horrors.

In spite of these reports, however, little actually improved in the child care field—other than that parents became increasingly uneasy about the dearth of child care choices available to them, particularly for children in the birth-to-age-three group. Adding to the atmosphere of urgency was the passage of the Personal Responsibility and Work Opportunity Reconciliation Act of 1996, which required millions of mothers to leave the welfare rolls and join the paid labor force without providing a corresponding increase in available high-quality child care. In 1996, 150 brain scientists, child development and early education specialists, business leaders, and media representatives convened in Chicago for a major national meeting entitled *Brain Development in Young Children: New Frontiers in Research, Policy and Practice*. This meeting provided a research base for policy makers and child advocates, though material about brain research and its implications for those who care about children had not yet crossed the public's horizon in any significant way.

Representatives of the entertainment media also played a significant role in bringing child development topics to prominence. One example is the I Am Your Child Program developed in 1997 by the New York-based Families and Work Institute in conjunction with actor-director Rob Reiner. Comedian Robin Williams and other celebrities including Whoopi Goldberg and Tom Hanks also hosted the effort. The television special was only one piece of a larger project to bring child development information to parents: Reiner has also developed a Web site (I Am Your Child, at iamyourchild.com) devoted to practical, hands-on parenting advice, public service announcements, CD-ROMs, and a videotape series.

Like many other media productions, the I Am Your Child efforts have had both positive and negative consequences. Much of the material produced is subject to the same kinds of oversimplification and exaggeration that have characterized scores of magazine and newspaper articles. The title of one of the I Am Your Child booklets, for example ("The First Years Last Forever"), is an overly strong interpretation of the more tempered notion that a child's early experiences influence subsequent development. The program's focus on infancy reinforces the justifiably criticized idea that a developmental door swings shut after the age of three, essentially halting learning and development.

But the show and its spin-off materials have reached parents and bestowed an imprimatur that tells parents that nurturing an infant through close, responsive interactions is both scientifically sound (based in brain research) and hip (endorsed by stars like Whoopi Goldberg). It has strengthened a media trend in which film and television stars—viewed by many people as friendly, accessible, and knowledgeable—give easy-to-handle parenting advice (read to your baby, hold your baby, have dinner with your kids).

The I Am Your Child campaign also continues to have a significant impact on social policy. The stated goals of the campaign include raising public awareness and promoting citizen involvement, as well as uniting and expanding the work being done on the national, state, and local levels to provide comprehensive, integrated early childhood development programs for young children. It was Reiner's idea to support programs focusing on health care, child care, parent education, and intervention programs in California by placing a fifty-cent tax on each pack of cigarettes sold in the state, along with comparable taxes on other tobacco products. Building on the nation's increasing antitobacco sentiment, growing concerns about threats to healthy childhood development and school readiness, and Reiner's own energetic and high-profile lobbying for the measure, Proposition 10 passed in November 1998 and took effect in January 1999 as the California Children and Families First Act (Grimes 1998). Ironically, even though much of the impetus for the effort was based on an exaggerated understanding of how brain research might be applied to early childhood education and intervention, the effort has had positive programmatic outcomes, which we'll describe in more detail in the Epilogue.

In 2000, President Bill Clinton and Hillary Rodham Clinton invited several neuroscience experts to Washington, D.C., to present recent findings on brain development in the first three years at the *White House Conference on Early Learning and the Brain.* A small army of journalists representing every conceivable print, broadcast, and Internet medium descended on the conference to report on the new findings and to interpret and reinterpret them to make them more accessible. One of the more responsible reports on brain research findings was published by the Families and Work Institute. *Rethinking the Brain: New Insights into Early Development* (Shore 1997) attempted to summarize and present key findings for professionals who work with young children. Although distortions of findings have certainly occurred—most often in the forms of overstatement of the findings or their implications—the media has been pivotal in bringing the issue of early brain development before the public and in advancing the policy agenda. Once an esoteric topic for neuroscientists, the influences on the growth of very young children's learning capacities have become material for conversations at dinner tables and play groups.

The Media's Role in Shaping Opinion and Policy

In 1980, one of the country's leading media specialists noted that an average of sixty-three network news stories a year covered children and youth (Gerbner 1980). Today, of course, such a count would be far higher. As family policy analyst Susan Muenchow (1996) notes, coverage of issues pertinent to children and families is widespread. But what role does such coverage play in the process of shaping child and family policy and service-provision efforts?

The media are ostensibly neutral, but in fact they have a profound effect on how the public and lawmakers view and act on the problems families face and the solutions they seek. Even if we were to submit that lawmakers are supposed to be ideologically neutral—and this is certainly not the case—media coverage of issues and events would still be a powerful shaper of attitudes and behaviors. Merely because time and space are limited in print and on the airwaves relative to the amount of material that might receive coverage, the editors and news anchors who select which stories will run, and in what context, wield enormous power. The media's lack of space and time contributes pivotally to what the public does and does not see (Graber 1989).

Moreover, the traditional model of presenting news stories almost invariably emphasizes certain details over others, relies heavily, as we have noted, on a crisis-oriented approach to reporting, and tends to confirm, rather than challenge, the public's perception of the status quo. Reporting on drug abuse is a case in point. Although research indicates that drug use among Americans is actually declining, stories on the dangers of and threats posed by drug use persistently confirm what most people believe: that drug use is on the rise. Reporting on crime reflects a similar distortion of what statistics actually show (Hall 1998; Horgan 1993; Zigler and Hall 1997).

The power of the media to reach millions of people at once, however, makes it an invaluable tool for child advocates—just as it is a crucial tool for those who lobby against actions that would improve the lives of children and families. A *Headline News* report on CNN or a heartrending family story on *Oprah* has the power to affect the outcome of a legislative debate, the choices parents make for their children, even a national election. At times, the mere threat of media coverage has spurred policy makers to action (Graber 1989).

Media may be used positively to encourage people to become involved in public affairs at many levels. Public participation in the U.S. Census, for instance, has significant power to affect funding for much of the social infrastructure in states and communities, yet many thousands of citizens and noncitizen residents remain uncounted each time a census is taken. When the U.S. Census Bureau undertook to insure the success of the 2000 census, the bureau implemented a major media campaign to overcome public resistance. Through newspaper advertisements, radio announcements, and television spots, the census received constant media exposure. According to preliminary findings of a major independent study being conducted at InterSurvey, a private company in Menlo Park, California, the 2000 census promotion and mobilization campaign was instrumental in increasing the public's awareness, understanding, and participation in the count.

Another case in point is the antismoking campaign waged by public health organizations, which has been successful at least in part by influencing new laws regarding smoking, bringing about advertising restrictions, and altering popular views regarding the social acceptability of smoking in public places or even in front of one's children. By inundating the public with antismoking messages in the form of warning labels on cigarette packs, public service announcements, press releases, televised special reports, and the like, the collaboration between public health entities and the media has significantly raised public concern and has resulted in policy initiatives restricting smoking in public places, even if it has not yet eradicated smoking.

Brain-based child development stories, no matter how simplistic or hyperbolized, do seem to have caused a shift in how parents perceive both the nature of early development and their role in fostering it. Interest in materials purporting to increase infant intelligence through scientific stimulation—the purchase of classical music recordings and allegedly educational toys for babies, enrollment in infant enrichment classes like "Baby and Me"—skyrocketed after the release of *Starting Points*. Interest in brain development and how parents can employ its lessons spurred a temporary but powerful boom in branches of the magazine industry based on a close analysis of parents' interests: *Parents, Parenting, Child, American Baby, Scholastic Parent and Child, Working Mother,* and other publications met parents' needs for a service-based approach to child development research. And throughout this period, the relationship between the social scientist and the journalist shaped public perceptions.

The Scientist and the Journalist

The relationship between social science and journalism is steeped in irony. Both the scholar and the journalist have as their goals uncovering and disseminating information about their subjects: What is the effect of spending many hours in child care at an early age, for instance, or what factors appear to contribute to better outcomes following child abuse or neglect? The question for both, in the present case, concerns how a young child's brain develops and which variables affect this course of development. Both the scientist and the journalist are investigators; both are interested in getting their findings—*new* findings—in front of an audience, and in doing so before their colleagues do or in a format that makes a unique contribution.

Beyond these similarities, however, we find differences that impinge on the effectiveness of both the reporter and the scholar. Fundamental contrasts in the ways journalists and scientists uncover and tell a story arise over issues like language: a developmental psychologist, for instance, would prepare a manuscript for a specialty journal in a passive voice ("Little is known about . . . ") stressing aggregate findings ("75 percent of subjects reached criterion on the task," or "the 332 subjects cried an average of 2.8 hours a day"). The journalist can have a greater impact on an audience by speaking in an active voice and focusing on individuals: "Sue Swanson, a thirty-four-year-old mother of two, struggles daily to hold together a patchwork of day care arrangements," or "Cassandra, fifteen, feels hopeful that she can overcome these obstacles and become the first person in her family to graduate from high school." The scholar often describes the norm: how much crying, the average age at which a developmental milestone is reached, the percentage of children vaccinated by a given age. The journalist will use this information, too, but will make it more real and accessible to the audience by adding a human face: "Emily's parents even took turns by nights, one sleeping, one staying up to deal with the four-month-old's incessant crying," or "But when Eric still hadn't said his first words at eighteen months, his parents insisted that their pediatrician refer them to a speech and language therapist."

The structure of popular publications that target parents both relies heavily on research in child development and manifests a certain distrust of academia. Newspaper and magazine editors seek out freelance writers with backgrounds in a given field, like child development, even though they may doubt their ability to distill their scholarly information into a format digestible by their readers. Similarly, even scholars who are eager for their work to attract media attention are leery of journalists who may misunderstand, misinterpret, or oversimplify research findings. They are inclined to fear a publication process in which they have little control of the final product. After all, describing one's research in a lengthy journal article in which the work is explained in detail and placed in a scholarly and historical context is very different from describing the same work to a journalist who may use only a line or two of interview material and who may then draw new or unexpected implications from that work.

Scholars are seldom trained to interact with journalists. Accustomed to describing their work at length and in detail, many are unused to summarizing the methods and findings of their research for general readers. The specialized language of research can be off-putting as well, as scholars and editors fear (with some justification) that the nuances of a study or larger body of work will be lost in the translation from academic-ese to the vernacular. Scholars are often frustrated, too, by the short turnaround time of popular articles and by having to provide interviews on the spur of the moment. Although this is changing as media awareness invades even the most closeted, ivory-tower scholarly communities, it remains the case that relatively few academicians are accustomed to thinking of their work in terms of the media-friendly "sound bites" so often demanded—in short order—by journalists. In turn, journalists who may be guided as much by their interest in promoting children's issues and interests (a style Thompson and Nelson 2001 refer to as "campaign journalism") are quick to make use of research findings that support—or appear to support—child advocacy goals.

What Has Gone Wrong?

Following the release of *Starting Points,* the subsequent flurry of news and parenting articles reflected a slant that tended to convey to parents a sense of urgency, even panic, over what young children needed, when they needed it, and what could happen if they didn't get it. Every difference between journalists and social scientists, and every disparity between the linguistic and procedural styles of the two groups, came into play as brain-based child development information was reported:

- In most cases, the length of articles so severely limits the detail that can be included that the finer points of the brain research cannot be covered.
- The format of the popular article lends itself to oversimplification. Readers too busy to scan more than text boxes or photo captions or headlines get a skewed picture—either too frightening or too reassuring.
- Reporting on the issue often takes place too soon, and provides a static rather than dynamic picture of brain research and its implications.

- Research is "new" to journalists unfamiliar with the existing body of work on neurological development and is described as such even if the research took place years or even decades earlier.

- Because the public perceives the newer findings as qualitatively different from earlier behavioral and observational research, journalists make little attempt to integrate neurological findings into the canon of research. Instead, the newer or more highly technical work is taken out of context and set against earlier work, even if, as in the case of brain research, extant neurological findings are more likely to confirm than to contradict what we have long believed about the importance of the early years.

The body of popular journalistic work that emerged from this arena in the mid-1990s was often misleading and confusing, not only for parents, but also for policy makers. In a special child-oriented issue of *Time*, one reporter in 1997 issued a virtual mandate to policy makers to respond to brain research with early intervention programs: "The 'new' insights [into brain development] have begun to infuse new passion into the political debate over early education and day care. There is an urgent need, say child development experts, for preschool programs designed to boost the brain power of youngsters born in impoverished rural and inner city households. Without such programs, they warn, the current drive to curtail welfare costs by pushing mothers with infants and toddlers back into the workforce may well backfire" (Nash 1997, 51).

Another reporter adds specific advice for the creation or strengthening of day care policy: "With the new scientific evidence [included in *Starting Points*] to bolster it, the logic for spending money on early-childhood development programs may seem incontrovertible (Collins 1997, 62).

The concern is not simply that the scientific picture is far more complex than its representation in the media, or that journalists are inaccurate (sometimes simply generalizing from existing knowledge to issues that have not been studied or cannot be studied well). More important, however, is that valuable public interest in early childhood may evaporate as quickly as it has emerged if parents, practitioners, and policy makers conclude that they were misled about how they could contribute to optimizing early development, especially if simplified interpretations and applications of research on early brain development do not yield expected outcomes for enhanced intellectual and socioemotional growth (Thompson and Nelson 2001).

The backlash was inevitable. Following a cooling-off period and the publication of books like John Bruer's *Myth of the First Three Years: A New Understanding of Early Brain Development and Lifelong Learning* (1999) and Alvin Rosenfeld and Nicole Wise's *Hyper-Parenting: Are You Hurting Your Child by Trying Too Hard?* (2000), parents began to feel skeptical about brain research and what it might mean for their children. *Time,* the same magazine that trumpeted, at the height of the brain-research frenzy, "From birth, a baby's brain cells proliferate wildly, making connections that may shape a lifetime of experience. The first three years are critical" (Nash 1997, 48), in 2001 ran a cover story proclaiming, "So you want to raise a superkid . . . throw away those flash cards, relax and let kids be kids: A how to (and how-not-to) guide for parents" (*Time,* 30 April 2001). Excerpts from this issue not only debunk many of the earlier issue's assertions but frighten parents in new ways: "Want a brain child? . . . Is [perfecting your child] really a wise thing to attempt? What if you were to get a smarter but meaner kid?" (*Time* 2001, 5). As the new millennium began, parents were being urged to eschew trendy black-and-white toys in favor of letting their kids go back to banging pots and pans on the kitchen floor, to read books to their toddlers instead of giving them computer games, and to provide crayons and dress-up clothes as a means of promoting creativity and language development (Kluger and Park 2001).

As we have noted earlier, the history of developmental psychology is characterized by a series of pendulum swings from overoptimism to despair (see box, "That Was Then, This Is Now"). The nature of IQ and what influences it, the efficacy of intervention and primary prevention efforts, the promise of family policy—all these areas of study have manifested wild swings. As the field moves, in these areas and others, from one extreme to another, two things happen. First, it brings along with it the parents, and the practical information they expect to receive as a benefit of the research, typically in a time frame that lags

That Was Then, This Is Now

Then: "Music . . . excites the inherent brain patterns and enhances their use in complex reasoning tasks" (Begley 1997, 38).

Now: "The myth: A more stimulated brain is a smarter one. Not true. Neurons grow explosively before age 5, but many may shut down after that. Stimulation can help babies learn skills, but overall aptitude is unchanged" (Kluger and Park 2001, 50).

Then: "Parenting has been oversold. You have been led to believe that you have more of an influence on your child's personality than you really do" (Harris 1998, 6).

Now: "When it comes to your child—a child you know better than your mother and mother-in-law do, better often than pediatricians do, better than teachers and caregivers do, and yes, better than I do—you're a parenting expert, too" (Murkoff 2000, 22).

Then: "Singing or playing music to a baby can increase their abilities to learn language and process information. This can be done as early as when the baby is in the womb, and the type of music can vary from lullabies to children's songs to music for adults" (Heller 1996, 58).

Now: "The myth: Listening to music can boost creativity. Nope. The so-called Mozart effect doesn't enhance artistic skills but may improve spatial skills. The effect is just temporary, though, and seen only in adults" (Kluger and Park 2001, 51).

several steps behind the scholarly origins of the advice. Second, as we pass from left to right, from despair to hope, we pass through brief but regular periods of common sense and moderation. As we write this, we see signs that we are coming into such a period. The cycle will recur again, and again we will read or watch on the news exaggerated versions of what we believe to be true about how our children develop and how we can best support them as they do, but these periods of moderation will, we hope, ground parents and policy makers in useful and productive ways.

10

Epilogue
Implications of the Infant Brain Debate

The more things change, the more they remain the same. A theme we have sounded throughout this book has been the predictability of the pendulum swings affecting the field of child development and how these swings have affected how we intervene in the lives of children and families. The impact on child study of what is often called "the brain research," however, strikes us as being somewhat different from the other paradigm shifts that have changed what we know, or believe we know, about children and families, and the most appropriate and efficacious ways of intervening positively in their lives.

Previous alterations in our thinking about children (some of which, of course, proved to be dead ends) were typically shifts in direction: children were blank slates, ready to be shaped by their environments and our input; children were genetically hardwired to do and learn the things they needed to grow and learn. Environmental stimulation boosted intellect and development; parents should *create* additional stimulation to make their children better and smarter. Parents were important shapers of their children's lives, then parents weren't important, then parents were important again. In each of these and many other cases, child development scholars second-guessed themselves (or each other); the implications of their shifts in thinking trickled down to parents in ways that sometimes contradicted the advice they had previously derived from such scholarship.

The impact of research on neurobiology and neurochemistry and the imaging techniques that have allowed us to see into the functioning human brain, however, has been different, albeit no less significant. This revolution has focused less on the message than on the media delivering it. The findings of the new research have had profound implications for medical science, specifically for the treatment of brain and central nervous system injuries and illness. But for child development study, the case has been rather different. In fact, it seemed at first as if scholars in our field didn't know quite what to make of the material on neurological development: much of the media coverage had to stretch a little to describe just what *new* information and ideas could be derived from incorporating this body of research into decades' worth of observational and behavioral research.

Where We Stand Now

Several years have passed since the White House conference on brain development, the birth of the I Am Your Child campaign, the publication of the first special issues of *Time* and *Newsweek* and scores of other articles on what this new (or new to the general public) research might mean for parenting and education. Several books describing the neurological and genetic events of the early years of life have contributed to our understanding of—and the controversy over—what this material really means. The bottom line?

■ Brain research, still in its infancy, has so far simply confirmed what decades of social science research have told us: that the young child's experience of the world has a profound impact on early—and continuing—development.

■ Parents play a profound role in their child's development. But a caregiving situation that emphasizes warmth, continuity of care, love, and respect gives infants and young children the elements they need for healthy and sound cognitive, social, and physical development without the need for special toys, music, or classes.

■ Growth and development do not stop after infancy or
toddlerhood or the school-age years, and, with few exceptions having largely to do with sensory systems, windows of
opportunity for learning and growth do not slam shut at
preset intervals. Everything we continue to learn about
human growth and development—through both observational and neurological research—confirms our earlier understanding that the early years of life are of critical importance for laying the foundation for a lifetime of learning
and loving but that development and learning continue
throughout life.

One other important outcome has emerged from the ways we
and others have tried to make sense of the implications of brain research for a field that previously derived its findings largely from social
science. This, of course, relates to the policy implications of the rapidly
developing areas of neuroimaging and neurochemistry and what they
tell us about human development. Concern arose among policy scholars early on as the interpretation, and sometimes the misinterpretation, of new data pointed toward or away from the need to provide
supports and interventions for children and families. The dust has not
settled as rapidly in this area as it has in the developmental science
arena, but it is clear that the major implication for policy is not unlike
the outcomes for child study. Sound, empirically derived policies providing for safe and appropriate early care, education, health care, and
parent support are critical components of the way we can strengthen
families, communities, and the nation as a whole.

We have alluded many times before to the changing nature of
children's policies (Hall, Kagan, and Zigler 1996; Zigler and Hall 2000;
Zigler, Hopper, and Hall 1993) and are well aware of the forces external
to the fields of child and family study that shape policy initiatives and
the budgets proposed to implement them. In the 1960s, for instance,
public optimism regarding the promise of early intervention, coupled
with the robust American economy, permitted the creation and reasonably eager acceptance of a wide variety of broad-based social programs aimed at ameliorating poverty, educational risk, social incompe-
tence, and at improving access to health care. Those same programs

(including Head Start) were endangered, however, as fiscal and ideological constraints were brought to bear on every stage of the policy
process.

In the 1990s, public opinion again swung in favor of child and
family support, which had waned somewhat in the 1970s as a consequence of both the natural ebb and flow of interest in children and of
the economic constraints that resulted, in part, from funding the Viet-
nam War. Optimism blossomed anew, as children's issues achieved
new prominence in the public eye, and new research provided both social science and "hard" science evidence for the efficacy and cost effectiveness of family support initiatives. As the twentieth century drew to
a close and the new millennium began, a number of factors once again
changed the context in which we make, apply, and assess family policy.
One of these, of course, was the "welfare reform" movement that shifted
the way we approach service provision for poor and near-poor families
(Zigler and Hall 2000); another was the shift from the Democratic and
socially liberal Clinton administration to the more fiscally and socially
conservative Republican administration of George W. Bush.

Yet another factor was the beginning of an economic recession
from which, as of this writing, we have not yet emerged. Even as we put
the finishing touches on the manuscript for this book, we can already
see the handwriting on the wall. As America wages war on terrorism in
response to the actions of 11 September 2001, we believe that we can
predict some of the effects these circumstances will have on the American zeitgeist, on our perspectives and priorities when it comes to
supporting children and families, and on our economic and political
ability to mount effective responses to the needs we endorse as being
worthy of intervention.

In the legislative, judicial, and executive branches of the federal
government, the focus on trying to safeguard the nation and its citizens
from terrorism both abroad and at home has shifted attention from
many other policy concerns, including meeting the needs of children
and families. The needs of children—for consistent, nurturing care,
for good health, for high-quality education, for safe and culturally rich
communities, for a wide range of promising opportunities as they
grow—do not ebb and flow with the vagaries of world affairs. If anything, our nation (like others) has an even greater need, in times of cri-

sis, to develop the conditions that will optimize the capacity of our citizens to manifest physical and mental health, to bring the benefits of solid and innovative education programs to bear on their work and their ability to support the communities that nurtured them as infants and children.

We are not sanguine, however, about the nation's willingness or ability to increase investments in the programming and funding that (as decades of traditional research have shown and new, higher-technology research seems to confirm) would contribute to such outcomes. Instead, it seems likely that the needs of children and families will slip further down on the nation's agenda. These issues, in our opinion, have never—even in the best times of peace and prosperity—received the attention they merit. We mentioned earlier in this chapter the importance of remaining aware of the nonchild-oriented forces that affect child policy; the economics and machinery of war are among the most powerful.

Does this mean that the advocates for children and families, among whom we count ourselves, and among whom we hope readers of this volume will also find themselves, will take a hiatus from trying to improve the lot of our nation's children? It does not. But it does mean that parents themselves, philanthropic foundations, and our state and local governments will have to work harder to fill the relative vacuum that we see at the federal level with respect to genuine concern for addressing the problems of which we speak here. In that regard, the lessons from research, both traditional and groundbreaking, will play as important a role in policy formulation as it has ever played.

Policy Principles

As astounding as today's technological advances in the study of brain science seem to us today, it is important to place them in context: it is likely that fifty to a hundred years from now, and perhaps sooner, we will have diagnostic and research techniques for brain study that make today's PET and CT scans look as primitive as Stone Age trephining. Of course, we can no more wait patiently for these advances than we waited for those that form the core of this book in our efforts to make policy decisions for children. So it becomes essential to cultivate a small canon of principles we can use to frame policy decisions in any era. We hope these will apply to the situations that demand policy answers both today and in the near—and not so near—future.

A Research Foundation

First, we believe that policy debate, such as that which arose over the implications of brain research in the 1990s, is a good and essential activity. Policy itself, however, should always be guided both by research and by our best knowledge. Inherent in all of our work is a commitment to building policy based on a solid, empirical understanding of what we know about assessing and meeting the needs of children and families.

Acting Expeditiously

Second, an absence of complete knowledge of these issues should not lead to paralysis. We could not wait for fMRI techniques to be developed before we designed policies that would enhance educational readiness and cognitive development in the twentieth century; nor can we wait for the next new machine for peeking into the human brain to further our work. Neither a dearth of data nor some awkwardness associated with marrying the benefits of separate bodies of data should deter us. Our mandate is to support the creation of the best policy of which we are capable given the tools at hand.

The entire thrust of this volume has been an attempt to integrate often startling new evidence into an existing corpus of research and theory pertaining to the optimization of social, physical, and cognitive child development. To date, our interpretation of the data provided by new neuroimaging techniques points to its high degree of compatibility with the findings from years, even centuries, of behavioral and observational research on human development. Indeed, even the most startling new discoveries—evidence of adult neurogenesis, for instance —are remarkably at home side by side with earlier research (Gould et al. 1999). Both point to the primacy of the parent-child relationship and the role it plays in the development of robust skills in a number of areas, and to the active part in this development played by an infant previously thought to have been a helpless, unformed organism (Gopnik, Meltzoff, and Kuhl 1999). We are confident that before very long—indeed, probably by the time this book is in your hands—even newer technological advances will put new tools in our hands. In the meantime, we must still develop sound social policies.

Acting in Context

Third, our work is predicated on the assumption that although the construction of individual policies and programs may be helpful, they must be nested within a more cohesive policy framework for maximum effectiveness. The weakness of categorical programs, the inefficiencies of dysfunctional systems, and the lack of coordination among support services have become apparent. Twenty-first-century policy construction must be grounded in a vision that transcends individual services. Incremental policies can then be created within the context of an integrated approach that more effectively meet the needs of children and families.

The literature on early childhood intervention efforts and family support efforts are replete with well-documented examples of models for optimizing program effects. This can be achieved through the use of one-stop-shopping programs in which parents find a variety of related services under one programmatic umbrella or even one physical roof. The School of the 21st Century is one such model, in which community schools represent the hub of a network of services, including prenatal care, parent education, early and continuing developmental screening, child care referrals, training and support for local family day care providers, and others (Finn-Stevenson and Zigler 1999).

Another model is represented by programs in which high-quality early childhood education or broad-based intervention efforts create a snowball effect, in which one early success begets others that in turn increase the likelihood of enhanced success in other areas as the participants develop. A study of children from low-income families in the Chicago area demonstrates the promise of programs that follow a high-quality preschool program with an intervention targeting school-age graduates of the preschool component. The Chicago Longitudinal Study tracked about nine hundred participants in the Chicago school district's Child-Parent Center Program. Beginning at about age three, the participating children were compared with five hundred children matched on a variety of socioeconomic factors who attended different early intervention programs. Longitudinal follow-up studies indicate that children who received the Child-Parent Center Program intervention were less likely to be arrested as juveniles and were 29 percent more likely to complete high school than their comparison group peers. Program children were also significantly less likely to be retained in grade (Reynolds 2001). The social and economic implications of such research are profoundly important both in their own right and for the support they offer to a long line of studies showing similar outcomes (such as Pfannensteil, Seitz, and Zigler 2001).

Forming Alliances

Similarly, and with greater relevance for the topic at hand, we must be willing to forego intellectual turf battles, to cross the boundaries of various disciplines, and to create a network of interdisciplinary frameworks for the understanding of the whole human being. Too long we in the social sciences have emulated the blind men exploring the elephant, each seeing only a portion of the whole, and that incompletely. Those in both the social and physical sciences who care about children must be willing to construct workable models of collaboration. Reliance on disparate theoretical perspectives, increasing fragmentation of both fields by a growing tendency toward subspecialization, and competition for research and treatment dollars can all produce turf battles (Eisenberg 1985). Many workers, however, are managing to arrange scholarly relationships that satisfy the needs of both neurology specialists and psychologists while optimizing outcomes for children (Hall 1991).

Unexpected Outcomes

Last, we need to consider an important but sticky question concerning one outcome of the controversy over how current brain research can be applied to child study. Even though, as we have discussed at several points in this volume, the media treatment of some admittedly arcane neuroscience has resulted in many distortions of the limited data available, the results for young children have, ironically, been very positive in many cases. We hope we have demonstrated throughout this volume our respect for accurate reporting of scientific data through the popular media, and our concern for misinterpretation and misunderstandings when reports are, for the sorts of reasons we described in Chapter 9, inaccurate or less than complete. That said, we admit that the neuroscience research issues reported in often simplistic ways have inadvertently accomplished several things that more cautious reporting might not have done.

Parents

First, the research catapulted children's issues and child development to the front pages of news magazines and newspapers in a virtually unprecedented way. The rather sensationalist tone of many of the articles, referring to "whiz kids" and "brainy babies" and often accompanied by photos of tots in laboratory smocks or diminutive versions of Mozart's breeches and powdered wigs amused some and offended many—but they got parents' attention.

The publications that cater to the interests of parents are not just selling infant formula, designer babywear, sport-utility vehicles, and children's toys in the glossy advertisements that support the magazines. They are also selling an image or, rather, two images. The first is the dream child—healthy, precocious, well rounded, with chubby feet already firmly planted on the road to success. The second image, of course, is the role model for the parents themselves: caring, responsive, up on the latest child development research, and committed to doing whatever it takes to optimize their child's eventual success and happiness. There is no getting around the fact that the popular coverage of brain research in the past five years has generated a good deal of guilt and anxiety in parents who feel they may have missed an important window of learning opportunity or who lack the money to sign their toddlers up for Suzuki violin lessons or baby Gymboree classes.

At the same time, however, other parents have found reassurance in the notion that the experiences of the early years *are* terribly important to future development and that the love, care, and attention they pour into their little ones will likely bear fruit in all realms of development. Parents urged by magazine articles to talk to their tiny infants, even read to them well before they can appreciate the nuances of *Goldilocks and the Three Bears* or *The Cat in the Hat*, are indeed nurturing language development and laying the groundwork for later reading. Beneath all the hyperbole of Mozart and flash cards lay far more than a kernel of truth about the nature and importance of appropriate early stimulation. Parents got the message.

Programs

Second, program developers got the message, too. In California, Proposition 10, the California Children and Families First Initiative, increased the state's tax on cigarettes and other tobacco products by fifty cents and used the funds to establish a system of services and public awareness campaigns promoting good outcomes for California children. Head Start, the California State Preschool Program, and an Early Mental Health initiative were among the recipients of funds from the hundreds of millions of dollars raised by Proposition 10. All of these programs were based on a marriage of traditional but current developmental science and an up-to-the-minute understanding of how brain science can inform early childhood development programs. As one proponent of the program stated: "Proposition 10 will give our youngest children the healthy foundation they need to succeed—in school and in life. Scientific evidence proves that the care a child receives from the prenatal [period] through the first years of life is critical to the child's brain growth and development. It has a profound affect on whether the child will become a productive, well-adjusted adult" (Grimes 1998, 2).

Although the language may be a bit simplistic and the context lacking (the implication is that the early years are important to the exclusion of other periods of human development), the bottom line is sound. The programs implemented or fortified by the funding and commitment provided by Proposition 10 tend to be broad-based, solidly researched programs like those we have described in this book, adhering to the developmental principals we know to enhance development and to ameliorate risk of social, cognitive, and educational failure. Recall that director, actor, and children's advocate Rob Reiner, who is often called the father of Proposition 10, was soundly criticized for his nationally broadcast network television program on the needs of children. His attempt to combine a user-friendly tutorial on the neurology of early childhood with a program of comedic entertainment hosted by actor Tom Hanks may not have been rigorous science, but it accomplished its purposes. The intervention and support programs that emerged from Proposition 10 may have been motivated by good intentions and a sometimes simplistic understanding of the principals involved, but the programs that have emerged are sound and promising.

We have noted the early impetus for applying brain research to child development study and practice was provoked in 1994 with the Carnegie Corporation's publication of *Starting Points*. It seems appropriate that another Carnegie Corporation report brackets this period of exploration and controversy in our field. *Starting Now: Acting on Today's Best Ideas to Nurture, Teach and Protect America's Young Children* (Shore 2001) reemphasizes the foundation's earlier recommendations for programmatic and legislative actions that should be taken on behalf of children:

- Promote responsible parenthood
- Ensure good health and protection
- Guarantee high-quality child care
- Mobilize communities to support young children and their families

The Carnegie report emphasizes the need to rely on current, well-integrated research, the applications of which can serve families and children. The focus is on building political will, so that appropriate programs embracing and nurturing all aspects of child development are more likely to be funded, implemented, maintained, and evaluated. *Starting Now* lauds public information campaigns that can carry the message about how easy it is to promote child development directly to parents and caregivers and that recommend private and public-sector partnerships aimed at improving conditions for children, particularly if these programs incorporate new insights gleaned from recent research.

Alabama's Civitan International Research Center has also promoted an agenda that incorporates material from both social and bio-

logical sciences. The center confirms the importance of brain development research as a support for education programs for children from
birth to five and urges the building of strong coalitions on behalf of
children and families. Like California's Proposition 10 (but without the
tax-based funding element), Alabama's Zero to Three initiative builds
on programs like I Am Your Child to facilitate cooperation among state
departments responsible for education, human resources, rehabilita-
tion services, child care, and others to help develop successful, cost-
effective efforts to support Alabama's families. Certainly the rationale
for these programs has been at times simplistic, but the bottom-line
messages have not been harmful and in many cases have been demonstrably helpful.

Politics

The third surprise outcome of the overblown press depiction of the
brain development research has come in the form of pressure placed on
legislators and other policy developers. It is true that concerns were
also raised about the negative impact of this material on policy development, particularly when a few scholars (such as Bruer 1999) used
their own take on brain research to downplay the importance of early
intervention programs. Fortunately, the absurdity of such arguments
was quickly attacked:

> In *The Myth of the First Three Years,* however, Bruer crosses
> his own bridge and burns it, taking his correct observation
> that the neuroscience of early childhood is, in a sense, in its
> own infancy, and leaping to the absurd conclusion that
> what happens to a child in the early years is of little conse-
> quence to subsequent intellectual development. He also
> suggests that intervening in the lives of very young children
> at risk for poor outcomes in school and adulthood will have
> no effect. . . . We are particularly concerned that . . . policy
> makers will see Bruer's argument as an excuse to ignore the
> growing interest and demand for policies and services that
> support babies, toddlers and their families. [Zero to Three
> 1999]

Once most of the dust had settled on this thoroughly debunked facet of the controversy, the calls came for policy makers to redouble their efforts on behalf of children (for example, Collins 1997; McCall and Groark 2000; Meisels and Shonkoff 2000; C. T. Ramey and S. L. Ramey 1998; and Shonkoff 2000) and to promote "applied developmental science" (Lerner, Fisher, and Wienberg 2000).

We have seen many shifts and crises in the fields of developmental science and family policy, and we shall almost certainly see others. Between the periods of upheaval, however, the messages that trickle down from our ivory towers of study and research into the hands and homes of parents, policy makers, media pundits, and the scholars of the future do not really change so very much.

We still cherish and nurture our children as best we can and use the available research base and the most up-to-date technology to learn about and care for them. Some things change little: we believe that children benefit from being in a loving, stable nuclear family, that parents need to be physically and emotionally available to the child, that this family in turn benefits from being a part of a stable, supportive community. Evidence tells us that support and intervention in the early years are critical but that this period is not the only time that helps to define how we will evolve as individuals, nor is it the only period during which course corrections may be made and help given to improve children's lives and optimize their potential.

Last, we believe now, as we did ten years ago before the rumors of remarkable happenings in developmental neuroscience trickled in to upset, delight, and astound us, that an investment in children is an investment in the future strength of individuals, of families, of communities, and of our nation as a whole. The only difference is that the research, practice, and science paths we must take in order to make these investments is a richer, fuller, more promising one for the collaborations that will emerge from our new knowledge.

References

Aber, J. L., and D. Cicchetti. 1984. The socio-emotional development of maltreated children: An empirical and theoretical analysis. In H. Fitzgerald, B. Lester, and M. Yogman, eds., *Theory and research in behavioral pediatrics,* 2:147–205. New York: Plenum Press.

Aber, J. L., and S. M. Jones. 1997. Indicators of positive development in early childhood: Improving concepts and measures. In R. Hauser, B. Brown, W. Prosser, and M. Stagner, eds., *Indicators of children's well-being,* 122–136. New York: Russell Sage.

Administration for Children and Families. 2001. What is child maltreatment? www.calib.com/nccanch/pubs/factsheets/childmal.cfm.

Alaimo, K., M. A. McDowell, R. R. Briefel, A. M. Bischof, C. R. Caughman, C. M. Loria, and C. L. Johnson. 1994. Dietary intake of vitamins, minerals, and fiber of persons ages two months and over in the United States: Third national health and nutrition examination survey, phase 1, 1988–1991. Advance Data No. 258, 1–26, 3 November. Washington, D.C.: U.S. Department of Health and Human Services, Centers for Disease Control and Prevention.

Alexander, K. K. 2001. Is spanking ever OK? *Parents,* May, 90–98.

Als, H., and L. Gilkerson. 1995. Developmentally supportive care in the neonatal intensive care unit. *Zero to Three* 21(1): 2–9.

American Academy of Pediatrics. 2000. Policy statement: Corporal punishment in schools (RE9754). *Pediatrics* 106: 58.

Andrews, M., M. Nord, G. Bickel, and S. Carlson. 2000. *Household food security in the United States, 1999.* Food Assistance and Nutrition Research Report No. 8. Washington, D.C.: U.S. Department of Agriculture, Economic Research Service.

Anisfeld, M. 1991. Neonatal imitation. *Developmental Review* 11(1): 60–97.

Annie E. Casey Foundation. 2001. *American children faring better.* Baltimore: Annie E. Casey Foundation.

Ariès, P. 1962. *Centuries of childhood.* New York: Random House.

Arnsten, A. 1999. Development of the cerebral cortex: XIV. Stress impairs prefrontal cortical function. *Journal of the American Academy of Child and Adolescent Psychiatry* 38(2): 220–222.

Baker v. Owen. 1975. 395 F. Supp. 294, 96 S. Ct. 210.

Baker, A. J. L., C. S. Piotrkowski, and J. Brooks-Gunn. 1998. The effects of the Home Instruction Program for Preschool Youngsters (HIPPY) on children's performance at the end of the program and one year later. *Early Childhood Research Quarterly* 13: 571–588.

Baltes, P. B., F. Ditman-Kohli, and R. A. Dixon. 1984. New perspectives on the development of intelligence in adulthood: Toward a dual-process conception and a model of selective optimization with compensation. In P. B. Baltes and O. G. Brim, Jr., eds., *Lifespan development and behavior*, 6:33–76. New York: Academic Press.

Barnet, A. B., and R. J. Barnet. 1998. *The youngest minds: Parenting and genes in the development of intellect and emotion.* New York: Simon and Schuster.

Barnett, W. S. 1995. Long-term effects of early childhood programs on cognitive and school outcomes. *Future of Children* 5(3): 25–50.

Bauman, M., and T. L. Kemper. 1985. Histoanatomic observations of the brain in early infantile autism. *Neurology* 35: 866–874.

———. 1994. Neuroanatomic observations of the brain in autism. In M. L. Bauman and T. L. Kemper, eds., *The neurobiology of autism*, 216–229. Baltimore: Johns Hopkins University Press.

Beardslee, W. R., P. H. Wolff, and I. Hurwitz. 1982. The effects of infantile nutrition on behavioral development: A follow-up study. *American Journal of Clinical Nutrition* 35: 1437–1441.

Bee, H. L., K. E. Barnard, S. J. Eyres, C. A. Gray, M. A. Hammond, A. L. Speitz, C. Snyder, and B. Clark. 1982. Prediction of IQ and language skill from prenatal status, child performance, family characteristics, and mother-infant interaction. *Child Development* 53: 1134–1156.

Begley, S. 1997. How to build a baby's brain. *Newsweek,* special edition, spring–summer, 38–43..

———. 1996. Your child's brain. *Newsweek,* 19 February, 34–39.

Belle, D. 1997. Varieties of self-care: A qualitative look at children's experiences in the after-school hours. *Merrill-Palmer Quarterly* 43: 478–496.

Belsky, J. 1985. Experimenting with the family in the newborn period. *Child Development* 56: 407–414.

———. 1986. Infant day care: A cause for concern? *Zero to Three* 6: 1–6.

Belsky, J., G. B. Spanier, and M. Rovine. 1983. Stability and change across the transition to parenthood. *Journal of Marriage and the Family* 45: 567–577.

Benady, S. 2000. Mapping the brain in four dimensions. *Financial Times,* 10 April, 16.

Benes, F. M. 1994. Developmental changes in stress adaptation in relation to psychopathology. *Development and Psychopathology* 6(4): 723–739.

Benton Foundation. 1998. Effective language for discussing early childhood education and policy. Washington, D.C.: Benton Foundation.

Berg, L. 2000. Intellectual development in adulthood. In R. J. Sternberg, ed., *Handbook of intelligence,* 117–137. Cambridge: Cambridge University Press.

Bernard, S., and J. Knitzer. 1999. *Map and track: State initiatives to encourage responsible fatherhood.* New York: National Center for Children in Poverty.

Berrueta-Clement, J. R., L. J. Schweinhart, W. S. Barnett, A. S. Epstein, and D. P. Weikart. 1984. *Changed lives: The effects of the Perry Preschool Program on youths through age nineteen.* Ypsilanti, Mich.: High/Scope Press.

Bertenthal, B., and J. Campos. 1990. A system approach to the organizing effects of self-produced locomotion during infancy. In C. Rovee-Collier and L. P. Lipsitt, eds., *Advances in infancy research,* 6:2–60. Norwood, N.J.: Ablex.

Besharov, D. J. 1999. *America's disconnected youth: Toward a preventive strategy.* Washington, D.C.: CWLA Press.

Besharov, D. J., and P. Germanis. 1999. Is WIC as good as they say? *Public Interest* 134 (winter): 21–36.

———. 2001. Rethinking WIC: An evaluation of the Women, Infants and Children Program. La Vergne, Tenn.: AEI Press.

Blake, C. L. 1997. Mitochondral chain function in Parkinson's disease. *Moving Disorders* 12, 1: 3–8.

Blake, J., and B. de Boysson-Bardies. 1992. Patterns in babbling: A cross-linguistic study. *Journal of Child Language* 19: 51–74.

Blank, H., K. Schulman, and D. Ewen. 1999. Executive summary. *Seeds of success: State prekindergarten initiatives, 1998–1999.* Washington, D.C.: Children's Defense Fund.

Blood, A. J., and R. J. Zatorre. 2000. Intensely pleasurable responses to music correlate with activity in brain regions implicated in reward and emotion. *Proceedings of the National Academy of Sciences* 98: 11818–11823.

Bloom, B. S. 1964. *Stability and change in human characteristics.* New York: Wiley.

Bolton, P. 1983. Drugs of abuse. In D. F. Hawkins, ed., *Drugs and pregnancy: Human teratogenesis and related problems,* 51–62. Edinburgh: Churchill/Livingston.

Boo, K. 2001. After welfare. *New Yorker,* 9 April, 92–107.

Boswell, J. 1998. *The kindness of strangers: The abandonment of children in western Europe from late antiquity to the Renaissance.* New York: Pantheon Books.

Bouchard, T. J., and M. McGue. 1981. Familial studies of intelligence: A review. *Science* 212: 1055–1059.

Bourgeois, J., P. Goldman-Rakic, and P. Rakic. 1995. Formation, elimination, and stabilization of synapses in the primate cerebral cortex. In M. S. Gazzaniga, ed., *The new cognitive neurosciences,* 45–53. Cambridge, Mass.: MIT Press.

Boyer, E. 1991. *Ready to learn: A mandate for the nation.* Special report: Carnegie Foundation for the Advancement of Teaching. Princeton, N.J.: Princeton University Press.

Brazelton, T. B. 1986. Issues for working parents. *American Journal of Orthopsychiatry* 56: 14–25.

Brazelton, T. B., and S. I. Greenspan. 2000. *The irreducible needs of children: What every child must have to grow, learn, and flourish.* New York: Perseus.

Brazelton, B., B. Koslowsky, and M. Maine. 1974. The origins of reciprocity: The early mother-infant interaction. In M. Lewis and L. Rosenblum, eds., *The effect of the infant on the care giver,* 49–76. New York: Wiley.

Breakey, G., and B. Pratt. 1991. Healthy growth for Hawaii's Healthy Start: Toward a systematic statewide approach to the prevention of child abuse and neglect. *Zero to Three* 4: 6–12.

Bretherton, I. 1985. Attachment theory: Retrospect and prospect. *Monographs of the Society for Research in Child Development,* 50: 3–35.

Brody, D. J., J. L. Pirkle, R. A. Kramer, K. M. Flegal, T. D. Matte, E. W. Gunter, and D. C. Paschal. 1994. Blood lead levels in the U.S. population: Phase 1 of the Third National Health and Nutrition Examination Survey, 1988 to 1991. *Journal of the American Medical Association* 272: 277–283.

Bronfenbrenner, U. 1975. Is early intervention effective? In E. L. Struening and M. Guttentag, eds., *Handbook of evaluation research,* 2:519–603. Beverly Hills, Calif.: Sage.

———. 1979. *The ecology of human development: Experiments by nature and design.* Cambridge, Mass.: Harvard University Press.

———. 1988. Strengthening family systems. In E. Zigler and M. Frank, eds., *The parental leave crisis: Toward a national policy,* 143–160. New Haven and London: Yale University Press.

Brown, A. S., S. Tapert, F. Granholm, and D. C. Delis. 2000. Neurocognitive functioning and adolescents: Effects of protracted alcohol use. *Alcoholism Clinical Experience and Research* 24: 164–171.

Brown, B. 1999. Optimizing expression of the common human genome for child development. *Current Directions in Psychological Science* 8(1): 37–41.

Brown, J. L. 1998. *New scientific evidence on cognitive development: Why nutrition comes up an ace.* Address given at the School of the 21st Century Annual Conference, 20–23 July, Yale University Bush Center in Child Development and Social Policy, New Haven.

Brownell, K. 2001. Public policy to change the American diet: A heated controversy. Luncheon series, 19 January, Yale University Bush Center in Child Development and Social Policy, New Haven.

Bruer, J. T. 1997. Education and the brain: A bridge too far. *Education Researcher* 26(8): 4–16.

———. 1998a. The brain and child development: Time for some critical thinking. *Public Health Reports* 113: 387–397.

———. 1998b. Brain science, brain fiction. *Educational Leadership,* November, 13–18.

———. 1999. *The myth of the first three years: A new understanding of early brain development and lifelong learning.* New York: Free Press.

Bryant, D., and K. Maxwell. 1997. The effectiveness of early intervention for disadvantaged children. In M. J. Guralnick, ed., *The effectiveness of early intervention,* 23–46. Baltimore: Paul H. Brookes.

Buckner, R. L., and S. E. Petersen. 1998. Neuroimaging. In W. Bechtel and G. Graham, eds., *A companion to cognitive science,* 413–424. Blackwell Companions to Philosophy. New York: Blackwell.

Buckner, R. L., S. E. Petersen, J. G. Ojanann, F. M. Milzin, R. L. Squire, and M. E. Raichle. 1995. Functional and anatomical studies of explicit and implicit memory retrieval tasks. *Journal of Neuroscience* 15: 12–29.

Burghardt, J., and B. Devaney. 1995. School nutrition dietary assessment study: Summary and discussion. *American Journal of Clinical Nutrition* 61: 252S–257S.

Butler, N. R., H. Goldstein, and E. M. G. Ross. 1972. Cigarette smoking in pregnancy: Its influences on birthweight and perinatal mortality. *British Medical Journal* 4: 573–575.

Cabrera, N. J., and H. E. Peters. 2000. Public policies and father involvement. *Marriage and Family Review* 29: 295–314.

Cabrera, N. J., C. S. Tamis-LeMonda, R. H. Bradley, S. Hofferth, and M. E. Lamb. 2000. Fatherhood in the twenty-first century. *Child Development* 71: 127–136.

Caffey, J. 1946. Multiple fractures in the long bones of infants suffering from chronic subdural hematoma. *Journal of Roentgenology* 56: 163–173.

Cahn, R., and W. Cahn. 1972. *No time for school, no time for play: The story of child labor in America.* New York: Julian Messner.

Caldwell, B. 1987. Professional child care. In B. Caldwell, ed., *Group care for young children: A supplement to parental care,* 214. Lexington, Mass.: Toronto.

Campbell, F. A., E. Pungello, S. Miller-Johnson, M. Burchinal, and C. T. Ramey. 2001. The development of cognitive and academic abilities: Growth curves from an early childhood educational experiment. *Developmental Psychology* 37: 231–242.

Campbell, F. A., and C. T. Ramey. 1994. Effects of early intervention on intellectual and academic achievement: A follow-up study of children from low-income families. *Child Development* 65: 84–698.

———. 1995. Cognitive and school outcomes for high-risk African-American students at middle adolescence: Positive effects of early intervention. *American Education Research Journal* 32: 743–772.

Campbell, F. A., C. T. Ramey, E. Pungello, J. Sparling, and S. Miller-Johnson. 2002. Early childhood education: Young adult outcomes from the Abecedarian Project. *Applied Developmental Science* 6: 42–57.

Capizzano, J., K. Tout, and G. Adams. 2000. *Child care patterns of school-age children with employed mothers.* Occasional Paper No. 41. Washington, D.C.: Urban Institute.

Carlson, M., and E. Earls. 1999. Psychological and neuroendocrinological sequelae of early social deprivation in institutionalized children in Romania. In C. S. Carter, B. Lederhendler, and B. Kirkpatric, eds., *Integrative*

Neurobiology of Affiliation, 419–428. Annals of the New York Academy of Science, vol. 807.

Carnegie Corporation. 1994. *Starting points: Meeting the needs of our youngest children.* New York: Carnegie Corporation.

———. 1996. *Years of promise: A comprehensive learning strategy for America's children.* Report of the Task Force on Learning in the Primary Grades. New York: Carnegie Corporation.

Casper, L. M. 1997. My daddy takes care of me! Fathers as care provider. *Current Population Reports,* 70-59. Washington, D.C.: U.S. Bureau of the Census.

Center on Hunger, Poverty and Nutrition Policy. 1998. Statement on the link between nutrition and cognitive development in children. Brochure. Tufts University, School of Nutrition.

Centers for Disease Control and Prevention. 2000. State-specific changes in singleton preterm births among black and white women—United States, 1990 and 1997. *Morbidity and Mortality Weekly Report* 49(37): 837–840.

Chabris, C. F. 1998. IQ since "The bell curve." *Commentary,* August, 33–41.

———. 1999. Brief exposure to music does not increase intelligence. *Nature* 5: 1–3.

Chavez, A., C. Martinez, and T. Yaschine. 1975. Nutrition, behavioral development, and mother-child interaction in young rural children. *Federation Proceedings* 34(7): 1574–1582.

Chen, Z., and R. S. Siegler. 2000. Intellectual development in childhood. In R. Sternberg, ed., *Handbook of intelligence,* 92–216. New York: Cambridge University Press.

Child Welfare League of America. 2001. Statement from Shay Bilchik: Keeping a promise to America's abused and neglected children. Press release, 1 November.

Children's Defense Fund (CDF). 1998. *Child care challenges.* Washington, D.C.: Children's Defense Fund.

Chugani, H. T. 1994. Development of regional brain glucose metabolism in relation to behavior and plasticity. In G. Dawson and K. W. Fischer, eds., *Human behavior and the developing brain,* 153–175. New York: Guilford Press.

———. 1996. Neuroimaging of developmental nonlinearity and developmental pathologies. In R. W. Thatcher, G. R. Lyon, J. Rumsey, and N. Krasnegor, eds., *Developmental neuroimaging: Mapping the development of brain and behavior,* 187–196. San Diego, Calif.: Academic Press.

———. 1998. A critical period of brain development: Studies of cerebral glucose utilization with PET. *Preventive Medicine* 27: 184–188.

Chugani, H. T., D. A. Hovda, J. R. Villablanca, and M. E. Phelps. 1996. Cerebral metabolism following neonatal or adult hemineodecortication in cats: I. Effects on glucose metabolism using [14C]2-deoxy-D-glucose autoradiography. *Journal of Cerebral Blood Flow and Metabolism* 16(1): 134–146.

Cicchetti, D. In press. How a child builds a brain: Insights from normality and psychopathology. In W. Hartup and R. Weinberg, eds., *Child psychology in retrospect and prospect.* Minnesota symposia on child psychology, vol. 35. Mahwah, N.J.: Lawrence Erlbaum.

Cicchetti, D., and V. K. Carlson, eds. 1989. *Child maltreatment: Theory and Research on the causes and consequences of child abuse and neglect.* New York: Cambridge University Press.

Cicchetti, D., and F. A. Rogosch. Unpubl. ms. Diverse patterns of neuroendocrine activity in maltreated children. Mt. Hope Family Center.

———. 1997. The role of self-organization in the promotion of resilience of maltreated children. *Development and Psychopathology* 9: 799–817.

Cicchetti, D., and S. L. Toth. 2000. Child maltreatment in the early years of life. In J. D. Osofsky and H. E. Fitzgerald, eds., *WAIMH handbook of infant mental health,* vol. 4: *Infant mental health in groups at high risk,* 255–294. New York: John Wiley and Sons.

Clark, A. S., and M. L. Schneider 1993. Prenatal stress has long-term effects on behavioral responses to stress in juvenile rhesus monkeys. *Developmental Psychobiology* 26: 293–304.

Clarke, A. M., and A. D. B. Clarke. 1977. *Early experience: Myth and evidence.* New York: Free Press.

Coates, D. 1996. Early childhood evaluation. A report to the Parkway School District Board of Education, Chesterfield, Mo.

Cohen, L. B., and P. Salapatek. 1975. *Basic visual processes.* Vol. 1: *Infant perception: From sensation to cognition.* New York: Academic Press.

Cohen, S. E. 1982. Maternal employment and mother-child attachment. In J. Belsky, ed., *In the beginning,* 82–97. New York: Columbia University Press.

Coley, R. L., and P. L. Chase-Lansdale. 2000. Fathers' involvement of their own children over time. *Poverty Research News* 4: 12–14.

Collins, J. 1997. The day care dilemma. *Time,* 3 February, 58–62.

Commission on Family Leave. 1996. *A workable balance: Report to Congress on family and medical leave policies.* Washington, D.C.

Connecticut Task Force on Family and Medical Leave. 2000. *Final report to the Labor and Public Employees Committee.* Hartford, Conn.

Consortium for Longitudinal Studies. 1983. *As the twig is bent: Lasting effects of preschool programs.* Hillsdale, N.J.: Lawrence Erlbaum.

Cook, J., and J. L. Brown. 1994. *Two Americas: Comparisons of U.S. child poverty in rural, inner city, and suburban areas.* Medford, Mass.: Tufts University, School of Nutrition.

Coontz, S. 1997. *The way we really are: Coming to terms with America's changing families.* New York: Basic Books.

Coplin, J. W., and A. C. Houts. 1991. Father involvement in parent training for oppositional child behavior: Progress or stagnation? *Child and Family Behavior Therapy* 13: 29–51.

Cost, Quality, and Child Outcomes (CQCO) Study Team. 1995. *Cost, quality, and child outcomes in child care centers: Public report.* 2d ed. Denver: Center for Research in Economic and Social Policy, University of Colorado at Denver.

————. 1999. *The children of the Cost, Quality, and Outcomes Study go to school: Executive summary.* Denver: Center for Research in Economic and Social Policy, University of Colorado at Denver.

Courchesne, E. 1991. Neuroanatomic imaging in autism. *Pediatrics* 87: 781–790.

Crabtree, J. W., and A. H. Riesen. 1979. Effects of the duration of dark rearing on visually guided behavior in the kitten. *Developmental Psychobiology* 12: 291–303.

Crain, W. C. 1985. *Theories of development.* Englewood Cliffs, N.J.: Prentice Hall.

Currie, J. 2000. Early childhood intervention programs: What do we know? Working paper from the Children's Roundtable. Washington, D.C.: Brookings Institute.

Dalton, T. C. 1995. McGraw's alternative to Gesell's maturationist theory. in T. C. Dalton and V. W. Bergenn, eds., 1995. *Beyond heredity and environment: Myrtle McGraw and the maturation controversy,* 127–152. Boulder, Colo.: Westview Press.

————. 1998. Myrtle McGraw's neurobehavioral theory of development. *Developmental Review* 18: 472–503.

Darlington, R. B., J. M. Royce, A. S. Snipper, H. W. Murray, and I. Lazar. 1980. Preschool programs and later school competence of children from low-income families. *Science* 208: 202–204.

Daro, D. 1993. Child maltreatment research: Implications for program design. In D. Cicchetti and S. Toth, eds., *Child abuse, child development, and social policy,* 331–367. Norwood, N.J.: Ablex.

Daro, D., and K. Harding. 1998. Healthy Families America: Using research to enhance practice. *Future of Children* 8(1): 4–22.

Deater-Deckard, K., R. Pinkerton, and S. Scarr. 1996. Child care quality and children's behavioral adjustment: A four-year longitudinal study. *Journal of Child Psychology and Psychiatry and Allied Disciplines* 37: 937–948.

DeBellis, M. D., M. Keshavan, D. B. Clark, B. J. Casey, J. Giedd, A. M. Boring, K. Frustaci, and N. D. Ryan. 1999. Developmental traumatology. Part II: Characteristics of trauma and psychiatric symptoms and adverse brain development in maltreated children and adolescents with post-traumatic stress disorder. *Biological Psychiatry* 45: 1271–1284.

DeBellis, M. D., and F. W. Putnam. 1994. The psychobiology of childhood maltreatment. *Child and Adolescent Psychiatric Clinics of North America* 3: 663–678.

de Hann, M., A. Oliver, and M. H. Johnson. 1998. Electrophysiological correlates of face processing by adults and six-month-old infants. *Cognitive Neuroscience Society 1998 Annual Meeting Abstract Program,* 36.

Dennis, W. 1960. Causes of retardation among institutionalized children in Iran. *Journal of Genetic Psychology* 96: 47–59.

———. 1973. *Children of the crèche.* New York: Appleton-Century-Crofts.

Devaney, B., L. Bilheimer, and J. Schore. 1991. *The savings in Medicaid costs for newborns and their mothers from prenatal participation in the WIC program.* Vol. 2. Alexandria, Va.: U.S. Department of Agriculture.

Devaney, B. L., M. R. Ellwood, and J. M. Love. 1997. Programs that mitigate the effects of poverty on children. *Future of Children* 7(2): 88–112.

Diamond, A. 1988. Differences between adult and infant cognition: Is the crucial variable presence or absence of language? In L. Weiskranz, ed., *Thought without language,* 337–370. New York: Oxford University Press.

———. 2000. Close interrelation of motor development and cognitive development and the cerebellum and prefrontal cortex. *Child Development* 71: 44–56.

Dickinson, A. 2001. Mothers against guns. *Time,* 13 June, 32–34.

Dolins, J. C., and K. K. Christoffel. 1994. Reducing violent injuries: Priorities for pediatrician advocacy. *Pediatrics* 94: 638–651.

Dornbusch, S. M., P. L. Ritter, P. H. Leiderman, D. F. Roberts, and M. J. Fraleigh. 1987. The relation of parenting style to adolescent school performance. *Child Development* 58: 1244–1257.

Duggan, A. K., E. C. McFarlane, A. M. Windham, C. A. Rohde, D. S. Salkever, L. Fuddy, L. A. Rosenberg, S. B. Buchbinder, and C. C. J. Sia. 1999. Evaluation of Hawaii's Healthy Start Program. *The Future of Children: Home Visiting, Recent Program Evaluations* 9(1): 66–90.

Early childhood development and learning: What new research on the brain tells us about our youngest children. 1997. White House conference, Washington, D.C., 17 April.

Early Learning Development Bill. 2000. S. 2866 106th Cong., 2d sess.

Early Learning Right in the Crib. 1967. *Readers' Digest.*

Early Learning Trust Fund Act. 1999. S. 749, 106th Cong., 1st sess.

Education Commission of the States. 1996. Bridging the gap between neuroscience and education. Denver, Colo.: Education Commission of the States.

———. 1997. Brain research has implications for education. Denver, Colo.: Education Commission of the States.

Egan, T. 2002. In bid to improve nutrition, schools expel soda and chips. *New York Times,* 20 May, A1, 16.

Egeland, B., and D. Brunnquell. 1979. An at-risk approach to the study of child abuse: Some preliminary findings. *Journal of the American Academy of Child Psychiatry* 18: 219–235.

Eisenberg, L. 1985. What is the science basis for pediatrics? *Journal of Developmental and Behavioral Pediatrics* 6: 188–189.

Emens, E. F., N. W. Hall, C. Ross, and E. Zigler. 1996. Preventing juvenile delinquency. In E. F. Zigler, S. L. Kagan, and N. W. Hall, eds., *Children, families, and government: Preparing for the twenty-first century,* 308–332. New York: Cambridge University Press.

Erikson, E. 1959. Identity and the life cycle. *Psychological Issues* I, monograph no. I.

———. 1963. *Childhood and society.* New York: Norton.

Estrada, P., W. F. Arsenio, R. D. Hess, and S. D. Holloway. 1987. Affective quality of the mother-child relationship: Longitudinal consequences for children's school-relevant cognitive functioning. *Developmental Psychology* 23: 210–215.

Ezzo, G., and R. Bucknam. 1998. *On becoming babywise.* Portland, Oreg.: Multnomah.

Ezzo, G., and A. M. Ezzo. 1998. *On becoming babywise.* New York: PRWIS.

Farber, E., M. Alejandro-Wright, and S. Muenchow. 1988. Managing work and family: Hopes and realities. In E. Zigler and M. Frank, eds., *The parental leave crisis: Toward a national policy,* 38–54. New Haven and London: Yale University Press.

Farran, D. C. 2000. Another decade of intervention for children who are low income or disabled: What do we know now? In J. P. Shonkoff and S. J. Meisels, eds., *Handbook of early childhood intervention,* 510–548. 2d ed. New York: Cambridge University Press.

Federal Interagency Day Care Requirements (FIDCR). 1968. U.S. Department of Health, Education and Welfare: U.S. Department of Health, Economic Opportunity: U.S. Department of Labor. Pursuant to Sec. 522(d) of the Economic Opportunity Act. Washington, D.C.: U.S. Government Printing Office.

———. 1972. Revisions prepared by the Office of Child Development, U.S. Department of Health, Education and Welfare.

———. 1980. Fed. Reg., Part 5, 45(55), 17870, 17885, 19 March.

Federal Interagency Forum on Child and Family Statistics. 1998. Nurturing fatherhood: Improving data and research on male fertility, family formation, and fatherhood. Washington, D.C.: U.S. Government Printing Office.

Feshbach, S. 1980. Child abuse and the dynamics of human aggression and violence. In G. Gerbner, C. J. Ross, and E. F. Zigler, eds., *Child abuse: An agenda for action,* 121–143. New York: Oxford University Press.

Field, T. M., S. M. Schanberg, F. Scafidi, C. R. Bauer, N. Vega-Lahr, R. Garcia, J. Nystrom, and C. M. Kuhn. 1986. Tactile/kinesthetic stimulation effects on preterm neonates. *Pediatrics* 77: 654–658.

Finn-Stevenson, M., and E. Zigler. 1999. *Schools of the twenty-first century: Linking child care and education.* Boulder, Colo.: Westview Press.

Fox, N. A., S. D. Calkins, and M. A. Bell. 1994. Neural plasticity and development in the first two years of life: Evidence from cognitive and socioemotional domains of research. *Developmental Psychopathology* 6(4): 677–696.

Fraker, T. M. 1990. *The effects of food stamps on food consumption: A review of the literature.* Alexandria, Va.: U.S. Department of Agriculture, Food and Nutrition Service.

Frank, M. 1988. Cost, financing, and implementation mechanisms of parental leave policies. In E. Zigler and M. Frank, eds., *The Parental Leave Crisis: Toward a National Policy,* 315–325. New Haven and London: Yale University Press.

Frank, M., and E. F. Zigler. 1996. Family leave: A developmental perspective. In E. F. Zigler, S. L. Kagan, and N. W. Hall, eds., *Children, families, and government: Preparing for the twenty-first century,* 117–131. New York: Cambridge University Press.

Frank Porter Graham Child Development Center. 1998. The Carolina Abecedarian Project: Overview, design, findings. www.fpg.unc.edu/overview/abc/abcfind.htm.

Friedman, D. 1987. *Family supportive policies: The corporate decision making process.* New York: Conference Board.

Friedman, S., and M. Sigman. 1992. *The psychological development of low-birthweight children.* Norwood, N.J.: Ablex.

Gale, W. G., and I. Sawhill. 1999. The best return on the surplus. *Washington Post,* 17 February.

Galinsky, E., and J. T. Bond. 1998. *Business work-life study.* New York: Families and Work Institute.

Galinsky, E., C. Howes, S. Kontos, and M. Shinn. 1994. *The study of children in family and relative care: Highlights of findings.* New York: Families and Work Institute.

Gallagher, J. J., R. Rooney, and S. Campbell. 1999. Child care licensing regulations and child care quality in four states. *Early Childhood Research Quarterly* 14: 313–333.

Galler, J. R., F. Ramsey, G. Solimano, and W. Lowell. 1983. The influence of early malnutrition on subsequent behavioral development: II. classroom behavior. *Journal of the American Academy of Child Psychiatry* 22: 16–22.

Gallese, V., L. Fadiga, L. Fogassi, and G. Rizzolatti. 1996. Action recognition in the premotor cortex. *Brain* 119(2): 593–609.

Gallup Organization. 1997. Family values differ sharply around the world. Princeton, N.J.: Gallup Organization.

Gelles, R. J. 1996. *The book of David: How preserving families can cost children's lives.* New York: Basic Books.

Gerbner, G. 1980. Children and power on television: The other side of the picture. In G. Gerbner, C. J. Ross, and E. F. Zigler, eds., *Child abuse: An agenda for action,* 239–248. New York: Oxford University Press.

Gerbner, G., C. J. Ross, and E. F. Zigler, eds. Child abuse: An agenda for action. New York: Oxford University Press.

Gesell, A. 1928. *Infancy and human growth.* New York: McMillan.

Giedd, J. N., J. Blumenthal, and N. O. Jeffries. 1999. Brain development during childhood and adolescence: A longitudinal MRI study. *Neuroscience* 2(10): 861–863.

Gladwell, M. 2000. Baby steps: Do our first three years of life determine how we'll turn out? *New Yorker,* 10 January, 80–87.

Glaser, D. 2000. Child abuse and neglect and the brain—A review. *Journal of Child Psychology and Psychiatry* 41(1): 97–116.

Goals 2000: Educate America Act of 1994. Pub. L. No. 103-227, 108 U.S.C. 125 1994.

Goldberg, W. A., and M. A. Easterbrooks. 1984. Role of marital quality in toddler development. *Developmental Psychology* 20: 504–514.

Goldman-Rakic, P. S., J.-P. Bourgeois, and P. Rakic. 1997. Synaptic substrate of cognitive development: Life-span analysis of synaptogenesis in the prefrontal cortex of the nonhuman primate. In N. Krasnegor and G. R. Lyon, eds., *Development of the prefrontal cortex: Evolution, neurobiology, and behavior,* 27–47. Baltimore: Paul H. Brookes.

Goldstein, A. 2001. It took three dead babies. *Time* www.time.com/time/reports/mississippi/welfare.html.

Gomby, D. S., P. L. Culross, and R. E. Behrman. 1999. Home visiting: Recent program evaluations—Analysis and recommendations. *Future of Children* 9(1): 4–26.

Gopnik, A., and A. N. Meltzoff. 1997. *Words, thoughts, and theories.* Cambridge, Mass.: MIT Press.

Gopnik, A., A. N. Meltzoff, and P. K. Kuhl. 1999. *The scientist in the crib: Minds, brains, and how children learn.* New York: William Morrow.

Gordon, A., and L. Nelson. 1995. *Characteristics and outcomes of WIC participants and nonparticipants: Analysis of the 1988 National Maternal and Infant Health Survey.* Princeton, N.J.: Mathematica Policy Research.

Gould, E., A. J. Reeves, M. S. Graziano, and C. G. Gross. 1999. Neurogenesis in the neocortex of adult primates. *Science* 286: 548–552.

Gould, E., P. Tanapat, N. Hastings, and T. Shors. 1999. Neurogenesis in adulthood: A possible role in learning. *Trends in Cognitive Sciences* 3: 186–192.

Goyette-Ewing, M. In press. Children's after-school arrangements: A study of self-care and developmental outcomes. *Journal of Prevention and Intervention in the Community, Special Issue on Families.*

Graber, D. A. 1989. *Mass media and American politics.* Washington, D.C.: Congressional Quarterly.

Grafman, J., and I. Littman. 1995. Reorganizing the importance of deficiencies in executive functions. *Lancet* 354: 1921–1923.

Grantham-McGregor, S. 1995. A review of studies of the effect of severe malnutrition on mental development. *Journal of Nutrition* 125: 2233S—2238S.

Greene, A. D., and K. A. Moore. 1999. Nonresident father involvement and child well-being among young children in families on welfare. *Marriage and Family Review* 29: 2–3.

Greenleaf, B. K. 1978. *Children through the ages: A history of childhood.* New York: Harper and Row.

Greenough, W. T. 1975. Experiential modification of the developing brain. *American Scientist* 63: 37–46.

Greenough, W. T., and J. Black. 1992. Induction of brain structure by experience: Substrates for cognitive development. In M. Gunnar and C. A. Nelson, eds., *Developmental neuroscience,* 155–200. Minnesota symposia on child psychology, vol. 24. Hillsdale, N.J.: Lawrence Erlbaum.

Greenough, W. T., J. E. Black, and C. S. Wallace. 1987. Experience and brain development. *Child Development* 58: 539–559.

Greenspan, S. 2002. *The secure child: Helping children feel safe and confident in a changing world.* New York: Perseus.

Greenspan, S. I., and B. L. Benderly. 1997. *The growth of the mind and the endangered origins of intelligence.* Reading, Mass.: Addison-Wesley.

Grimes, J. 1998. Materials on Proposition 10: State and county early childhood development programs. Sacramento, Calif.: California Budget Project.

Gunnar, M. 1992. Reactivity of the hypothalamic pituitary-adrenocortical system to stressors in normal infants and children. *Pediatrics* 90: 491–497.

Gunnar, M. R., and R. G. Barr. 1998. Stress, early brain development, and behavior. *Infants and Young Children* 11(1): 1–14.

Gunnar, M. R., M. Broderson, M. Nachmias, K. Buss, and J. Rigatuso. 1996. Stress reactivity and attachment security. *Developmental Psychobiology* 29: 191–204.

Gunnar, M. R., M. Larson, L. Hertsgaard, M. Harris, and L. Broderson. 1992. The stressfulness of separation among nine-month-old infants: Effects of social context variables and infant temperament. *Child Development* 63: 290–303.

Gunnar, M. R., and C. Nelson. 1994. Event-related potentials in year-old infants predict negative emotionality and hormonal responses to separation. *Child Development* 65: 80–94.

Gunnar, M. R., K. Tout, M. deHaan, and S. Pierce. 1997. Temperament, social competence, and adrenocortical activity in preschoolers. *Developmental Psychobiology* 31(1): 66–85.

Guralnick, M. J. 1997. Second-generation research in the field of early intervention. In M. J. Guralnick, ed., *The effectiveness of early intervention,* 3–20. Baltimore: Paul H. Brookes.

Hall, N. 1991. Pediatrics and child development. In F. S. Kessel, M. H. Bornstein, and A. J. Sameroff, eds., *Contemporary constructions of the child: Essays in honor of William Kessen,* 209–224. Hillsdale, N.J.: Lawrence Erlbaum.

Hall, N. W. 1998. What you need to know today to keep your child drug-free to-morrow. *Parents,* January, 67–72.

———. In press. That was then and this is now: New insights into infant brain development. *American Baby.*

Hall, N. W., S. L. Kagan, and E. Zigler. 1996. The changing nature of child and family policy: An overview. In E. Zigler, S. L. Kagan, and N. W. Hall, eds., *Children, families and government: Preparing for the twenty-first century,* 3–9. New York: Cambridge University Press.

Halpern, R. 2000. Early intervention for low-income children and families. In J. P. Shonkoff and S. J. Meisels, eds., *Handbook of early childhood intervention,* 361–386. 2d ed. New York: Cambridge University Press.

Hambidge, M. 2000. Human zinc deficiency. *Journal of Nutrition* 130: 1344S—1349S.

Hamburg, D. 1987. *Fundamental building blocks of early life.* New York: Carnegie Corporation.

Hanway, J. 1785. *A sentimental history of chimney sweeps.* London: n.p.

Happy Baby. 1998. The world's first infant stimulation shirt. http://thehappybaby.com.

Harris, D. 2001. Paying for family leave. *Parenting,* February, 143–145.

Harris, J. R. 1998. *The nurture assumption: Why children turn out the way they do—Parents matter less than you think and peers matter more.* New York: Free Press.

Harris, K., F. F. Furstenberg, Jr., and J. K. Marmer. 1998 Parental involvement with adolescents in intact families: The influence of fathers over the life course. *Demography* 35: 201–216.

Harris, W. W. 1997. Richmond Award acceptance speech. *Pediatrics* 102: 621–624.

Hart, B., and T. R. Risley. 1995. *Meaningful differences in the everyday experience of young American children.* Baltimore: Paul H. Brookes.

Hayes, C. D., J. L. Palmer, and M. J. Zaslow, eds. 1990. *Who cares for America's children: Child care policy for the 1990s.* Washington, D.C.: National Academy Press.

Healthy Families America. 2002. Program facts and features. Chicago: Prevent Child Abuse America Corporation.

Healthy Steps. 2001. Healthy Steps success stories as told by Healthy Steps specialists. www.healthysteps.org.

Hebb, D. O. 1949. *The organization of behavior.* New York: Wiley.

Heckman, J. J. 2000. Policies to foster human capital. *Research in Economics* 54: 3–56.

Helfer, R. E., and H. C. Kempe. 1968. *The battered child.* Chicago: University of Chicago Press.

Heller, L. J. 1996. From babble to baby talk. *Parents,* January, 58.

Henrich, C., N. Fedoravicius, M. Finn-Stevenson, and L. Desimone. 2002. *Na-*

tional evaluation of the School of the 21st Century: Preliminary report. New Haven: Bush Center in Child Development and Social Policy.

Hernandez, D. J. 1993. *America's children: Resources from family, government, and the economy.* New York: Russell Sage.

———. 1997. Poverty trends. In G. Duncan and J. Brooks-Gunn, eds., *Consequences of growing up poor,* 18–34. New York: Russell Sage Foundation.

Herrnstein, R. J., and C. Murray. 1994. *The bell curve: Intelligence and class structure in American life.* New York: Free Press.

Hertsgaard, L., M. R. Gunnar, M. F. Erickson, and M. Nachmias. 1995. Adrenocortical responses to the Strange Situation in infants with disorganized/ disoriented attachment relationships. *Child Development* 66: 1100–1106.

Hess, R. D., S. D. Holloway, W. P. Dickson, and G. G. Price. 1984. Maternal variables as predictors of children's school readiness and later achievement in vocabulary and mathematics in sixth grade. *Child Development* 55: 1902–1912.

Hetherington, E. M., and M. Stanley-Hagan. 1986. Divorced fathers: Stress, coping and adjustment. In M. E. Lamb, ed., *The father's role: Applied perspectives,* 103–134. New York: Wiley.

Hetzel, B. S. 2000. Iodine and neuropsychological development. *Journal of Nutrition* 130: 493S—495S.

Heymann, J. 2001. *The widening gap: Why America's working families are in jeopardy and what can be done about it.* Cambridge, Mass.: Harvard University Press.

Hicks, L. E., and R. A. Langham. 1985. Cognitive measure stability in siblings following early nutritional supplementation. *Public Health Reports* 100(6): 656–662.

HIPPY. 2002. Program description and outcomes. www.hippyusa.org/research.html.

Hobbes, N. 1980. Knowledge transfer and the policy process. In G. Gerbner, C. J. Ross, and E. Zigler, eds., *Child abuse: An agenda for action.* New York: Oxford University Press.

Hockfield, S., and P. J. Lombroso. 1998a. Development of the cerebral cortex: IX. Cortical development and experience: I. *Journal of the American Academy of Child and Adolescent Psychiatry* 37(9): 992–993.

———. 1998b. Development of the cerebral cortex: X. Cortical development and experience: II. *Journal of the American Academy of Child and Adolescent Psychiatry* 37(10): 1103–1105.

Hofferth, S. L., A. Brayfield, S. Deich, and P. Holcomb. 1991. *National child care survey, 1990.* Urban Institute Report 91-5. Washington, D.C.: Urban Institute.

Holland, R. 1998. This is your brain . . . on White House data. *Southwind,* 21 January.

Hopper, P., and E. Zigler. 1988. The medical and social science basis for a national infant care leave policy. *American Journal of Orthopsychiatry* 58: 324–338.

Horgan, C. D. 1993. Substance abuse: The nation's number one health problem—Key indicators for policy. Princeton, N.J.: Robert Wood Johnson Foundation.

Horn, J. M., J. C. Loehlin, and L. Willerman. 1979. Intellectual resemblance among adoptive and biological relatives: The Texas Adoption Project. *Behavior Genetics* 9: 177–207.

Howes, C., D. A. Phillips, and M. Whitebook. 1992. Thresholds of quality: Implications for the social development of children in center-based child care. *Child Development* 63: 449–460.

Hubel, D. H., and T. N. Weisel. 1970. The period of susceptibility to the physiological effects of unilateral eye closure in kittens. *Journal of Physiology* 206: 419–436.

Hunt, J. M. 1961. *Intelligence and experience.* New York: Ronald Press.

———. 1971. Parent and child centers: Their basis in the behavioral and educational sciences. *American Journal of Orthopsychiatry* 41: 13–38.

Husaini, M. A., L. Karyadi, Y. K. Husaini, B. Sandjaja, D. Kayadi, and E. Pollitt. 1991. Developmental effects of short-term supplementary feeding in nutritionally-at-risk Indonesian infants. *American Journal of Clinical Nutrition* 54: 799–804.

Huttenlocher, J., W. Haight, A. Bryk, M. Seltzer, and T. Lyons. 1991. Early vocabulary growth: Relation to language input and gender. *Developmental Psychology* 27(2): 236–248.

Huttenlocher, P. R. 1990. Morphometric study of human cerebral cortex development. *Neuropsychologia* 28: 517–528.

———. 1994. Synaptogenesis, synapse elimination, and neural plasticity in human cerebral cortex. In C. A. Nelson, ed., *Threats to optimal development: Integrating biological, psychological, and social risk factors,* 35–54. Minnesota symposia in child psychology, vol. 27. Hillsdale, N.J.: Lawrence Erlbaum.

Huttenlocher, P. R., and A. S. Dabholkar. 1997. Regional differences in synaptogenesis in human cerebral cortex. *Journal of Comparative Neurology* 387: 167–178.

Hyman, I. A., and J. H. Wise. 1979. *Corporal punishment in American education: Readings in history, practice, and alternatives.* Philadelphia: Temple University Press.

Idjradinata, P., and E. Pollitt. 1993. Reversal of developmental delays in iron-deficient anaemic infants treated with iron. *Lancet* 341: 1–4.

Ingraham v. Wright. 1977. 430 S. Ct. 651.

Janowsky, J. S., and R. Carper. 1996. Is there a neural basis for cognitive transitions in school-age children? In A. J. Sameroff and M. M. Haith, eds., *The Five to Seven Year Shift,* 32–66. Chicago: University Chicago Press.

Jason, M. 1999. Developmental cognitive neuroscience. In M. Bennett, ed., *De-*

velopmental psychology: Achievements and prospects. Ann Arbor, Mich.: Psychology Press.

Jansen, E. M., and W. C. Low. 1994. Plasticity and reorganization in neural injury and neural grafting. In C. A. Nelson, ed., *Threats to development: Integrating biological, psychological, and social risk factors,* 55–68. Minnesota Symposia on Child Psychology, vol. 27. Hillsdale, N.J.: Lawrence Erlbaum.

Jensen, A. R. 1969. How much can we boost IQ and scholastic achievement? *Harvard Educational Review* 39: 1–123.

Johnson, M. H. 1999a. Cortical plasticity in normal and abnormal cognitive development: Evidence and working hypotheses. *Development and Psychopathology* 11: 419–437.

———. 1999b. Developmental cognitive neuroscience. In M. Bennett, ed. *Developmental psychology: Achievements and prospects,* 147–162. Ann Arbor, Mich.: Psychology Press.

Jones, K., and D. Smith. 1973. Recognition of the fetal alcohol syndrome in early infancy. *Lancet* 2: 999–1001.

Jordan, L. 1999. Recent family and medical leave proposals and European leave laws. Office of Legislative Research, Connecticut General Assembly. Hartford, Conn.: Office of Legislative Research.

Kagan, J. 2000. Three seductive ideas. Cambridge, Mass.: Harvard University Press.

Kagan, S. L., E. Moore, and S. Bredekamp, eds. 1995. *Reconsidering children's early development and learning: Toward shared beliefs and vocabulary.* Washington, D.C.: National Education Goals Panel.

Kagan, S. L., and M. J. Neuman. 1997. Defining and implementing school readiness: Challenges for families, early care and education, and schools. In R. P. Weissberg, T. P. Gullotta, R. L. Hampton, B. A. Ryan, and G. R. Adams, eds., *Healthy children 2010,* vol. 9: *Establishing preventive services,* 61–96. Thousand Oaks, Calif.: Sage.

Kamerman, S. B. 2000a. International developments in early childhood education and care: The report of a consultative meeting. Available at: www. childpolicy.org.

———. 2000b. Parental leave policies: An essential ingredient in early childhood early education and care policies. *Social Policy Report* 14(2): 3–16.

Kamerman, S. B., and A. J. Kahn. 1991. *Child care, parental leaves, and the under threes.* Westport, Conn.: Auburn.

Kanner, L. 1942. Autistic disturbances of affective contact. *Neurons Child* 2: 217–250.

Karoly, L. A., P. Greenwood, S. S. Everingham, J. Hoube, R. Kilburn, C. P. Rydell, M. Sanders, and J. Chiesa. 1998. *Investing in our children: What we know and don't know about the costs and benefits of early childhood interventions.* Santa Monica, Calif.: Rand.

Karr-Morse, R., and M. S. Wiley. 1997. *Ghosts from the nursery: Tracing the roots of violence.* New York: Atlantic Monthly Press.

Karweit, N. L. 1994. Can preschool alone prevent early learning failure? In R. E. Slavin, N. L. Karweit, and B. A. Wasik, eds., *Preventing early school failure: Research, policy, and practice,* 58–77. Boston: Allyn and Bacon.

Kaufman, J., B. Birmaher, J. Perel, R. E. Dahl, S. Stull, D. Brent, L. Trubnick, M. Al-Shabbout, and N. D. Ryan. 1997, under review. Serotonergic functioning in depressed abused children: Clinical and familial correlates. *Biological Psychiatry.*

Kaufman, J., and D. Charney. 2000. Effects of early stress on brain structure and function: Implications for understanding the relationship between child maltreatment and depression. *Development and Psychopathology* 13: 451–471.

Kaufman, J., P. M. Plotsky, C. B. Nemeroff, D. S. Charney. 2000. Effects of early adverse experiences on brain structure and function: Clinical implications. *Society of Biological Psychiatry* 48: 778–790.

Kaufman, J., and E. F. Zigler. 1996. Child abuse and social policy. In E. F. Zigler, S. L. Kagan, and N. W. Hall, eds., *Children, families, and government: Preparing for the twenty-first century,* 233–255. New York: Cambridge University Press.

Kempe, C., F. Silverman, B. Steele, W. Droegmueller, and H. Silver. 1962. The battered child syndrome. *Journal of the American Medical Association* 181: 17–24.

Kemperman, G., H. G. Kuhn, and F. H. Gage. 1997. More hippocampal neurons in adult mice living in an enriched environment. *Nature* 386: 493–495.

Kenealy, P., and A. Monseth. 1994. Music and IQ tests. *Psychologist* 7: 346.

Kessen, W. 1965. *The child.* New York: Basic Books.

Kessler, D. B. 1999. Failure to thrive and pediatric undernutrition: Historical and theoretical context. In D. B. Kessler and P. Dawson, eds., *Failure to thrive and pediatric undernutrition: A transdisciplinary approach,* 3–18. Baltimore: Paul H. Brookes.

Keyserling, M. D. 1972. *Windows on day care.* New York: National Council of Jewish Women.

Kinsbourne, M., and M. Hiscock. 1983. Development of lateralization of the brain. In D. Musser, ed., *Handbook of child development,* 2:250–261. New York: John Wiley.

Kirkpatrick, K. 1999. U.S. parents want help with newborns: Lack of experience and skill seen as reason for increased child abuse and neglect. 1999 Public Awareness Survey. Chicago: Prevent Child Abuse America.

Kirlik, A. 1998. Everyday life environments. In W. Bechtel and G. Graham, eds., *A companion to cognitive science,* 702–712. Blackwell Companions to Philosophy. New York: Blackwell.

Kitzman, H., D. L. Olds, C. R. Henderson, C. Hanks, R. Cole, R. Tatelbaum, K. McConnochie, K. Sidora, D. W. Luckey, D. Shaver, K. Engelhardt, D.

James, and K. Barnard. 1997. Effects of prenatal and infancy home visitation by nurses on pregnancy outcomes, childhood injuries, and repeated childbearing: A randomized controlled trial. *Journal of the American Medical Association* 278: 644–652.

Kluger, J., and A. Park. 2001. The quest for a super kid. *Time,* 20 April, 50–55.

Knitzer, J. 2000. Using mental health strategies to move the early childhood agenda and promote school readiness. New York: National Center for Children in Poverty.

Knitzer, J., and S. Page. 1998. Map and track: State initiatives for young children and families. New York: National Center for Children in Poverty.

Kolb, B. 1989. Brain development, plasticity, and behavior. *American Psychologist* 44: 1203–1212.

Kolb, B., and I. Wishaw. 1985. *Fundamentals of human neuropsychology.* 2d ed. New York: Freeman.

Kopp, C. 1992. Trends and directions in studies of developmental risks. In M. Gunnar and C. A. Nelson, eds., *Developmental neuroscience,* 1–33. Minnesota symposia on child psychology, vol. 24. Hillsdale, N.J.: Lawrence Erlbaum.

Kotulak, R. 1997. *Inside the brain: Revolutionary discoveries of how the mind works.* Kansas City, Mo.: Andrews McMeel.

Kuhl, P. 2000. The role of experience in early language development: Linguistic experience alters the perception and production of speech. In N. A. Fox, L. A. Leavit, and J. G. Warhol, eds., *The role of early experience in infant development.* Pediatric Round Table: Johnson and Johnson Pediatric Institute.

Lakshmi, I. 1996. Setting up a children's beat. Paper presented at Poynter Institute Journalism Conference, 18 April, Hartford, Conn.

Lally, J. R., P. L. Mangione, and A. S. Honig. 1988. The Syracuse University Family Development Research Project: Long-range impact of an early intervention with low-income children and their families. In D. R. Powell and I. E. Siegel, eds., *Parent education as early childhood intervention: Emerging directions in theory, research, and practice,* 79–104. Norwood, N.J.: Ablex.

Lamb, M. E. 1997. *The role of the father in child development.* New York: Wiley.

Lamb, M. E., K. J. Sternberg, and M. Prodromidis. 1992. Nonmaternal care and the security of infant-mother attachment: A reanalysis of the data. *Infant Behavior and Development* 15: 71–83.

Lazar, I., and R. Darlington. 1979. Summary report: Lasting effects after preschool. A report by the central staff of the Consortium for Longitudinal Studies. Publication No. OHDS 79-30179. Washington, D.C.: Department of Health, Education, and Welfare.

Lazar, I., R. Darlington, H. Murray, J. Royce, and A. Snipper. 1982. Lasting effects of early education. *Monographs of the Society for Research in Child Development,* serial no. 195, 47(2–3): 1–51.

Lazarov, M., and A. Evans. 2000. Breastfeeding: Encouraging the best for low-income women. *Zero to Three* 21(1): 15–23.

LeMenestrel, S. 2000. What do fathers contribute to children's well-being? Washington, D.C.: Child Trends.

Lerner, B. 1998. Sometimes spanking can't be beat. *Wall Street Journal,* 21 April, A22.

Lerner, C., and A. L. Dombro. 2000. Learning and growing together: Understanding and supporting your child's development. Arlington, Va.: Zero to Three.

Lerner, R. M. 2002. *Adolescence: Development, diversity, context, and applications.* Englewood Cliffs, N.J.: Prentice Hall.

Lerner, R. M., C. B. Fisher, and R. A. Weinberg. 2000. Toward a science for and of the people: Promoting civil society through the application of developmental science. *Child Development* 71: 11–20.

Levenstein, P., S. Levenstein, J. A. Shiminski, and J. E. Stolzberg. 1998. Long-term impact of a verbal interaction program for at-risk toddler: An exploratory study of high school outcomes in a replication of the Mother-Child Home Program. Journal of Applied Developmental Psychology, 19.

Levenstein, P., J. M. O'Hara, and J. Madden. 1983. The Mother-Child Home Program of the Verbal Interaction Project. In *As the twig is bent,* 121–140. Hillsdale, N.J.: Lawrence Erlbaum.

Levine, S. 2000. The price of child abuse. Hidden, lifelong costs. *U.S. News and World Report,* 9 April, 58.

Levitsky, D. A., and R. H. Barnes. 1972. Nutritional and environmental interactions in behavioral development of the rat: Long-term effects. *Science* 176: 68–72.

Lewis, J., C. Mallouh, and V. Webb. 1989. Child abuse, delinquency, and violent criminality. In D. Cicchetti and V. K. Carlson, eds., *Child maltreatment: Theory and research on the causes and consequences of child abuse and neglect,* 707–721. New York: Cambridge University Press.

Lewis, M. 1992. Individual differences regarding response to stress. *Pediatrics* 90: 487–490.

Lichtman, J. 1999. National Partnership for Women and Families lauds president's bold initiative to make family leave more affordable. Press release, National Partnership for Women and Families, Washington, D.C., 24 May.

Liederman, P. H. 1983. Social ecology and child birth: The Newborn Nursery as an environmental stressor. In N. Garmezy and M. Rutter, eds., *Stress, coping and development in children,* 113–123. New York: McGraw Hill.

Lombroso, P. J., and K. D. Pruett. 2002. *Critical periods regarding CSN development.* New Haven: Yale University, Child Study Center.

Lombroso, P. J., and R. Sapolsky. 1998. Development of the cerebral cortex: XII.

Stress and brain development: I. *Journal of the American Academy of Child and Adolescent Psychiatry* 37(12): 1337–1339.

Lozoff, B., G. M. Brittenham, A. W. Wolf, D. K. McClish, P. M. Kuhnert, R. Jiminez, L. A. Mora, I. Gomez, and D. Krauskoph. 1987. Iron deficiency anemia and iron therapy effects on infant developmental test performance. *Pediatrics* 79: 981–995.

Lozoff, B., E. Jimenez, J. Hagen, E. Mollen, and A. W. Wolf. 2000. Poorer behavioral and developmental outcome more than ten years after treatment for iron deficiency in infancy. *Pediatrics* 105(4): e51.

Lucas, A., R. Morley, T. J. Cole, S. M. Gore, P. J. Lucas, P. Crowle, R. Pearse, A. J. Boon, and R. Powell. 1990. Early diet in preterm babies and developmental status at eighteen months. *Lancet* 335: 1447–1481.

Lucas, A., R. Morley, T. J. Cole, G. Lister, and C. Leeson-Payne. 1992. Breast milk and subsequent intelligence quotient in children born preterm. *Lancet* 339: 261–264.

Maccoby, E. 1992. The role of parents in the socialization of children: An historial review. *Developmental Psychology* 28: 1006–1017.

———. 2000. Parenting and its effects on children, on reading and misreading behavioral genetics. *Annual Review of Psychology* 51: 1–27.

Marsten, A. S., J. J. Hubbard, S. D. Gest, A. Tellegen, N. Garmezy, and M. Ramirez. 1999. Competence in the context of adversity: Pathways to resilience and maladaptation from childhood to late adolescence. *Development and Psychopathology* 11: 143–169.

Maurer, A., and J. S. Wallerstein. 1987. The influence of corporal punishment on crime. http://silcon.com/~ptave/maurer1.htm.

McCall, R. B. 1977. Childhood IQs as predictors of adult educational and occupational status. *Science* 197: 482–493.

McCall, R. B., and C. J. Groark. 2000. The future of applied child development research and public policy. *Child Development* 71: 197–204.

McCall, R. B., L. Larsen, and A. Ingram. In press. The science and policies of early childhood education and family services. In A. J. Reynolds, M. C. Wang, and H. J. Walberg, eds., *Early childhood programs for a new century: Issues in children's and families lives.* The University of Illinois at Chicago Series on Children and Youth. Washington, D.C.: CWLA Press.

McGraw, M. 1943. *The neuromuscular maturation of the human infant.* New York: Haffner.

McGue, M. 1994. Why developmental psychology should find room for behavioral genetics. In C. A. Nelson, ed., *Threats to optimal development: Integrating biological, psychological, and social risk factors,* 121–139. Minnesota symposia on child psychology, vol. 27. Hillsdale, N.J.: Lawrence Erlbaum.

McGue, M., and D. Lykken. 1992. Genetic influence on risk of divorce. *Psychological Science* 3: 368–373.

McLaren, L. 1988. Fostering mother-child relationships. *Child Welfare* 67: 353–365.

McLoyd, V. 1998. Socioeconomic disadvantage and child development. *American Psychologist* 53: 185–204.

McVicker Hunt, J. 1961. *Intelligence and experience.* New York: Ronald Press.

Meisels, S. J., and J. P. Shonkoff. 2000. Early childhood intervention: A continuing evolution. In J. P. Shonkoff and S. J. Meisels, eds., *Handbook of early childhood intervention,* 3–34. 2d ed. New York: Cambridge University Press.

Metallinos-Katsaras, E., and K. S. Gorman. 1999. Effects of undernutrition on growth and development. In D. B. Kessler and P. Dawson, eds., *Failure to thrive and pediatric undernutrition: A transdisciplinary approach,* 3–18. Baltimore: Paul H. Brookes.

Meyers, A., and N. Chawla. 2000. Nutrition and the social, emotional, and cognitive development of infants and young children. *Zero to Three* 21(1): 5–12.

Miller, J. O. 1970. Cultural deprivation and its modification: Effects of intervention. In H. C. Haywood, ed., *Social-cultural aspects of mental retardation: Proceedings of the Peabody-NIMH Conference,* 451–489. New York: Meredith.

Milunsky, A., H. Jick, S. S. Jick, C. L. Bruell, D. S. MacLaughlin, K. J. Rothman, and W. Willett. 1989. Multivitamin/folic acid supplementation in early pregnancy reduces the prevalence of neural tube defects. *Journal of the American Medical Association* 262: 2847–2852.

Minuchin, P. 1985. Families and individual development: Provocations from the field of family therapy. *Child Development* 56: 289–302.

Montague, P. R., and P. Dayan. 1998. Neurobiological modeling. In W. Bechtel and G. Graham, eds., *A companion to cognitive science,* 526–541. Blackwell Companions to Philosophy. New York: Blackwell.

Moon, R. Y., K. M. Patel, and S. J. Shaefer. 2000. Sudden infant death syndrome in child care settings. *Pediatrics* 106: 295–300.

Morgan, B. L. G., and M. Winick. 1985. Pathologic effects of malnutrition on the central nervous system. In H. Sidransky, ed., *Nutritional pathology—pathobiochemistry of dietary imbalances,* 161–206. New York: Dekker.

Morris, R. G., and C. L. Worsley. 2002. Neuropsychology of Alzheimer's disease. In V. S. Ramachandran, ed., *Encyclopedia of the human brain,* 1:512–565. New York: Academic Press.

Morton, J., and M. H. Johnson. 1991. A two process theory of infant face recognition. *Physiological Review* 98(2): 164–181.

Muenchow, S. 1996. The role of the media in child and family policy. In E. F. Zigler, S. L. Kagan, and N. W. Hall, eds., *Children, families and government: Preparing for the twenty-first century,* 394–408. New York: Cambridge University Press.

Mullen, P., J. Martin, S. Anderson, S. Romas, and G. Herbison. 1996. The long-term impact of the physical, emotional and sexual abuse of children: A community study. *Child Abuse and Neglect* 20: 7–21.

Mundale, J. 1998. Brain mapping. In W. Bechtel and G. Graham, eds., *A companion to cognitive science*, 129–139. Blackwell Campanions to Philosophy. New York: Blackwell.

Murkoff, H. 2000. The real parenting expert is . . . you. *Newsweek*, fall—winter, special edition, 20–22.

Myers, A. F., A. E. Simpson, M. Weitzman, B. L. Rogers, and H. Kayne. 1989. School breakfast program and school performance. *American Journal of Public Health* 143: 1234–1239.

Nachmias, M., M. R. Gunnar, S. Mangelsdorf, and R. Parritz. 1996. Behavioral inhibition and stress reactivity: Moderating role of attachment security. *Child Development* 67: 508–522.

Nash, J. M. 1997. Fertile minds. *Time,* 3 February, 47–53.

National Academy of Science. 1990. Effects of gestational weight gain on outcome in singleton pregnancies. In *Nutrition during pregnancy, part 1: Nutritional status and weight gain*, 176–211. Washington, D.C.: National Academy Press.

National Association for the Education of Young Children. 1997. Early years are learning years. Washington, D.C.: National Association for the Education of Young Children.

National Center for Children in Poverty (NCCP). 2000. *Child poverty in the States: Levels and trends from 1979 to 1998.* New York: NCCP.

National Center for Early Development and Learning. 1998. Teachers: 48% of children have transition problems. *Kindergarten Transitions* 1: 1.

National Center for Education Statistics (NCES). 1996. *Child care and early education program participation of infants, toddlers, and preschoolers.* NCES 95-824. Washington, D.C.: U.S. Department of Education.

National Center for Environmental Health (NCEH). 2001. *CDC's Lead Poisoning Prevention Program* CDC lead fact sheet. www.cdc.gov/nceh/lead/factsheets/leadfcts.htm

National Commission on Children. 1991. *Beyond rhetoric: A New American agenda for children and families.* Washington, D.C.: U.S. Government Printing Office.

National Council of Jewish Women (NCJW). 1999. *Opening a new window on child care: A report on the status of child care in the nation today.* New York: NCJW.

National Education Goals Panel (NGEP). 1997. *Getting a good start in school.* Washington, D.C.: U.S. Government Printing Office.

National Education Goals Report. 1994. Washington, D.C.: U.S. Department of Education.

National Institute of Child Health and Development (NICHD). 1997. Infant child care and attachment security: Results of the NICHD Study of Early Child Care. *Child Development* 68: 860–879.

———. 1998. *NICHD study of early child care, executive summary.* NIH Pub. No. 98-4318. Washington, D.C.: National Institutes of Health.

National Partnership for Women and Families. 1999a. Family leave initiative. Press release, Washington, D.C., 3 February.

———. 1999b. Family and Medical Leave Act is working for America. Press release, Washington, D.C., 14 July.

———. 1999c. Campaign for family leave income launched today. Press release, National Partnership for Women and Families, Washington, D.C., 10 June.

———. 1999d. Family leave income: Picking up speed. *National Partnership for Women and Families News,* spring–summer.

———. 2000. Public support for family leave benefits growing. Press release, Washington, D.C., 4 October.

———. 2001. Work and family: Some mid-sized employers are already providing the equivalent of FMLA leave. Press release, Washington, D.C., 23 May.

National Research Council. 1982. *Alternative dietary practices and nutritional abuses in pregnancy: Summary report.* Committee on Nutrition of the Mother and Preschool Child, Food and Nutrition Board, Commission on Life Sciences. Washington, D.C.: National Research Council.

———. 1999. *How people learn.* Washington, D.C.: National Academy Press.

Nelson, C. A. 1999a. How important are the first three years of life? *Applied Developmental Science* 3(4): 235–238.

———. 1999b. Neural plasticity regarding human development. *Current Directions in Psychological Science* 8: 42–45.

———. 2000. The neurobiological bases of early intervention. In J. P. Shonkoff and S. J. Meisels, eds., *Handbook of early childhood intervention,* 204–227. 2d ed. New York: Cambridge University Press.

Nelson, C. A., and F. E. Bloom. 1997. Child development and neuroscience. *Child Development* 68(5): 970–987.

Newman, J., J. H. Rosenbach, K. L. Burns, B. C. Latimer, H. R. Matochia, and E. Rosenthal-Vogt. 1995. An experimental test of the "Mozart effect": Does listening to his music improve spatial ability? *Perceptual and Motor Skills,* 81: 1379–1387.

Newman, S., T. B. Brazelton, E. Zigler, L. W. Sherman, W. Bratton, J. Sanders, and W. Christeson. 2000. *America's child care crisis: A crime prevention tragedy.* Washington, D.C.: Fight Crime: Invest in Kids.

Newsweek. 1997. Your child from birth to three. Special ed., spring–summer.

Nowakowski, R. S., and N. L. Hayes. 2000. New neurons: Extraordinary evidence or extraordinary conclusion? *Science* 288: 771.

Office of the President. 1999. New tools to help parents balance work and family: Memorandum for the heads of executive departments and agencies. 24 May.

Olds, D. 1992. Home visitation for pregnant women and parents of young children. *American Journal of Diseases in Children* 146: 704–708.

Olds, D. L., J. Eckenrode, C. R. Henderson, H. Kitzman, J. Powers, R. Cole, K. Sidora, P. Morris, L. M. Petitt, and D. Luckey. 1997. Long-term effects of home visitation on maternal life course and child abuse and neglect: Fifteen year follow-up of a randomized trial. *Journal of the American Medical Association* 278: 637–643.

Olds, D. L., and C. R. Henderson. 1989. The prevention of maltreatment. In D. Cicchetti and V. K. Carlson, eds., *Child maltreatment: Theory and research on the causes and consequences of child abuse and neglect,* 722–762. New York: Cambridge University Press.

Olds, D., C. R. Henderson, Jr., R. Cole, J. Eckenrode, H. Kitzman, D. Luckey, L. Pettitt, K. Sidora, P. Morris, and J. Powers. 1998. Long-term effects of nurse home visitation on children's criminal and antisocial behavior: Fifteen-year follow-up of a randomized trial. *Journal of the American Medical Association* 280: 1238–1244.

Olds, D. L., C. R. Henderson, H. Kitzman, J. J. Eckenrode, R. E. Cole, and R. C. Tatelbaum. 1999. Prenatal and infancy home visitation by nurses: Recent findings. *Future of Children* 9(1): 44–65.

Olds, D. L., C. R. Henderson, H. Kitzman, J. Eckenrode, R. Cole, R. Tatelbaum, J. Robinson, L. M. Petitt, R. O'Brien, and P. Hill. 1993. Prenatal and infancy home visitation by nurses: A program of research. www.welfareacademy.org/conf/papers/olds/prenatal.cfm

Olds, D., P. Hill, J. Robinson, N. Song, and C. Little. 2000. Update on home visiting for pregnant women and parents of young children. *Current Problems in Pediatrics* 30: 109–141.

Olds, D. L., and H. Kitzman. 1993. Review of research on home visiting for pregnant women and parents of young children. *Future of Children* 3(3): 53–92.

Olweus, D. 1980. Stability of aggressive reaction patterns in males: A review. *Psychological Bulletin* 86: 852–875.

Ounce of Prevention Fund. 1996. Starting smart: How early experiences affect brain development. Chicago: Ounce of Prevention Fund.

Parke, R. D. 1981. *Fathers.* Cambridge, Mass.: Harvard University Press.

Parker, L. 2000. The federal nutrition programs: A safety net for very young children. *Zero to Three* 21(1): 29–36.

Patterson, G. R. 1982. *Coercive family process.* Eugene, Oreg.: Castalia.

Patterson, G. R., L. Bank, and M. Stoolmiller. 1990. The preadolescent's contribution to disrupted family processes. In G. Adams and T. Gullotta, eds., *Childhood to adolescence: A transition period,* 107–133. New York: Saxx.

Pear, R. 1999. Dispute over plan to use jobless aid for parental leave. *New York Times,* 8 November.

Pederson, F. A., R. L. Cain, M. Zaslow, and G. J. Anderson. 1982. Variation in infant experiences associated with alternative family roles. In L. Laosa and I. Sigel, eds., *Families as learning environments for children*, 123–149. New York: Plenum.

Peisner-Feinberg, E. S., M. R. Burchinal, R. M. Clifford, M. Culkin, C. Howes, S. L. Kagan, N. Yazejian, P. Byler, and J. Rustici. 1999. *The children of the Cost, Quality, and Outcomes Study go to school: Technical report.* Chapel Hill, N.C.: Frank Porter Graham Child Development Center, UNC— Chapel Hill.

Perry, B. D. 1997. Incubated in terror: Neurodevelopmental factors in the "cycle of violence." In J. D. Osofsky, ed., *Children in a violent society*, 124–149. New York: Guilford Press.

Perry, B. D., R. A. Pollard, T. L. Blakley, W. L. Baker, and D. Vigilante. 1995. Childhood trauma, the neurobiology of adaptation, and "use-dependent" development of the brain: How "states" become "traits." *Infant Mental Health Journal* 16(4): 271–289.

Perry, B. D., and J. Marcellus. 1998. The impact of abuse and neglect on the developing brain. Scholastic. http://teacher.scholastic.com/professional/bruceperry/abuse_neglect.htm.

Perry, B. D., and J. E. Pate. 1994. Neurodevelopment and the psychobiological roots of post-traumatic stress disorder. In L. F. Koziol and C. E. Stout, eds., *The neuropsychology of mental disorders: A practical guide*, 129–146. New York: Charles C. Thomas.

Peth-Pierce, R. 2000. *A good beginning: Sending America's children to school with the social and emotional competence they need to succeed.* Report from the Child Mental Health Foundations and Agencies Network. Bethesda, Md.: National Institutes of Mental Health.

Pfannenstiel, J. 1989. New Parents as Teachers project: A follow-up investigation. Overland Park, Kans.: Research and Training Associates.

Pfannenstiel, J., T. Lambson, and V. Yarnell. 1991. Second wave study of the Parents as Teachers program. Overland Park, Kans.: Research and Training Associates.

Pfannenstiel, J., V. Seitz, and E. Zigler. 2001. Promoting school readiness: The role of the Parents-as-Teachers Program. Manuscript submitted for publication.

Pfannenstiel, J., and D. Seltzer. 1989. New Parents as Teachers: An evaluation of an early parent education program. *Early Childhood Research Quarterly* 4: 1–18.

Phillips, D. 1987. *Quality child care: What does the research tell us?* Washington, D.C.: National Association for the Education of Young Children.

Phillips, D., K. McCartney, and S. Scarr. 1987. Child care quality and children's social development. *Developmental Psychology* 23: 537–543.

Phillips, D., and E. Zigler. 1987. The checkered history of federal child care regulations. In E. Z. Rothkopf, ed., *Review of research in education,* 14:3–41. Washington, D.C.: American Educational Research Association.

Plomin, R. 1990. *Nature and nurture: An introduction to behavioral genetics.* Pacific Grove, Calif.: Brooks/Cole.

Pollitt, E. 1994. Poverty and child development: Relevance of research in developing countries to the United States. *Child Development* 65: 283–295.

Pollitt, E., M. Golub, K. Gorman, S. Grantham-McGregor, D. Levitsky, B. Schurch, B. Strupp, and T. Wachs. 1996. A reconceptualization of the effects of undernutrition on children's biological, psychosocial, and behavioral development. *Social Policy Report* 10(5): 1–22. Ann Arbor: University of Michigan, Society for Research in Child Development.

Pollitt, E., K. S. Gorman, P. Engle, R. Martorell, and J. Rivera. 1993. Early supplementary feeding and cognition: Effects over two decades. *Monographs of the Society for Research in Child Development* 58(7), serial no. 238.

Pollitt, E., and S. Oh. 1994. Early supplementary feeding, child development, and health policy. *Food and Nutrition Bulletin* 15(3): 208–214.

Poole, S. R., M. C. Ushkow, and P. R. Nader, eds. 1991. The role of the pediatrician in abolishing corporal punishment in schools. *Pediatrics* 88: 162–176.

Posner, J. K., and D. L. Vandell. 1994. Low-income children's after-school care: Are there beneficial effects on after-school programs? *Child Development* 65: 440–456.

Provence, S. 1989. Infants in institutions revisited. *Zero to Three* 14(3): 1.

Provence, S., and A. Naylor. 1983. *Working with disadvantaged parents and their children: Scientific and practice issues.* New Haven and London: Yale University Press.

Pruett, K. 1987. *The nurturing father.* New York: Warner Books.

———. 1999. *Me, myself and I: How children build their sense of self.* New York: Goddard.

———. 2000a. The coming backlash to early intervention. Luncheon series, January, Yale University Bush Center in Child Development and Social Policy, New Haven.

———. 2000b. *Fatherhood: Why father care is as essential as mother care for your child.* New York: Free Press.

Quigley, M. E., K. Sheehan, M. M. Wilkes, and S. S. Yen. 1979. Effects of maternal smoking on circulating catecholamine levels and fetal heart rates. *American Journal of Obstetrics and Gynecology* 6: 685–690.

Rakic, P. 1985. Limits of neurogenesis in primates. *Science* 227: 154–156.

———. 2000. Adult corticogenesis: A review of the evidence. Unpublished manuscript, Yale University School of Medicine.

Rakic, P., J.-P. Bourgeois, and P. S. Goldman-Rakic. 1994. Synaptic development of the cerebral cortex: Implications for learning, memory, and mental illness. In J. van Pelt, M. A. Corner, H. B. M. Uyslings, and F. H. Lopes da Silva, eds., *Progress in brain research*, 102:27–243. Amsterdam: Elsevier Science.

Ramey, C. T., and F. A. Campbell. 1984. Preventive education for high-risk children: Cognitive consequences of the Carolina Abecedarian Project. *Special Issue: American Journal of Mental Deficiency* 88: 515–523.

———. 1991. Poverty, early childhood education, and academic competence: The Abecedarian experiment. In A. C. Huston, ed., *Children in poverty*, 190–221. New York: Cambridge University Press.

Ramey, C. T., and S. L. Ramey. 1998. Early intervention and early experience. *American Psychologist* 53(2): 109–120.

———. 1999. *Right from birth: Building your child's foundation for life*. New York: Goddard.

Ramey, S. L., and C. T. Ramey. 1998. *Alabama's young children: How their futures can be brighter*. Birmingham, Ala.: A+ Research Foundation.

———. 1999. *Going to school: How to help your child succeed*. New York: Goddard.

Ramey, C. T., K. O. Yeates, and E. J. Short. 1984. The plasticity of intellectual development: Insights from preventive intervention. *Child Development* 55: 1913–1925.

Rauch, S., B. van der Kolk, R. Fisler, N. Alpert, S. Orr, C. Savage, A. Fischman, M. Jenike, and R. Pittman. 1996. A symptom provocation study of post-traumatic stress disorder using positron tomography and script-driven imagery. *Archives of General Psychiatry* 53: 380–387.

Rauscher, F., G. L. Shaw, and K. N. Ky. 1993. Music and spatial task performance. *Nature* 365: 611.

———. 1995. Listening to Mozart enhances spatial-temporal reasoning: Towards a neurophysiological bias. *Neuroscience Letters* 185: 44–47.

Rauscher, F., G. L. Shaw, L. Levine, E. Wright, W. R. Dennis, and R. Newcomb. 1997. Music training causes long-term enhancement of preschool children's spatial-temporal reasoning. *Neurological Research* 19: 2–7.

Raver, C. C., and E. Zigler. 1997. Social competence: An untapped dimension in evaluating Head Start's success. *Early Childhood Research Quarterly* 12(4): 363–385.

Reaves, J. 2001. Our kids have guns: Now what do we do about it? *Time*, 13 June, 27–29.

Reich, R. B. 1999. The other surplus option. *New York Times*, 11 August, A19.

Rescorla, L. A., S. Provence, and A. Naylor. 1982. The Yale Child Welfare Research Program: Descriptions and results. In E. F. Zigler and E. W. Gordon, eds., *Day care: Scientific and social policy issues*, 183–199. Boston: Auburn House.

Resner, J. 1997. Hollywood goes gaga. *Time*, 3 February, 62.

Reynolds, A. 1998. Developing early childhood programs for children and families at risk: Research-based principles to promote long-term effectiveness. *Children and Youth Services Review* 20: 503–523.

————. 2000. *Success in early intervention: The Chicago Parent-Child Centers.* Lincoln: University of Nebraska Press.

————. 2001. Early childhood intervention cuts crime, dropout rates. *Journal of the American Medical Association* 282: 428–442.

Reynolds, A., E. Mann, W. Miedel, and P. Smokowski. 1997. The state of early childhood intervention: Effectiveness, myths and realities, new directions. *Focus: Newsletter of the Institute for Research on Poverty of the University of Wisconsin–Madison* 19(1): 1–7.

Ricci, J. A., and S. Becker. 1996. Risk factors for wasting and stunting among children in Metro Cebu, Phillipines. *American Journal of Clinical Nutrition* 63: 966–975.

Richardson, J. L., D. Dwyer, K. McGuigan, W. B. Hansen, C. Dent, C. A. Johnson, S. Y. Sussman, B. Brannon, and B. Flay. 1989. Substance use among eighth-grade students who take care of themselves after school. *Pediatrics* 84: 556–566.

Risch, N., D. Spiker, L. Lotspeich, N. Nouri, D. Hinds, J. Hallmayer, L. Kataydjieva, P. McCague, S. Dimicelli, and T. Pitts. 1999. A genomic screen of autism: Evidence for a multifocus etiology. *American Journal of Human Genetics* 65: 493–507.

Rizzolatti, G., L. Fadiga, V. Gallese, and L. Fogassi. 1996. Premotor cortex and the recognition of motor actions. *Brain Research* 3: 131–141.

Rose, C. 1999. Scientists debate importance of first three years. Channel 13, New York, broadcast, 20 September.

Rose, D., J. Habicht, and B. Devaney. 1998. Household participation in the Food Stamp and WIC programs increases the nutritional intakes of preschool children. *Journal of Nutrition* 128: 548–555.

Rosemond, J. 1994. *To spank or not to spank: A parent's handbook.* New York: Andrews McMeel.

Rosenfeld, A., and N. Wise. 2000. *Hyper-parenting: Are you hurting your child by trying too hard?* New York: St. Martin's.

————. 2001. *The overscheduled child: Avoiding the hyperparenting trap.* New York: Griffin.

Rosenzweig, M. R., E. L. Bennett, and M. C. Diamond 1972. Brain changes in response to experience. *Scientific American* 226: 22–29.

Rossi, P. H. 1998. *Feeding the poor: Assessing federal food aid.* Washington, D.C.: AEI Press.

Roy, K. 2000 Fathers on the margins of work and family: The paternal involvement project. *Poverty Research News* 4: 15–18.

Royce, J. M., I. Lazar, and R. B. Darlington. 1983. Minority families, early education, and later life chances. *American Journal of Orthopsychiatry* 53: 706–720.

Rush, D., J. Leighton, N. Sloan, J. M. Alvir, and G. C. Garbrowski. 1988a. Review of the past studies of WIC. *American Journal of Clinical Nutrition* 48: 394–411.

Rush, D., J. Leighton, N. Sloan, J. M. Alvir, D. G. Horvitz, W. B. Seaver, G. C. Garbowski, S. S. Johnson, R. A. Kulka, J. W. Devore, M. Holt, T. G. Virag, M. B. Woodside, and D. S. Shanklin. 1988b. Study of infants and children. *American Journal of Clinical Nutrition* 48: 439–483.

Rutter, M. 1998. English and Romanian adoptees study team: Development catchup, and deficit, following and after severe global early deprivation. *Journal of Child Psychology and Psychiatry* 39: 465–476.

St. Pierre, R. G., and J. I. Layzer. 1998. Improving the life chances of children in poverty: Assumptions and what we have learned. *Society for Research on Child Development Social Policy Research Report* 4: 1–23.

Salovey, P., and J. D. Mayer. 1989–1990. Emotional intelligence. *Imagination, Cognition, and Personality* 9: 185–211.

Sameroff, A. J., and M. J. Chandler. 1975. Reproductive risk and the continuum of caretaking casualty. In F. D. Horowitz, ed., *Review of child development research*, 1100–1139. Chicago: University of Chicago Press.

Sameroff, A. J., and M. M. Haith, eds. 1996. *The Five to Seven Year Shift.* Chicago: University of Chicago Press.

Sapolsky, R. 1996. Stress, glucorcorticoids and damage to the neurons system: The current confusion. *Stress* 1: 1–9.

Sawhill, I. V. 1999. *Investing in children.* Brookings Children's Roundtable Policy Brief No. 1, April. Washington, D.C.: Brookings Institution.

Scarr, S. 1992. Developmental theories for the 1990s: Development and individual differences. *Child Development* 63: 1–19.

———. 1997. Why child care has little impact on most children's development. *Current Directions in Psychological Science* 6: 143–147.

Scarr, S., and K. McCartney. 1983. How people make their own environments: A theory of genotype-environment effects. *Child Development* 54: 424–535.

Schlaggar, B. L., T. Brown, M. Lugar, K. M. Visscher, F. Miezin, and S. E. Petersen. 2002. Functional neuroanatomical differences between adults and school-age children in the processing of single words. *Science* 296: 1476–1479.

Schore, A. N. 1994. Affect regulation and the origin of the self: The neurobiology of emotional development. Hillsdale, N.J.: Lawrence Erlbaum.

———. 2000. Neuroscience perspectives on brain development from the domains of language and educational experience. Plenary speech, Head Start's Fifth National Conference: Developmental and Contextual Transitions of Children and Families: Implications for Research, Policy, and Practice. 29 June, Washington, D.C.

Schorr, L. B. 1988. *Within our reach: Breaking the cycle of disadvantage.* New York: Doubleday.

Schweinhart, L. J., H. V. Barnes, and D. P. Weikart. 1993. Significant benefits: The High/Scope Perry Preschool study through age twenty-seven. Monographs of the High/Scope Educational Research Foundation No. 10. Ypsilanti, Mich.: High/Scope Press.

Schweinhart, L. J., J. R. Berrueta-Clement, W. S. Barnett, A. S. Epstein, and D. P. Weikart. 1985. Effects of the Perry Preschool Program on youths through age nineteen: A summary. *Topics in Early Childhood Special Education* 5: 26–35.

Schweinhart, L. J., and D. P. Weikart. 1998. High/Scope Perry Preschool Program effects at age twenty-seven. In J. Crane, ed., *Social programs that work,* 148–162. New York: Russell Sage Foundation.

Seitz, V. 1990. Intervention programs for impoverished children: A comparison of educational and family support models. *Annals of Child Development* 7: 73–103.

Seitz, V., W. D. Abelson, E. Levine, and E. Zigler. 1975. Effects of place of testing on the Peabody Picture Vocabulary Test scores of disadvantaged Head Start and non—Head Start children. *Child Development* 46: 481–486.

Seitz, V., and N. H. Apfel. 1994. Parent-focused intervention: Diffusion effects on siblings. *Child Development* 65: 677–693.

Seitz, V., L. Rosenbaum, and N. H. Apfel. 1985. Effects of family support intervention: A ten-year follow-up. *Child Development* 56: 376–391.

Sherry, B. 1999. Epidemiology of inadequate growth. In D. B. Kessler and P. Dawson, eds., *Failure to thrive and pediatric undernutrition: A transdisciplinary approach,* 19–36. Baltimore: Paul H. Brookes.

Shonkoff, J. 2000. Science, policy, and practice: Three cultures in search of a shared mission. *Child Development* 71: 181–187.

Shonkoff, J. P., and S. J. Meisels. 1990. Early childhood intervention: The evolution of a concept. In S. J. Meisels and J. P. Shonkoff, eds., *Handbook of early childhood intervention,* 3–32. New York: Cambridge University Press.

———. 2000. Preface. In J. P. Shonkoff and S. J. Meisels, eds., *Handbook of early childhood intervention,* xvii–xviii. 2d ed. New York: Cambridge University Press.

Shonkoff, J. P., and D. A. Phillips, eds. 2000. *From neurons to neighborhoods: The science of early childhood development.* Washington, D.C.: National Academy Press.

Shore, R. 1997. *Rethinking the brain: New insights into early development.* New York: Families and Work Institute.

———. 2001. *Starting now: Acting on today's best ideas to nurture, teach, and protect America's young children.* New York: Carnegie Corporation of New York.

Sia, C. 1992. The medical home: Pediatric practice and child advocacy in the 1990s. *Pediatrics* 90: 419–423.

Siegel, D. 1999. *The developing mind: Toward a neurobiology of interpersonal experience.* New York: Guilford.

Sigman, M., C. Neumann, M. Baksh, N. Bwibo, and M. A. McDonald. 1989. Relationship between nutrition and development in Kenyan toddlers. *Journal of Pediatrics* 115: 357–364.

Sigman, M., and A. H. Parmelee. 1974. Visual preferences of four-month-old premature and full-term infants. *Child Development* 45(4): 959–965.

Silva, A., R. Paylor, J. M. Wehmner, and S. Tonegawa. 1992. Impaired spatial learning in alpha-calcium-calmodulin kinase II mutant mice. *Science* 257: 201–206.

Simeon, D. T., and S. Grantham-McGregor. 1990. Nutritional deficiencies and children's behavior and mental development. *Nutrition Research Reviews* 3: 1–24.

Skeels, A. M. 1966. Adult status of children with contrasting life experiences: A follow-up study. *Monographs of the Society for Research in Child Development* 31(3).

Skolnick, A. 1991. *Embattled paradise: The American family in an age of uncertainty.* New York: Basic Books.

Smith, J. R. 1941. The frequency and growth of the human alpha rhythms during normal infancy and childhood. *Journal of Genetic Psychology* 53: 455–469.

Smith, S., ed. 1995. *Two generation programs for families in poverty: A new intervention strategy.* Vol. 9 of *Advances in applied developmental psychology.* Norwood, N.J.: Ablex.

Spangler, G., and K. E. Grossman. 1993. Biobehavioral organization in securely and insecurely attached infants. *Child Development* 64: 1439–1450.

Spear, L. P. 2000. The adolescent brain and age-related behavioral manifestations. *Neuroscience and Behavioral Reviews* 24: 417–463.

Spitz, H. R. 1986. *The raising of intelligence: A selected history of attempts to raise retarded intelligence.* Hillsdale, N.J.: Lawrence Erlbaum.

Sroufe, L. A. 1979. The coherence of individual development: Early care, attachment and subsequent developmental issues. *American Psychologist* 34: 194–210.

———. 1988. A developmental perspective on day care. *Early Childhood Research Quarterly* 3: 238–291.

Steele, K. M., T. Ball, and R. Runk. 1997. Listening to Mozart does not enhance backwards digit span performance. *Perceptual and Motor Skills* 84: 1179–1184.

Steele, K. M., K. E. Bass, and M. D. Crook. 1999. The mystery of the Mozart effect: Failure to replicate. *Psychological Science* 10(4): 366–369.

Stein, B. E., M. T. Wallace, and T. R. Stanford. 1998. Single neuron electrophysiology. In W. Bechtel and G. Graham, eds., *A companion to cognitive sci-*

ence, 433–449. Blackwell Companions to Philosophy. New York: Blackwell.

Steinberg, L. 1986. Latchkey children and susceptibility to peer pressure: An ecological analysis. *Developmental Psychology* 22: 433–439.

Steiner, G. Y. 1981. *The futility of family policy.* Washington, D.C.: Brookings Institute.

Stern, D. 1974. Mother and infant at play: The diadic interaction involving facial, vocal and gaze behavior. In M. Lewis and L. Rosenblum, eds., *The effect of the infant on the care giver,* 45–67. New York: Wiley.

———. 1977. *The first relationship: Infant and mother.* Cambridge, Mass.: Harvard University Press.

———. 1985. *The interpersonal world of the infant: A view from psychoanalysis and developmental psychology.* New York: Basic Books.

Stern, E. S. 1948. The Medea complex: The mother's homicidal wishes to her child. *Journal of Mental Sciences* 94: 324–325.

Sternberg, R. J. 1999. The theory of successful intelligence. *Review of General Psychology* 3: 292–316.

Sternberg, R. J., and E. L. Grigorenko. 1999. Genetics of childhood disorders: I. Genetics and intelligence. *Journal of the American Academy of Child and Adolescent Psychiatry* 38: 486–488.

Stipek, D., and J. McCroskey. 1989. Investing in children: Government and workplace policies for children. *American Psychologist* 44: 416–423.

Stough, C., B. Kerkin, T. Bates, and G. Mangan. 1994. Music and spatial IQ. *Personality and Individual Differences* 17: 695.

Straus, M., and S. Mathner. 1996. Spanking no more effective than other forms of discipline. Chicago: Family Research Laboratory.

Sullivan, A. 2000. Hunger in the United States. Waltham, Mass.: Center on Hunger and Poverty, Heller School, Brandeis University.

Swatzwelder, H. S. 1998. Developmental differences in the acquisition and tolerance of ethanol alcohol. *Developmental Brain Research* 15(4): 311–314.

Taylor, L. 1997. Home visit program seeks to prevent child abuse. *Detroit Free Press,* 24 September, 8A.

Thompson, P. M., J. N. Giedd, and R. P. Woods. 2000. Growth patterns in the developing brain detected by using continuum mechanical tensor maps. *Nature* 404: 160–163.

Thompson, R. A. 1998. Early brain development and social policy. *Policy and Practice of Public Human Services* 56(2): 66–77.

Thompson, R. A., and C. A. Nelson. 2001. Developmental science and the media: Early brain development. *American Psychologist* 56: 5–15.

Tout, K., M. de Haan, E. Kipp-Campbell, and M. R. Gunnar. 1998. Social behavior correlates of adrenocortical activity in day care: Gender differences and time-of-day effects. *Child Development* 69: 1247–1262.

Touwen, B. C. L. 1995. A developmental neurologist's "homage." In T. C. Dalton and V. W. Bergenn, eds., *Beyond heredity and environment: Myrtle McGraw and the maturation controversy,* 271–283. Boulder, Colo.: Westview Press.

———. 1998. The brain and development of function. *Developmental Review* 18: 504–526.

U.S. Advisory Board on Child Abuse and Neglect. 1993. *Neighbors helping neighbors: A new national strategy for the protection of children. Growth report.* DHHS Stock No. 017-092-00106-1. Washington, D.C.: U.S. Government Printing Office.

U.S. Bureau of the Census. 1997. *Fertility of American women: June 1995 update.* Current Population Survey P20-499. Washington, D.C.: U.S. Bureau of the Census.

U.S. Congress. Office of Technology Assessment. 1990. *Neurotoxicity: Identifying and controlling poisons of the nervous system.* OTA-BA-436. Washington, D.C. : U.S. Government Printing Office.

U.S. Department of Education. 1987. *1986–1987—Elementary and secondary schools civil rights survey: National summary of projected data.* Washington, D.C.: Office of Civil Rights, U.S. Department of Education.

———. 1999. *Bringing education into the afterschool hours.* Washington, D.C.: U.S. Department of Education.

———. 2000. *21st Century Community Learning Centers: Providing quality afterschool learning opportunities for America's families.* Washington, D.C.: U.S. Department of Education.

U.S. Department of Education. State of Hawaii. 2000. *After-school Plus (A+)* program operations manual. August 1999. Honolulu: U.S. Department of Education.

U.S. Department of Health and Human Services. 1997. *National study of protective, preventive and reunification services delivered to children and their families.* Final report. Washington, D.C.: U.S. Government Printing Office.

———. 1999. *Highlights of findings.* www.act.dhhs.gov/programs/cb/publications/cm99.

———. 2000. *Healthy people 2010: Understanding and improving health.* Washington, D.C.: U.S. Department of Health and Human Services.

U.S. Department of Health and Human Services. Administration on Children, Youth and Families. 1998. *Head Start program performance measures: Second Progress Report.* Washington, D.C.: U.S. Department of Health and Human Services.

U.S. Department of Health, Education, and Welfare. 1979. *Smoking and Health: A Report of the Surgeon General.* Washington D.C.: Public Health Service.

U.S. Department of Labor. Bureau of Labor Statistics. 1997. *Current population survey.* Washington, D.C.: U.S. Department of Labor.

————. 2000. *Current population survey.* Washington, D.C.: U.S. Department of Labor.

U.S. General Accounting Office. 1995. *Early childhood programs: Promoting the development of young children in Denmark, France, and Italy.* Briefing Report to the Ranking Minority Member, Subcommittee on Children and Families, Committee on Labor and Human Resources, U.S. Senate, GAO/HEHS-95-45BR. Washington, D.C.: U.S. General Accounting Office.

————. 1997. *Head Start: Research provides too little evidence on impact of current program size* Report to the Chairman, Committee on the Budget, House of Representatives, GAO/HEHS-97-59. Washington, D.C.: U.S. General Accounting Office.

————. 1998a. *Head Start: Research insufficient to assess program impact* Testimony before the Subcommittee on Children and Families, Committee on Labor and Human Resources, U.S. Senate, and the Subcommittee on Early Childhood, Youth, and Families, Committee on Education and the Workforce, House of Representatives, GAO/T-HEHS-98-126. Washington, D.C.: U.S. General Accounting Office.

————. 1998b. *Head Start: Challenges faced in demonstrating program results and responding to societal changes.* Testimony before the Subcommittee on Early Childhood, Youth, and Families, Committee on Education and the Workforce, House of Representatives, GAO/T-HEHS-98-183. Washington, DC: U.S. General Accounting Office.

————. 1999. *Food Stamps Program: Various factors have led to declining participation.* GAO Publication No. RCED 99-185. Washington, D.C.: U.S. Government Printing Office.

Vandell, D. L., and L. Shumow. 1999. *After-school child care programs. Future of Children* 9(2): 64–80.

Verrengia, J. 2000. Nurturing may help intelligence. Associated Press, 19 July.

Wachs, T. D. 1995. Relation of mild-to-moderate malnutrition to human development: Correlational studies. *Journal of Nutrition* 125(8): 2245S–2254S.

Wallerstein, J., J. Lewis, and S. Blakeslee. 2000. *The unexpected legacy of divorce: A twenty-five-year longitudinal study.* Sunnyvale, Calif.: Hyperion.

Waters, E., and L. A. Sroufe. 1983. Social competence as a developmental construct. *Developmental Review* 3: 79–97.

Weikart, D. P., and L. J. Schweinhart. 1997. High/Scope Perry Preschool Program. In G. W. Albee and T. P. Gullotta, eds., *Primary prevention works: Issues in children's and families' lives,* 6:146–166. Thousand Oaks, Calif.: Sage.

Weininger, O. 1998. In the remote chance winking at your rebellious brat fails, try spanking. *Alberta Report* 25: 2.

Werker, J. F., and R. C. Tees. 1984. Cross-language speech perception: Evidence for perceptual reorganization during the first year of life. *Infant Behavior and Development* 7: 49–63.

Wertheimer, R. F. 1999. *Working poor families with children.* Washington D.C.: Child Trends.

West, P. 2001. Day care drivers may face tougher set of rules. Associated Press, 29 May.

White, B. L., and R. Held. 1966. Plasticity of sensorimotor development in the human infant. In J. F. Rosenblith and W. Allinsmith, eds., *The causes of behavior: Readings in child development and educational psychology,* 41–70. 2d ed. Boston: Allyn and Bacon.

White, S. H. 1965. Evidence of a hierarchical arrangement of learning processes. In L. P. Lewis and C. C. Spiter, eds., *Advances in child development,* 41–57. New York: Academic Press.

———. 1996. The child's entry into the age of reason. In A. J. Sameroff and M. M. Haith, eds., *The Five to Seven Year Shift,* 17–32. Chicago: University of Chicago Press.

Whitebook, M., C. Howes, and D. Phillips. 1998. *Worthy work, unlivable wages: The National Child Care Staffing Study, 1988–1997.* Washington, D.C.: Center for the Child Care Workforce.

Widom, C. 1989. Does violence beget violence? A critical examination of the literature. *Psychological Bulletin* 106 (28 March): 221–239.

Wilkie, J. R. 1993. Changes in U.S. men's attitudes toward the family provider role, 1972–1989. *Gender and Society* 7: 261–79.

Wiesel, T. 1982. Postnatal development of the visual cortex and the influence of environment. *Nature* 299: 583–591.

Wiesel, T., and D. Hubel. 1963. Single-cell responses in the striate cortex of kittens deprived of vision in one eye. *Journal of Neurophysiology* 28: 1003–1017.

Williams, W. 1994. Are we raising smarter children today? School and home-related influences on IQ. In U. Neisser, ed., *The Rising Curve: Long Term Gains in IQ and Related Measures,* 87–101. Washington, D.C.: American Psychological Association.

Wilson, T. L., and T. L. Brown. 1997. Reexamination of the effect of Mozart's music on spatial-task performance. *Journal of Psychology* 131(4): 365–370.

Winter, G. 2001. Some states fight junk food sales in schools. *New York Times,* 9 September, A9.

Winter, M. 1995. Home visiting: Forging the home-school connection. Washington, D.C.: U.S. Department of Education.

———. 2000. Parents as Teachers program overview. Personal communication, October.

Wisensale, S. K. 2000. Family leave policy: An assessment of the past, a look toward the future. Luncheon Series, 18 February, Yale University Bush Center in Child Development and Social Policy, New Haven.

———. 2001. *Family leave policy: The political economy of work and family in America.* New York: M. E. Sharpe.

Wolfe, D. A. 1993. Child abuse intervention research: Implications for policy. In

D. Cicchetti and S. L. Toth, eds., *Child abuse, child development and social policy,* 369–397. Norwood, N.J.: Ablex.

Women's Statewide Legislative Network. 1999. *The Family Leave Project: A strategy to advance the economic status of women, and to bring family and economic security to all Massachusetts workers.* Boston: Women's Statewide Legislative Nework.

Yehuda, S., and M. B. H. Youdim. 1989. Brain iron: A lesson from animal models. *American Journal of Clinical Nutrition* 50: 618–629.

Yeung, W. J., J. F. Sandrent, P. Davis-Kean, and S. L. Hofferth. 1998. Children's time with fathers in intact families. Paper presented at the annual meeting of the Populations Association of America, April 1998.

Yip, R. 1989. The changing characteristics of childhood iron nutritional status in the United States. In C. J. Filer, ed., *Dietary iron: Birth to two years,* 37–61. New York: Raven Press.

Yoshikawa, H. 1994. Prevention as cumulative protection: Effects of early family support and education on chronic delinquency and its risks. *Psychological Bulletin* 115: 27–54.

———. 1995. Long-term effects of early childhood programs on social outcomes and delinquency. *Future of Children* 5: 51–75.

Young, K. T., K. W. Marsland, and E. Zigler. 1997. The regulatory status of center-based infant and toddler child care. *American Journal of Orthopsychiatry* 67: 535–544.

Young, K. T., and E. Zigler. 1986. Infant and toddler day care: Regulation and policy implications. *American Journal of Orthopsychiatry* 56: 43–55.

Zero to Three. 1992. *Heart Start: The Emotional Foundations of School Readiness.* Washington, D.C.: Zero to Three: National Center for Infants and Todders.

———. 1999. Response to "The myth of the first three years." Press release, 11 September. Washington, D.C.: Zero to Three.

———. 2000. What grownups understand about child development: A national benchmark survey. Washington, D.C.: Zero to Three.

Zigler, E. 1967. Mental retardation. *Science* 157: 578–579.

———. 1969. Developmental versus difference theories of mental retardation and the problem of motivation. *American Journal of Mental Deficiency* 73: 536–556.

———. 1970a. The environmental mystique: Training the intellect versus development of the child. *Childhood Education* 46: 402–412.

———. 1970b. The nature-nurture issue reconsidered. In H. C. Haywood ed., *Social-cultural aspects of mental retardation,* 81–106. New York: Appleton-Century-Crofts.

———. 1987. From theory to practice. Address by the recipient of the 1986 Edgar A. Doll Award. *Psychology in Mental Retardation* APA Division 33 Newsletter, 13(2): 5–6.

———. 1988a. The IQ Pendulum. Review of H. Spitz, *The raising of intelligence. Readings* 3(2): 4–9.

———. 1998b. By what goals should Head Start be assessed? *Children's Services: Social Policy, Research, and Practice* 1: 5–17.

———. 1990. Foreword. In S. J. Meisels and J. P. Shonkoff, eds., *Handbook of early childhood intervention,* ix–xiv. New York: Cambridge University Press.

Zigler, E., W. D. Abelson, P. K. Trickett, and V. Seitz. 1982. Is an intervention program really necessary to raise disadvantaged children's IQ scores? *Child Development* 53: 340–348.

Zigler, E., and E. C. Butterfield. 1968. Motivational aspects of changes in IQ test performance of culturally deprived nursery school children. *Child Development* 39: 1–14.

Zigler, E. F., M. Finn-Stevenson, and K. W. Marsland. 1995. Child day care in the schools: The school of the twenty-first century. *Child Welfare* 124(6): 1301–1326.

Zigler, E., and M. Frank. 1988. *The parental leave crisis: Toward a national policy.* New Haven and London: Yale University Press.

———. 1996. Family leave. In E. Zigler, S. L. Kagan, and N. W. Hall, eds., *Children, families and government: Preparing for the twenty-first century,* 117–131. New York: Cambridge University Press.

Zigler, E. F., and E. P. Gilman. 1993. An agenda for the 1990s: Supporting families. In D. Blankenhorne, S. Bayme, and J. Bethke-Elshtain, eds., *Rebuilding the nest,* 212–232. Milwaukee, Wis.: Family Service America.

Zigler, E., and N. W. Hall. 1989. Physical child abuse in America: Past, present and future. In D. Cicchetti and V. K. Carlson, eds., *Child maltreatment: Theory and research on the causes and consequences of child abuse and neglect,* 38–75. New York: Cambridge University Press.

———. 1997. Drug abuse prevention efforts for young children: A review and critique. *American Journal of Orthopsychiatry* 67: 134–143.

———. 2000. *Child development and social policy.* Boston: McGraw-Hill.

Zigler, E. F., P. Hopper, and N. W. Hall. 1993. Infant mental health and social policy. In C. H. Zeanah, ed., *Handbook of infant mental health,* 480–492. New York: Guilford.

Zigler, E. F., and M. E. Lang. 1991. *Child care choices: Balancing the needs of children, families, and society.* New York: Free Press.

Zigler, E., and S. Muenchow. 1992. *Head Start: The inside story of America's most successful educational experiment.* New York: Basic Books.

Zigler, E., C. S. Piotrkowski, and R. Collins. 1994. Health services in Head Start. *Annual Review of Public Health* 15: 511–534.

Zigler, E., and S. J. Styfco. 1993. Strength in unity: Consolidating federal education programs for young children. In E. Zigler and S. J. Styfco, eds., *Head Start and beyond: A national plan for extended childhood intervention,* 111–145. New Haven and London: Yale University Press.

————. 1996. Head Start and early childhood intervention: The changing course of social science and social policy. In E. Zigler, S. L. Kagan, and N. W. Hall, eds., *Children, families, and government: Preparing for the twenty-first century,* 132–155. New York: Cambridge University Press.

————. 1997. A "Head Start" in what pursuit? IQ versus social competence as the objective of early intervention. In B. Devlin, S. E. Feinberg, D. Resnick, and K. Roeder, eds., *Intelligence, genes, and success: Scientists' response to "The bell curve,"* 283–314. New York: Springer-Verlag.

Zigler, E., C. Taussig, and K. Black. 1992. Early childhood intervention: A promising preventative for juvenile delinquency. *American Psychologist* 47: 997–1006.

Zigler, E., and P. K. Trickett. 1978. IQ, social competence, and evaluation of early childhood education programs. *American Psychologist* 33: 789–798.

Index